AF413607

There are stories that recount a life story, and then there are stories that transform the way we understand our own. In *Blow Up Your Life*, Áine Rock embodies a radical posture: that everything that happens—every rupture, every reckoning—is a gift, one that points her toward the life that is truly hers. With striking courage, she refuses to look away. This is a brave, unflinching, and deeply generous offering that invites every woman to meet her own life with the same honesty, and to discover what becomes possible when she does.

— SHERRI BROWN, Somatic practitioner and guide

Áine Rock writes with rare honesty about the moment a woman realizes the life she's built is no longer aligned with who she truly is. *Blow Up Your Life* is a powerful exploration of desire, burnout, and the cost of self-abandonment and more importantly what is possible when we listen to the wisdom of the body. This book is a permission slip and a guide for any woman ready to come home to herself and embody her highest potential.

— EMILY FLETCHER, Bestselling author of *Stress Less, Accomplish More* and Founder of Ziva

In *Blow Up Your Life*, Áine Rock dismantles the myth so many women have been taught that safety requires self-abandonment and instead reveals desire as a pathway to truth and liberation. With striking vulnerability, she shares a journey shaped by deep pain, resilience, and ultimately, the courageous choice to live a life that is fully her own. This book is both a personal reckoning and a cultural call forward, an invitation for any woman ready to come home to herself and rewrite her life from a place of inner sufficiency, truth, and deep, embodied knowing.

— DR. GERTRUDE LYONS, author of *Rewrite the Mother Code: From Sacrifice to Stardust – A Cosmic Approach to Motherhood* and host of *Rewrite the Mother Code* podcast

Blow Up Your Life is your new permission slip to demand the life you know is waiting for you. We don't all have to divorce our husbands to get there but we do need to rediscover the passion AND desire that makes this life so beautiful. Áine shares how to find that woman again and my God, it's good. You MUST read this book.

— JENNIFER PASTILOFF, National bestselling author of *On Being Human* and *Proof of Life*

When a woman stops apologizing for her desire, she becomes a force. *Blow Up Your Life* is an invitation to trust your desire, to honor your body, and to choose yourself with a new level of devotion. This is a woman walking herself home—and lighting the path for others to follow.

— REGENA THOMASHAUER, aka Mama Gena, *New York Times* bestselling author of *Pussy: A Reclamation*

Blow Up Your Life is a rare and powerful transmission—one that reminds us that the longing of your heart is not selfish, it's sacred. Through raw honesty, Áine Rock gives permission to peel back the layers and see where self-abandonment has been hiding beneath gratitude and commitment. What unfolds is both confronting and liberating. While the path carries grief and loss, it ultimately reorganizes your life around what is true, authentic, and fully your own.

— DR. SOPHIA TREVENNA, Author and intuitive business strategist

Áine Rock has written a sacred invitation back to the truth of who you are: a woman of desire, of power, of aliveness. *Blow Up Your Life* is the match, the mirror, and the permission slip all at once. If you're ready to stop living half-alive and start honoring what's been calling you… this is your moment.

— JESSICA ZWEIG, National bestselling author of *The Light Work*

BLOW UP YOUR LIFE

BLOW UP YOUR LIFE

ÁINE ROCK

The Wild Art of Wanting More

Cover design and illustrations by Caitlin Keegan
Jacket and interior design by Caitlin Keegan & Laura Boyle

Library of Congress Cataloging-in-Publication Data
Available on request

ISBN 978-1959524205 (hardcover)

Printed in the United States of America
First Edition
10 9 8 7 6 5 4 3 2 1

Dedication

For my children.
I walk this path not for you, but because of you —
and with you, always.
For my daughter especially —
may you always trust yourself.

Table of Contents

Prologue on Memory

This book weaves my story as it intersects with the lives of those around me. I am only telling my version—how I experienced it, how it landed in my body, how it shaped me.

Two people can sit in the same room and walk away with entirely different memories of the same conversation. I have not gone back to mine for accuracy. I have gone back for truth—my truth—the moments that formed my character, and the ones I eventually had to unlearn.

There is a tension I know well, between the codes of family and the desire to be fully expressed. Between loyalty and liberation. These can feel deeply at odds.

And yet we are living through a reckoning. We are learning how to tell the truth and how to protect the most vulnerable among us at the same time. I don't believe those things are opposites. I believe they require each other.

For me, using my voice to tell this story is not separate from the healing. It *is* the healing.

If you were there and remember it differently, I believe you. This is one woman's account of how she found her way back to herself—through the stories she carried, and those she finally chose to set down.

This is my version.

Aine

Introduction

The car was still, morning light filtering through the windshield. I heard my own breathing before I heard myself whisper.

"Where is my desire? And why don't I have any?"

I was sitting in the driver's seat of my SUV, a fuzzy robe pulled over my pajamas and a coffee getting cold in the console. I was in an empty lot, looking at my therapist through my phone; I wished I were anywhere but here.

When the world went into lockdown in 2020, my husband and I, along with our two children—who were seven and eleven at the time—hunkered into our three-story house in Chicago, each of us taking a corner for survival. I worked for hours in the basement; my husband took over the dining room. Our kids rotated their Zoom classes at the kitchen table. We stayed up too late binge-watching shows, drank wine, and tried to stay sane during masked grocery runs. By winter, we were ready for a jailbreak. Just before Christmas, we packed the car—two kids, two dogs, laptops, iPads—and drove twenty hours to Florida, to the small house my father left me when he died.

For three months we lived there. The space was home, school, and work. We took long walks to break up the sameness. We played cards at night, skipped math tests for beach days, and I found small slivers of peace during a time that pushed me to my edges daily.

The night before that therapy call, I had talked with an old friend from theater school, a woman whose wedding I had stood in years before. She lived down south now, training horses, raising a son just a bit younger than mine. Her husband wanted to explore his sexuality outside their marriage. She spoke calmly, but I could hear the heartbreak beneath it. They were staying together for their son, both dating other men. When I shared the news with my husband, we laughed about how we'd entered the season where marriages fall apart—weddings in your thirties, divorces in your forties. We said the words that always followed those foreboding conversations: *That'll never happen to us.*

But COVID tested every couple I knew. We were no exception.

That night, my husband asked if I was jealous that my friend was dating again. "Do you wish it were you?" he said. "Getting to date?"

We had a running joke that after fourteen years together, there was nothing new left to discover. But maybe it wasn't a joke at all. I let myself imagine it—someone new, a spark of possibility, a flicker of aliveness in my chest.

It was gone as quickly as it came.

Later that night, we lay in bed reading on opposite sides of our king-size bed, a pillow between us, our backs turned. We were as far from desire as two people could be. So, when I asked my therapist, "Where is my desire?" it felt like an ember falling from the sky, landing in my lap, and setting fire to my world. I could feel the shift the instant the words left my mouth. I knew I was playing with fire. But this was the catalyst, the truth I had been circling finally spoken.

On a podcast, I heard Brené Brown describe midlife as a moment when the universe whispers...*the armor you've built to survive is no longer useful. That it's actually keeping us from our gifts.*

Sitting there that morning, I finally understood what she meant. All my masks and mechanisms that had once kept me safe were keeping me stuck. It was time for me to lay down my armor and walk willingly into the fire of my own becoming.

Desire is the flame, the creative life energy that lives inside each of us. It is our inner navigation, the compass that leads us toward aliveness.

For many women, that flame has been dimmed, silenced, or snuffed out. It has been overridden by parents, culture, trauma, or quieted by the exhaustion of motherhood and the self-sacrifice that comes with caring for everyone else. Sometimes even birth itself—the primal opening—becomes the moment we learn to close. Desire gets delayed, excused, and pushed aside in favor of performance and obligation. It is softened by shame and sometimes erased entirely by religion.

But desire is not frivolous.
Desire is who we are.

It holds power, which is why it has been feared. For centuries, patriarchal systems have separated our sexuality from our creativity, sanitizing each of them. To remember that they are one and the same—that your creative energy and your erotic energy flow from the same source—is an act of reclamation.

This remembering takes courage. It asks for intention and often a deep undoing, a deconditioning of the voices that say you are too much, too needy, too sensual, too alive. Desire is divine. It is a knowing, a longing, a whisper from the soul guiding you home. Learning to trust it, and to follow it even when it moves against everything you have been taught, is nothing short of revolutionary.

And this revolution sparks the remembering. Desire becomes the fuel, the nourishment on which we thrive, and sometimes, as in my case, the accelerant that blows up your life.

There is no prescription or formula for blowing up your life. You will know when it is time.

You may try to dismantle it neatly, to control the unraveling, but some of us cannot find our way back to ourselves through careful deconstruction. We have buried our truth so deep, like an Easter egg in a Taylor Swift video, that even when someone else points to it, we are not sure it is real. For me, I could not ease my way into change. I had to strike the match.

I had to blow it all up and start again.

The Invitation

This book is an invitation to blow up your life.

Not as destruction for its own sake, but rather for the sacred burning that reveals what has been waiting underneath. A remembrance of your own desire, the one that is still glowing beneath the ash. The one guiding you back to yourself, if you are willing to follow it.

This is always where the story begins: the quiet moment before you blow it up. Once you name your desire, you cannot unknow it. It will keep asking to be heard, like it or not. It asks for more truth, more movement, more life. When the wanting is all you have. When you decide you are no longer willing to live half alive.

Desire has a way of demanding action. The question I had asked—*Where is my desire?*—had been following me for months, whispering under every surface of my life until it became impossible to ignore.

We don't all have big, dramatic wake-up calls, though I doubt any of us get through life without at least one tragedy, a personal or financial crisis, an illness, something that rocks our sense of tomorrow's predictability and safety. We often need a proverbial kick in the ass before we wake up and ask, *What do I actually want?*

If I know that I have this one life, what do I want to accomplish? What mark do I want to leave? Who do I want to be?

That wanting is the seed of desire. But often our desire, our longing, our inner navigation, in its most potent form, is ignored. Our conditioning sweeps our dreams and curiosities into the most convenient current, and we follow the path of least resistance. But what happens when we no longer want to anchor where we've been?

The week after my first realization that my marriage wasn't what I thought it was, I booked myself a hotel room for the weekend. We had moved to California by then, finally following a dream I'd carried for years. But a new place doesn't fix what's already breaking. It just gives it more room. As we started to face the possible end of our marriage, we took more and more time apart. He would travel back to the Midwest and when he came back, I would take a couple of days at an Airbnb or hotel—any way to get out of the same space.

So, I took the weekend and went to the city. I walked into the hotel bar, a modern, lush space overflowing with greenery in West Hollywood, and looked for my friend, Sophia.

We had been friends for twenty-five years through marriages, breakups, cross-country moves, and endless late-night calls. We would go months without talking and then, as best friends do, pick up right where we left off. Now we had found ourselves living in the same city for the first time in twenty years.

We sat down among the verdant radiance of the hotel patio.

"I'm leaving him," I said before she even had a chance to catch her breath.

Over the next few hours, I told her everything: how something in me had woken up, how I could finally see what I had been avoiding for years. Now that my eyes were open, there was no way to go back.

Sophia had been my maid of honor. She knew me before marriage, through marriage, and also motherhood. She had seen my relationship with my husband unfold from the beginning, and she wasn't surprised.

That surprised me.

As we sat at that breakfast, knowing the truth and sealing it with our lips, I could finally see that it was inevitable. I sensed a different life waiting for me, one of the woman I was becoming. The distance felt vast, the details impossible to imagine but I knew who I wanted to become.

Sophia and I talked about logistics—an apartment, time in the city—but what she was really offering me was something much older and more powerful. She was offering presence. Women have always held each other through thresholds like this, bearing witness to the death of one life and the birth of another. In a culture that isolates us, that teaches us to endure privately and perform resilience, the simple act of being seen in grief and joy becomes a quiet rebellion.

At first, it felt like a chance to reclaim a past version of myself. In truth, it was an invitation to step into a lineage of women who know how to hold one another with grace, not to fix or rescue, but to stand steady in the fire together. That kind of sisterhood does not just heal individuals, it pushes back against the systems that rely on our silence, our separation, and our self-abandonment.

In the months that followed, I noticed the way people responded. Some were shocked. Others weren't phased at all. One friend reminded me that before we had kids, I used to say we'd probably end up divorced. I have no memory of that, but it sounded like something the twenty-seven-year-old version of me would say.

Some friends slipped quietly out the side door, uncertain how to hold this new version of me. Others leaned in closer, steady in their witnessing, unafraid of my transformation.

This was one of the hardest parts: realizing that with awakening came its own kind of grief. When you change, not everyone comes with you. Some people only know how to love the woman you used to be.

I didn't grow up believing in perfect marriages. My parents were divorced, and so were most of my friends' parents. I had grown up through divorce and turmoil, and somewhere along the way, I decided I would make it work, no matter what. But now, standing in this new truth, I could hardly recognize the woman who had stayed so long in a life that no longer fit. Where had I gone? Why had it taken me so long to come back to myself?

"I can't spend one more minute pretending to be happy," I told Sophia. "Actually, I am happy—for the first time in years. I feel more myself than I ever have, and he doesn't like it. I stopped drinking, I'm microdosing mushrooms, I've lost weight, I feel vibrant, and I don't want to go back."

Three years later, while I straddled a lover on my leather couch in my new apartment, he asked, "How is it possible you didn't have sex for so many years? You are always in the mood."

"I was a different person," I said. "It's amazing what you can get used to."

Two years ago, I never could have imagined myself doing a boudoir photo shoot or joining a Zoom room full of women in lingerie, talking about pleasure and power. The idea of even owning lingerie, let alone dancing in it, felt foreign to me.

For years, I dreamed of being in California, of living by the ocean, and near the mountains. I was called there by an inexplicable wanting that I could not justify in the real terms of my life.

Two decades before, when I met my ex-husband in New York, my plan was to move to Los Angeles. I moved to New York from Toronto to go to theater school, and as soon as I could afford it, I was going to LA. But then love appeared. We moved to his home in Chicago, where he needed to go for work; it seemed like a short detour that couldn't hurt. The move required that I trade some of my ambition for the steadiness of our relationship, so I set my dreams of being on stage or in film aside.

I was in my mid-twenties, and I wanted to be loved most of all. So, I made the trade. As consciously as I could, yet, it was still a trade. When I look back, I wonder about the ways we sabotage our dreams when our wounds are at the helm. We sidestep, we delay, we put our dreams on hold for someday—someone.

I carefully and loudly justified this new version of the dream to friends that had watched me build my life in New York. My mind was set. There was no turning back.

Sometimes it feels impossible that I spent fourteen years in Chicago. That version of me feels so distant and unrelated, but she was me. I am her. That period of time was dynamic; I wasn't unhappy throughout. For the first few years, my life fell into a beautiful cadence. I worked, enjoyed my relationship, and became a mother. Those early years of motherhood were overwhelming and exhausting, and in the beautiful chaos of babies and toddlers, my dreams faded to the background.

Yet every so often, my old dream of living in California resurfaced. I'd catch a glimmer of it when I watched an award show or saw a film about LA, and I'd have a deep feeling that I wasn't where I was supposed to be. I felt a calling to be there. I brought it up to my husband, but without conviction. I wasn't someone who was willing to bet on themselves—not yet. It seemed impossible, the timing was never right. Between work, kids, and the tapestry of our lives, could we unravel it for a dream? My dream?

My clients have said similar things about their own lives:

"I've lowered my expectations."

"I've learned to live with this, and to stop letting my wild fantasies ruin all the goodness I have."

"I am grateful for what I have. Is it selfish to want more?"

Marriage is a funny thing. We spend our teens and twenties watching romance movies and dreaming of the perfect partnership. We've all heard, "Till death do us part," but we don't make a contingency plan for what happens when we experience the kind of growth or change that takes us in different directions. Where was the promise to grow and change together when we promised our lives? Where was the faith to leap together, to re-evaluate often, to tend to our own wounds? If those promises were part of choosing a life with another, then perhaps we wouldn't find ourselves trapped by the very thing we spent our lives wanting: a partner, a loving husband, a family.

When my father died and left me money, he gave me a temporary pass, a way out. And yet it still took me four years to muster the courage and the self-worth, and resilience to say, "I want this, and wanting is enough." Full stop.

What I had been doing all those years was abandoning myself. Unconsciously, I had been making a deal: I will betray myself for your love, because the loss of your affection, your love, feels so drastic and insurmountable to me, or to my nervous system (or more accurately, to the inner child) that I will abandon myself instead.

For two decades, I dismissed what I wanted because I couldn't make it fit into the life I had created, and then I couldn't ask my kids and my husband to give up or sacrifice their happiness for mine, and so I put mine at the bottom. But the result was that I found myself piled under a ton of resentment that I had created.

In the process of learning to honor and trust my dreams and desires, I went on a deep journey back to myself.

My therapist sometimes reflects on how much I've changed, and not just physically, but energetically. And it's insightful and helpful to have this reflection held up for me because we can't always see how our inner transformation looks from the outside.

Sure, I lost weight, I stopped drinking, I have a few more tattoos, but it's more subtle to know that my energy is different when I walk into the room, that I don't feel guarded or closed. Through healing, my capacity for grief has grown; I have integrated the parts of me that were so afraid, so masked. I'm not afraid of being alone, and I'm willing to advocate for my desire again, because I am willing to take up space.

The journey of my transformation began with one single question and the power it carried. A power I had cut myself off from completely.

You might be reading this and thinking, *I'm not that kind of woman.*

But here you are, reading a book about blowing up your life. So, maybe there is a part of her in you, too.

She was in me—buried under the good-mother mask, the wife costume, the woman trying to hold it all together. She was suffocated and almost gone. And if I'm honest, I used to judge the women who seemed free in their bodies, who spoke openly about desire.

Disapproval is the first clue that we are touching our own shadow. For me, it's my signal. Every time I thought, *I could never do that*, it was pointing me toward something I secretly wanted but didn't yet feel safe to claim.

I said I'd never get divorced. I did. I said I'd never have an affair. I did that, too. I said I'd never quit drinking. I stopped drinking for two years.

I guess "never" belongs to the versions of ourselves we outgrow. Along the way, I've shed every one of them—not recklessly, but intentionally.

Five years ago, I was the woman who had it all together on the outside: the marriage, the house, the coaching career, the constant motion. Inside, I was numb. My life looked full, but I felt empty. I spent hours in the basement of our three-story house in Chicago, writing about another version of my life—one with sunsets and mountains in California—and carrying a quiet longing I barely allowed myself to feel. I wanted to make an impact with my words, my ideas, my stories. I wanted to feel alive in my work, not just useful.

Eventually, I came to a breaking point, and I wondered: What if the key to more joy, more connection, more meaning wasn't harder work but more presence and pleasure? Five years ago, I would have rolled my eyes at the thought.

She was happier venting with girlfriends over wine about husbands who wanted sex and weren't getting any. She was hiding from herself—from shame, from grief, from the untended needs of her inner child—while trying to fit into a version of womanhood that looked big from the outside but felt small inside. But the more honest I became, the more I started to see what was possible.

Moving to California was the first step.

Admitting that I wanted to be free lit the fuse that got me there.

The more permission I gave myself to become her—the woman who led with pleasure—the closer I came to creating the life I had always imagined.

What I began leaning into wasn't a concept or a framework, but a question—one I couldn't shake.

How is intimacy tied to the success I'm seeking in my life and my business?

The intimacy I am referring to is with myself. One rich in connection to my body and my truth. One devoid of performance and productivity. I wanted to know the signals I had spent years overriding in the name of being capable, reliable, and "together."

The more I paid attention, the clearer my patterns became. When I felt connected—regulated in my nervous system, resourced in my body, honest about what I wanted—everything moved with ease. My decisions sharpened. My creativity expanded. My capacity to receive deepened.

When our nervous system is locked in survival—constantly in fight-or-flight—it limits our capacity to create, receive, and thrive. When we learn to alchemize the grief and anger that keep us stuck and turn them into power, pleasure becomes our ally in expansion.

By choosing a life that is no longer governed by old wounds, we blaze toward a story in which our truest selves are the loving guide. I walked through the fire with clear intention and a deep commitment to healing. I sat with my shadows, tended my inner child, stopped numbing, and mined the decades of pain I had been avoiding. I faced the grief of divorce and betrayal, and for the first time, I chose myself.

I did the work for that phase of life, and I will return to these practices when life inevitably asks more from me. That is the art of wanting more; it greets you where you are, all times in your life. I am no longer willing to trade my authenticity for anyone else's comfort. This is my one wild and precious life, and I will not waste another moment of it hiding in shame.

And I want the same for you, in whichever phase of life you're in, to reclaim intimacy with yourself, to reconnect with your creative and sexual energy as the sacred life force that draws you into harmony with nature, and to become magnetic to the life you truly desire.

A path reveals itself. An invitation to listen more closely to your body, your desires, and the places within you that already know the way forward. We don't begin by fixing or forcing anything. We begin by remembering.

I'm sharing my story so intimacy can be your teacher. Because in my missteps and my moments of grace, my unraveling and my victories, you may begin to recognize your own path. I don't believe transformation happens through instruction alone. For me, a story is worth a thousand lessons.

So, I've woven my own life into these pages—not as a prescription, but as an offering. Take what resonates. Leave what doesn't. Let it meet you where you are.

Let's begin.

✦ Desire Practice
The Beginning of Wanting More

W hat is desire?

Is it longing? Is it the insatiable need to build fantasies and romance around even the most barren landscape of love? Is it string lights of hope that we hang on one end of our life across decades spanning marriages, kids, and heartbreak?

Is it a crack to be filled with love? A seed planted deep within me, a craving, a dream, an unanswerable call, a voice that said, "More?" A tug in my heart that said, "Maybe?" A knowing traveled without map or supplies, urged my feet in the direction of my pleasure?

Desire emerged in my body, like a hunger, a need, I wanted to be touched, caressed, adored. I wanted to disrobe my armor and feel the curves and crevices of my body explored. Desire, like fire, grew with oxygen.

When I look at my body, she perks up.

I talk to my wetness, and she stirs.

When all the dos and don'ts, should's and shouldn'ts are silenced, I can hear my desire. She whispers softly in my ear; she calls me to the place where I can be wild. The place where my hips sway, my feet move, and my voice is never silenced. I stomp my feet and scream for the life

I could've had. For the lies and half-truths that buried my desire beneath shame and people pleasing.

She wants me to be savage, untamed, erotic, messy, cold, angry, hot, wet, pulsing with life—nature itself. She wants that for you, too.

My desire is life, flowing from place to place, finding her way, like water, rushing over all that there is. Sometimes I get trapped by a moment, a decade, a man, a life, but desire wants to be free. It unwraps the chains of duty. When I give myself permission to be—to feel, to rage, to love, and fuck—every shade of grey rises inside me. She was within me as I crossed through the door, she held me as I cried through the night, every person that I was, inconsolable with grief and love.

And she will be with me through the darkness until light peeks through the window and the sun promises a new day.

Now, it's your turn. Take out a journal, give yourself a quiet space, a timer, and permission to write whatever surfaces without your editor hat on.

What does your desire feel like?

What if you could have it? What would it cost you?

What else? Write for ten minutes about desire. Start with this:

If I'm being honest, I desire _______________________________ .

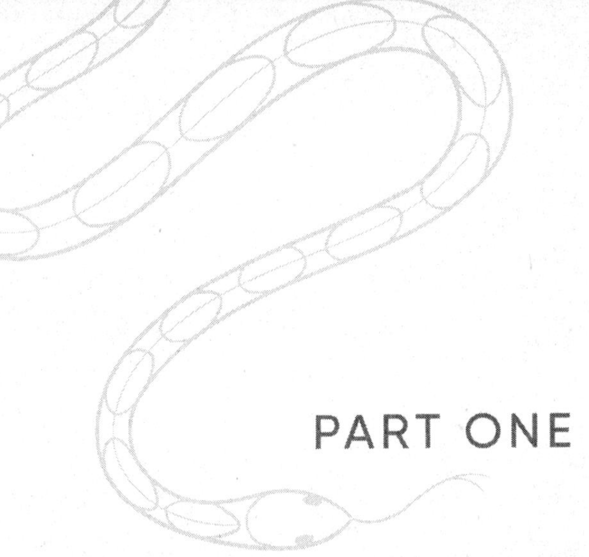

PART ONE

The Invitation: Reclaim Your Pain

✦ Invitation Meditation

Breathe deeply. Let yourself arrive.

Close your eyes. Find a comfortable seat, or lie down.

Honor your body honoring you for being here.

Take the time to open to this invitation.

You are here to discover what brings you pleasure.

Notice where you are right now, on this day.

Feel your breath.

Feel it expand and move your body.

Take a moment to notice any tightness or sense of holding.

Can you release it?

Bring your hand and place it over your womb.

Breathe. In and out.

Now move your hand to your pussy.

She is your portal—to the temple of your inner knowing.

Feel the warmth of her glow.

Rest your other hand on your heart

You've entered the sacred space of desire.

Cultivate curiosity and love.

Let yourself discover without reaching or judging.

Notice what arises.

What do you desire?

How do you desire to be met in your body, in self-pleasure, in reclaiming the sensual and erotic touch of receiving in your body, both with yourself and with a lover or partner?

If nothing arises, so be it.

The better you know yourself, the more you can ask for.

Inspiration is everywhere.

Begin in your body.

Your unique erotic blueprint is like a fingerprint.

It is only yours and it shifts depending on the light and shadows of moods, experiences, and capacity.

What does your intimacy recipe look like today?

Do you want to be playful?

Tantalized, teased, tossed around?

Do you want to be submissive or dominant?

Are you full of energy or in your softness?

Do you want to dance to music in the living room?

When do you feel most sensual?

Notice how this practice stays with you, and you will start to see examples of intimacy that feel edgy or interesting to you.

Start to wonder how you desire to be pleasured.

What feels safe?

What feels like it will expand your capacity?

Are you willing to try new things?

Are you leading or following?

Are you willing to be present with the energy that's available to you?

How about without agenda or performance?

What stories come up that block you?

Where do you feel them in your body as you breathe?

Come back to this meditation, any time that you need it, throughout the book or later. Feel a sense of wholeness that you are held and loved. Every cell in your body is perfectly aligned and ready to receive pleasure just as you are, exactly in this moment. No adjusting necessary.

You are exactly the woman capable and ready to receive pleasure and expand, just as you are able to expand your breath to receive more. Feel the pleasure of that breath and the relief of letting it go.

Take three deep breaths here, and as you finish the last exhale, let your eyes float open and come back.

Ask yourself: *Where will pleasure take me next?*

The Relearning

The moment I stumbled across his secret, the air left the room. It was ordinary and devastating all at once—the kind of truth that doesn't shout, but has the strength to rearrange everything you thought was real.

I remember staring at the words, reading them again, as if repetition could change their meaning. The part of me that wanted to be logical, to fix it, tried to take over, but my body already knew. My heart raced. My stomach clenched. My skin flushed hot.

In that moment, I understood how the body carries what the mind refuses to see.

My husband had been my partner for almost two decades. We had built a life, a family, a home. But standing there, holding the evidence of his betrayal, I felt like I was looking at a stranger.

Maybe I was.

For years, we started our mornings together: meditating, journaling, sharing coffee on opposite ends of the same couch. I had never once thought to look at what he had written until that day. Something inside me said, *Read it.*

I opened it.

On a random page I found a confession written in his handwriting—an affair. Eight years before.

I'm not proud of looking, but it felt inevitable, as if some higher truth needed to be known. Betrayal is cruel and sharp. It taps the marrow of love and makes you question everything—not just the other person, but yourself.

Who was it? When was this happening? Why had he stayed? What did he think he was protecting? And what part of me had known all along and chosen silence anyway?

Strangely enough, relief came first—the confirmation that the distance between us wasn't made up in my head. Then came anger, heartache, the hollow disorientation of realizing that the version of love I had been holding onto had already left.

That was the beginning of my relearning. Not the kind that happens in the mind, but the kind that begins in the body—in the truth you can't unsee once it's found you.

THE UNFORGIVABLE

The message came out of nowhere. On a gray afternoon in 2020, a Facebook notification appeared on my phone.

Are you mad at me?

Five words that paralyzed time.

It was him—the boy who had sexually abused me when I was nine years old. My body reacted before my mind caught up. My breath shortened. My hands went cold. The room tilted. I stared at the screen, unable to move, as if seeing a ghost.

Another notification blinked: *I heard you wrote about us in your diary.*

The words didn't match the man he must have been at that point. He was just a few years older than I was, both in our forties now, but in that moment staring at the screen it felt as if time had folded in on itself, the past suddenly alive and pulsing in my living room. That message cracked something open I had buried for decades.

When I was nine, we took my older cousin to Disney World. One night, for some reason I cannot recall, we were put in a bed together. It started as teasing and play but quickly turned sexual. I was sworn to silence and secrecy. And since I knew that it was wrong, that he had crossed a line, I kept that promise. Months later I moved in with his parents, my aunt and uncle, while my mother traveled with my stepfather. I was in fourth grade, and I walked down the quiet tree lined street to and from my public school. In the afternoons and weekends, my cousin would have sex with me in the basement. I didn't protest, but I understand now that I was too young to consent.

I lived in that environment for a year before my parents gathered me up to move to a new city again. I was saved from the circumstance but lived with the shame and confusion of a child dealing with adult sexuality.

A few years later, I wrote about it in my diary, grappling with my own demons of unworthiness and grief. And then my mother found that diary and read it. I can still see her face as she confronted me—panic, disbelief, shame—the air thick with something neither of us knew how to name. In her shock, she told her family. The fallout was brutal. I was a teenager whose life was falling apart, and now my secret was out. I didn't have language for what had happened, only the unspoken rule I had already internalized: stay quiet. The silence of my family was powerful. No adults ever took accountability or responsibility, and I moved on as best I could.

When that message landed in 2020, it felt like the universe pressing a finger directly on my oldest wound.

My daughter was nine years old at the time.

Every night as I tucked her in, I would look at her, small and childlike, and think, *How could anyone have looked at me and thought I was ready for sex?* It seemed impossible. And yet, I had lived it.

I started searching for old photographs, wanting to see the girl I had been. I needed to remember her face, her softness, her confusion. When I found them, I realized how young I was. How much she had carried, which was beyond her maturity.

I understood for the first time how early my desire had been twisted by shame and the need to stay safe. *Don't get caught, your world will fall apart. Your family will fall apart.* What a heavy burden for a child to carry. My relationship to pleasure had been shaped by those years—desire and danger fused together in my nervous system.

That was the beginning of my unlearning.

It would take decades to separate them—to reclaim desire as something sacred, innocent, powerful, mine. And in that reclamation, my life as I knew it began to fall apart.

The message, the remembering, the years of silence—all of it became the fire that burned away the version of me that had been performing safety for everyone else. The truth was never gone. It had simply been waiting for me to be ready to hold it.

THERAPY IS JUST THE START

The first thing my mom did when she read my diary, besides telling everyone in my family, was send me to therapy. To the best of my memory, it was group therapy. It wasn't very successful, and it didn't last very long.

Shortly after, my mother became preoccupied with my stepfather's drama, and my trauma got swallowed by hers. I stopped talking about it. I put on a tough face and got on with it. It was the first piece of armor I ever built.

I went to therapy again on my own in other chapters, like in college, when I found myself living with a volatile boyfriend. Again, when I was trying to leave a relationship while also managing my mother's alcoholism. Then, when I met my husband and was so afraid I was going to make a shitty choice, I hired a therapist for the first nine months of our relationship.

For the first twelve years of our marriage, I went without therapy, overlooking one of the most fundamental pieces of information about our relationship: I didn't particularly want to have sex. We did, obviously, and have two beautiful children, but it usually felt like a chore. Something to be scheduled. Neither of us had any language for intimacy or desire. We locked into a rhythm of duty, child rearing, and living a half-happy life.

By the time that Facebook message arrived in 2020, I had found and met my biological father. He had passed away two years prior, and left me an unexpected inheritance. I was burned out and exhausted from raising kids with my husband who was often gone, and the money allowed me to step away from my work in network marketing and decide what I wanted next. I hired a writing teacher, and twice a week I descended into my basement office to write.

Writing became a type of therapy, a way to find my innermost desires and dreams. It became a place that was just mine. By this time, I had mostly given up acting; it had been squeezed out by the realities and demands of life, but I found that writing was a lifeline to a creative part of me, a different version of me. I was given a prompt, wrote, and read my writing out loud. So often my words stirred up grief and longing in me that I didn't recognize, as if I was unlocking a part of my heart that had been kept away without a creative place to put it.

When that message arrived, I felt the foundation of my life shift. The cracks started small, but I could feel them spreading. It was like standing on unsteady ground during an earthquake, reaching for anything to hold on to.

His naïve curiosity floored me. His words landed in my inbox and sent my whole body into a trauma response. I found myself anxious and shaking, my heart and mind racing. I felt like I was drowning. Why had he sent me this message thirty years later? What did he want?

My writing coach recommended her therapist, and I left her a message the next day. She specialized in somatic work, using the body to move and heal trauma, which I knew nothing about; I just knew I needed help. I couldn't process this alone. With her guidance, I began to remember what I had buried: memories of the abuse, abandonment, and how it all still lived inside me.

I had blocked out most of it, leaving only fragments and flashes. I had turned the story into a footnote, something I could reference without feeling. I had rejected the idea of being a victim, armored myself with competence, and convinced myself I was fine. I had a family, a career, and a marriage. Surely, I had done enough healing.

And yet, beneath it all, my body was telling a different story.

COMPOUND SADNESS

There are times in life when the wheels come off. When pain is compounded, it feels like the perfect storm, and we are consumed by grief. When we wonder if the pain we're feeling is ever going to end. Humans are resilient, and it's in our resilience that we create the masks and characters that protect us when we don't have the tools and resources to cope with the compounded pain.

I think it's safe to say we've all experienced a time when it all piles on. When the simple platitude, *When it rains, it pours*, is never truer. And when it pours, we can shut down, and pretend it's not happening, use a way of coping (as adults this may look like addictions), or steer into the storm. The way of the Priestess is to see the storm as the initiation. As a woman, walking into a season of storms, you know that you're going to face the dark night of the soul. You're going to be asked to slay the dragons of your past and seek your own medicine. It won't be easy, but it will be worth it.

THE WILD SPIRIT OF THE HORSE:

I spent much of my childhood riding horses. Every Christmas, I wrote the same word on my wish list: *Pony*. It was all I ever wanted.

The summer I turned eight, my mother found a small riding school called Sunnybrook Farms just outside Toronto. You had to be nine to enroll, but I was tall, and they made an exception. That summer, I fell in love with the smell of hay and leather, the dust rising from hooves, the rhythm of breath between horse and girl. I rode tired old ponies at first—patient souls who had carried a hundred little girls before me around the same oval ring. Slowly, I graduated to the faster ones, learning to post with their gait, to trust my balance, to find a kind of freedom that only existed when we moved as one.

I brushed their manes for hours, whispered secrets into their soft ears, and dreamed of the day one of them might be mine. Every time we moved, which was often, the first thing I wanted to find was a barn.

And then, one Christmas, it happened. Beneath the tree sat a small toy pony with a note attached. My mother had found one through her hairdresser, of all places. He had a barn and horses, and a daughter just a few years older than I was, who had outgrown her pony.

A few days later, in the freezing cold of an East Coast winter, we drove through the snow to a tiny wooden barn on the outskirts of Ottawa. Inside stood Casey Jones, with a white blaze down his face, fur thick for winter, breath steaming in the cold. He was beautiful, stubborn, and mine. My mother arranged for him to stay there, and the daughter became one of my closest friends. We spent endless afternoons riding through snowy fields, two girls and their horses, tasting freedom for the first time.

We would move again, as we always did, and Casey came with us—to a bigger barn outside the city, where I graduated to taller, sleeker horses and higher jumps. For the next few years, I would spend every afternoon after school at the barn, and wake up before sunrise on weekends for horse shows. I lived and breathed horses. I dreamed of joining the Canadian Olympic show jumping team with my friends. I was fearless, devoted, and sure of the life ahead of me.

Then, everything unraveled.

My mother caught our trainer beating one of the horses behind the stalls. The horse had knocked down a fence during a competition, and the trainer's rage spilled over to the horse. He took him behind the stalls and beat him, where my mother stumbled upon them. She told the owner and he pulled his horse from the barn.

A few days later, my horse, Con, developed colic, a twisting of the intestine that can turn fatal within hours. By the time we got him to the hospital, stress had triggered another condition that left him beyond saving. We put him down within days. I was devastated.

Not long after, my mother discovered my stepfather was having an affair with one of the mothers from the barn. She changed the locks one day, and he was gone the next, leaving us with debt and silence. I was fourteen years old.

The grief was too heavy, too layered. I had lost my horse, my family, my footing in the world. When you're a teenager, and everything you love disappears at once, it feels easier to start over than to rebuild from the ruins.

I didn't ride again for almost twenty years.

Sometimes I wonder why. Maybe because horses had always represented freedom, and when I lost them, I lost the place inside me that believed in freedom, too. Nine was the year I started riding. It was also the year I was molested, and my world turned upside down. I fell in love with horses because they saved me from humans. At the barn, I could leave the house that felt unsafe, the strangers I called family, and the secret I carried. There, I wasn't a girl holding shame. I was a horse girl—capable, strong, fearless. I could jump fences taller than myself and land steady. She was who I wanted to be.

Now, decades later, as I write this book, I find myself dreaming of horses again. Of dropping my kids at the bus stop, driving to a barn, brushing down a mare the color of chestnuts, and riding through open trails with no destination. I dream of gathering women in the fields—sisters, mothers, daughters—to stand in stillness beside these magnificent creatures.

Horses carry an ancient medicine. They attune to our nervous system and invite our bodies to slow down to match their heartbeat.

They call forth the wild and untamed parts of us—the ones that still know how to trust instinct and presence. They saved me once, and I know they are still saving me now. Because, when standing beside a horse, there is no need to perform. No need to prove. I breathe in the quiet communion of two beings remembering what it means to be free.

When I look back now, I can see that the horses were my first teachers. Long before I had words for trauma or healing or embodiment, they showed me what it meant to listen without language. To trust the body's rhythm. To find safety in presence, not perfection.

They taught me how to ground when the world felt unsteady, how to breathe through fear, and how to lead without control. Every lesson I now teach—the power of the body's wisdom, the art of surrender, the truth that freedom begins inside us—was there all along, in those early mornings at the barn.

The horses were my first taste of sovereignty. A wild, steady reminder that the spirit cannot be broken, only hidden.

HOW DO YOU HEAL A CHILD?

My eleven-year-old son cried the other day over FaceTime, upset about going to a friend's house, feeling angry and powerless that his dad was not there, and I was leaving for the weekend. I spent an hour of my drive reassuring him and holding space for his anger.

After we hung up, I thought about how often I do the same thing for the little girl inside me—the one who still flares up when life feels uncertain, when love feels distant, when things feel out of my control.

You might know this feeling, too. That moment in an argument or misunderstanding when suddenly, without meaning to, your three-year-old self takes the wheel. The tantrum rises, the words spill out, and only later do you realize that it wasn't your adult-self reacting—it was a much younger part of you trying to be seen, heard, or held.

It can be helpful to slow down in those moments and ask gently, *What part of me is feeling this?* And then tend to that part of you the way you would for one of your children. It's usually my bratty little girl who feels abandoned and hurt. Or, it's the teenage part of me that's rebellious and confrontational.

This is the practice of reparenting. The softer you can be with these parts of you (just like your own children), the more they begin to trust that they are safe. They learn that the adult—the wise, grounded self—is here now, and she can handle what they cannot.

When we face and untangle these wounded parts of ourselves, we can start to see how they have helped us through life, we can see them as gifts, as the parts of ourselves left behind when things were too difficult or scary.

I find it helpful to carry a photo of my younger self with me, to remind me that she exists within me and that I can always tend to her needs. You can reparent that child in you, the way you wish you were parented, giving space to the big feelings and fears that may have been present.

Healing happens quietly. Not with fireworks or an epiphany, but in small, almost forgettable moments that felt like nothing at all. For me, it was the morning light spilling through the curtains of my new part-time apartment, the feeling of solitude of that apartment, and the choices that got me there. The way my breath caught when I realized there was no one waiting for me to make breakfast, no one to report to, no one to perform for. Just me, emotional and uncertain, but free. I was slowly leaving my marriage, renting an apartment in Los Angeles as the paperwork and mediation began but also, so, too, the healing.

For a long time, healing had been a concept I could talk about fluently—in therapy, in coaching sessions, in the pages of my journal. I was starting to see the pattern, tracing the wound back to its origin. But embodiment was different. Embodiment required feeling. It asked me to stay. To stop running from my own body, from my own truth.

There were mornings when I would wake up in my beautiful new space still heavy with grief, the kind that presses into your chest until you can't tell if it's sadness or simply the weight of remembering. But beneath the grief, there was something else—a flicker. A pulse of life that I hadn't felt in years. Some days, it came through music. I'd put on a song I loved and start moving—awkwardly at first, like a woman relearning her own body after decades of disconnection. My hips would resist, my breath would catch, and then something would break open. I would find myself laughing through tears, or crying through laughter, until I was just feeling again. That's when I started to notice how possibility sneaks in through the cracks.

Remember, it arrives quietly—in the steady rhythm of your breath, in the pull toward sunlight, in the way you start saying yes to things that used to scare you. I began writing again—not because I had something polished to say, but because I couldn't *not* write. Words poured out like they had been waiting for my permission. I stopped censoring myself. I let my truth take up space.

There were nights I would sit on the floor of my bedroom with a candle lit, drawing tarot cards with the full moon, whispering prayers to the woman I was becoming. I didn't know what she looked like yet, only that she felt lighter. She laughed louder. She trusted herself. She moved through the world as she belonged in her body.

Slowly, the edges of my life began to shift. I started meeting people who reflected the version of me I was growing into, not the one I was trying to escape. Women who were unafraid of their own power. Lovers who saw me, not the mask. Teachers who didn't tell me what to do but reminded me that I already knew. It was as if the universe had been waiting for me to choose myself—and once I did, everything rearranged to meet me there.

Healing didn't make me softer in the way I expected. It made me honest. It made me bold. It made me hungry for a life that matched the truth of who I was becoming. For the first time in my adult life, I could see beyond survival. I could imagine a life not built on responsibility and obligation, but on desire. On trust. On pleasure.

And once I saw it—once that door cracked open—there was no going back.

The promise of liberation, when we begin to heal our childhood wounds, is not that the past disappears or that we suddenly become someone new. It's that we finally come home to the person we were always meant to be, who was waiting patiently beneath all the roles, the performing, the pretending.

When we tend to those early wounds, something inside us softens. The tight grip we've kept on control starts to loosen. The small, scared child who learned to earn love by being good, or quiet, or invisible finally exhales. We stop living as though we need to hold it all together—be the caretaker, the overachiever, the one who makes sure everyone is okay.

We begin to live as the woman we always needed. The one who can hold us with compassion instead of criticism.

Healing doesn't mean the memories fade. It means they stop running the show. The same stories that once triggered shame begin to reveal their wisdom. The body that once flinched begins to trust touch again. The heart that once closed begins to open, cautiously at first, then more fully, as we realize that we are no longer trapped in the story. We are the storyteller.

There's a moment, somewhere in the middle of the healing, when you catch your reflection and realize that the ache you've carried isn't gone, but it no longer defines you. It has softened into a tenderness that reminds you how deeply you've loved, how bravely you've endured, how sacred you were. Liberation isn't a single event. It's the quiet awakening that happens when we no longer abandon ourselves. When we stop apologizing for our needs.

When we stop chasing safety in others and start finding it inside our own bones, there's a steadiness that arrives with an internal peace that doesn't depend on circumstances. You begin to trust your own rhythm again. You wake up with softness instead of panic, and you begin to see the light at the end of the tunnel. You begin to hear the quiet pulse of life beneath the noise. You begin to understand that your power was never lost; it was simply waiting for your permission to return.

The world feels different because *you* are different. The little girl who once felt unseen now lives inside a woman who sees everything. The one who was silenced now speaks, even if her voice shakes at first. The one who was shamed now moves through life with an unshakable sense of belonging.

That is the promise of healing—not perfection, but presence. Not erasure, but reclamation. It's the sacred return to yourself—to the body, to the truth, to the pleasure, to the life that was always yours to live.

✦ Younger You Meditation

Find a quiet moment and let yourself settle.

Feel your feet on the ground, your body supported, your breath slowing.

The weight of your legs anchors you; the lift of your spine reminds you that you are both rooted and rising.

Let the shoulders soften. Let the heart open.

Imagine a door at the center of your chest.

Perhaps there is a key, or perhaps the door opens easily at your touch.

Step through.

You find yourself in a place that feels like home—maybe a field of light, maybe a warm, glowing room.

This is your heart space. The air is gentle here, the light familiar.

Somewhere in this space, she waits for you—the younger you.

Notice her.

How old she is, what she's wearing, the way she looks back at you.

There is a current that flows between you, a knowing that has never been broken.

Move toward her.

Reach out a hand.

When your fingers meet, something ancient and tender moves through you both—memory, love, recognition.

Look into her eyes and see the stories she still holds.

The ways she learned to stay small.

The ways she tried to keep everyone else safe.

The courage it took to survive.

Let her know she's not alone anymore.

Tell her the truth you now carry: *You are safe. You are loved. You are seen. I will never leave you again.*

Gather her into your arms if you wish.

Feel the warmth of her body against yours, the shared heartbeat, the breath that moves as one.

Let your love pour through you, surrounding you both in a soft, golden light.

When it feels complete, look into her eyes once more.

Tell her she can rest now.

You will carry her forward.

As she walks back into the light, feel her peace settle into your own body.

You have brought her home.

Return your awareness to the present.

Feel your feet, your breath, the rhythm of your heart.

There is no separation now—only wholeness, only love.

And if tears rise, let them.

They are the water that softens the soil for new life to grow.

You have met yourself.

And you are home.

CHAPTER TWO

Wounded Mothers, Healing Daughters

The desire to become a mother came on suddenly, like something ancient waking inside me.

Living in New York, I had never pictured myself with children. My days were full of auditions, late nights, and big dreams. But when I moved to the Midwest, life slowed down. The rhythm of domesticity left space for something deep to rise. I was nearing thirty, and friends around us were having babies. My husband wanted to wait, since he was focused on his career and on finding a sense of readiness that I wasn't sure existed.

Then he had a cardiac arrest the day after our first-year anniversary. He was just thirty-two and the cause was a mystery. And it changed our lives forever.

When it became clear that he would survive, my longing to have a child went from someday to *now*.

We conceived easily, and I loved being pregnant. After the first few months of nausea, I felt more at home in my body than I ever had before. I had spent years trying to control or perfect my body, but pregnancy returned me to its wisdom. I felt embodied, connected, and feminine in a way that felt like remembering.

I had been teaching yoga for years, including prenatal classes, and this felt like an extension of that work. I studied hypnobirthing, read about natural labor, practiced my breathing and toning, and envisioned myself giving birth in water, surrounded by calm strength. I imagined the experience as a portal, a passage between worlds that would return me to myself.

Labor began gently and then grew long and hard. My daughter was face up, which caused intense back pain and slowed the process. Fifteen hours in, I was vomiting, exhausted, and ready to give up. My midwife warned that we might need to go to the hospital if things didn't shift soon.

My doula looked at me, her eyes steady, and said, "It's all you now, Mama. You can do this."

And I did.

An hour later, after guttural sounds and primal effort, she slid from my body, eight pounds of perfection.

No book or class could have prepared me for the reality of birth. It was a portal of pain and surrender, an initiation that pushed me to the edge of what I thought I could survive. I remember looking at myself in the mirror between contractions, sticky notes with affirmations taped all around, and thinking, *I might die, but I have to keep going.* And then, somehow, I did.

Birth is the first initiation into motherhood. It is the moment the maiden becomes the mother, a crossing from innocence into power. Every woman I have worked with has faced that moment—whether medicated or not—the moment she meets her own strength. Birth prepares us for the long initiation that follows—the daily surrender of motherhood.

My memories of those early years exist in a blur. The physical demands of motherhood were relentless. Between breastfeeding and recovery from birth, my body didn't feel like my own, but it was the psychological weight that surprised me most. The nights I spent rocking a colicky baby in the dark felt unreal: pacing the room, whispering prayers I did not know if I believed in, wondering if it would ever end.

I loved my children deeply. And at the same time, I felt overwhelmed by their constant needs, how my body and attention were no longer my own. Sitting in that rocking chair, listening to a baby cry against my chest, I would feel a quiet ache for something more. Often it took the shape of ambition. I wanted more success, more money, imagining that if I could just get ahead enough, I could buy back time, ease, presence. If I could solve the logistics, everything else would fall into place.

But in those moments, what I felt most clearly was a sense of being behind and stuck at the same time. Behind some invisible timeline of who I thought I should have been by then, and stuck inside a life that required me to be needed around the clock. I didn't have language for it then, but I can see now how familiar that feeling was. It was the beginning of a pattern I knew well. The quiet negotiation where my longing waited patiently while I told myself this was how it was supposed to be.

THE PRICE OF SILENCE

My mother was at my first birth. She caught my daughter as she came earthside, her hands the bridge between generations. There is so much goodness my mother passed to me: her tenderness, her romantic heart, her belief in magic and beauty. She wrote handwritten cards for every occasion, donated to charities when she could barely afford her own bills, and filled the house with music and books.

There are also wounds I chose not to pass on.

My mother was charismatic and loving, but she carried deep fear. She sought love from men who couldn't give it and hid her anger beneath grief and silence. She withdrew from conflict instead of standing in it. It took me years to see that her avoidance of anger had shaped me, too. I reached my forties before realizing that I had no real relationship with anger at all.

Where would I have learned it? My mother didn't know how to hold her own emotions, let alone mine.

As a child, I learned that silence was how women survived. When my stepfather's affairs finally became unbearable, and she locked him out of our apartment, our life fractured in an instant. Overnight, he was erased from our lives; I didn't see him again for years. There were no conversations that helped me make sense of what had happened, no shared language for the devastation that had torn through our home. Only silence.

I watched my mother fall apart under the weight of betrayal and grief, and at the same time, I watched her contain it. She did not rage. She did not speak the unspeakable. She carried the pain inward, as if endurance itself were a form of strength, as if not speaking of what had happened were a badge of honor. Survival, in our house, meant holding it together no matter the cost.

I absorbed her heartbreak and her strategy. I learned that love meant silence, that there was dignity in not needing, that pain was something you swallowed and lived with, ideally without anyone else getting access to your vulnerability. I learned that when your life broke apart, you did not ask anyone to help you hold the pieces. You carried them alone.

I am slowly beginning to understand how deeply that lesson shaped me. How easily I learned to internalize grief, to mute anger, and to disappear inside relationships rather than risk conflict or abandonment. My mother did what she knew how to do, and I learned how to master my emotions from her.

Even now, as we navigate a painful rupture in our relationship, I see the same pattern alive in her. She carries the pain of what she endured as something she did *for us*, her children. She holds her suffering as proof of love, as though the depth of what she survived is the measure of her devotion. I can feel how true that is for her—and how heavy it is for me to hold.

As Carl Jung said, "The greatest burden a child must bear is the unlived life of the parents."

When a mother's longing is swallowed instead of spoken, when grief is endured rather than expressed, it doesn't disappear. It lives on in the atmosphere of the relationship, shaping what can be said, what's allowed, and what must remain silent. My mother's endurance was an act of love but also a transmission of pain. She was in pure survival mode, providing us with safety by carrying the unbearable in silence. And in doing so, she taught me that love meant suffering quietly, that devotion required self-erasure. It is so subtle it's almost imperceptible, because it's not taught in language but in observation. This is the inheritance I am working to interrupt—not by rejecting her, but by choosing a different truth, by making room for grief and loss with as much compassion as I can. I want to create a life where truth is spoken, grief is shared, and desire is not something we apologize for.

HEALING THE WOUND

Healing the mother wound means recognizing this inheritance—not with blame, but with accountability and compassion. Our mothers did the best they could with the tools they had. At some point in this work, we have to free ourselves of their judgement, of their limitations, and do our own work to be free.

It is not only our daughters who need this healing. We are raising sons who deserve to integrate the full range of their emotions without fear or shame. I remember a moment during a group workshop when a young man was struggling to express his anger. He trembled, terrified of his own power. His mother had muted his anger, punished him for it, and he had buried it at a high cost.

I thought of my own son then: his big feelings, his frustration, the way he used to rage and roar when he was little. I used to beg him to calm down, to be reasonable, but his brain wasn't ready for reason. But I didn't know how to meet him in that storm.

Now we have a foam bat in the living room. Anyone in the house can use it to hit the couch when they need to release something that feels too big to contain. When my son gets angry, he can grab the bat, smash the couch, and yell. I ask for a warning first, but otherwise I just stand by and hold space for him. I don't flinch. I don't rush to quiet him. I wait until the storm passes.

Sometimes, after the shouting, he ends up in tears. Frustration melts into grief. I sit with him while he cries, knowing I can't fix everything, but I can hold myself steady through it. I can show him that anger and tenderness can exist in the same breath.

I'm always a mom. I believe being a mother is one of the most fundamental and spiritual experiences available to a woman, but every woman doesn't need to have their own child to experience the benefits of it. Loving the children in our lives can be a portal to a new level of healing. For mothers, the first part of pregnancy is filled with anticipation and fear, both of what is happening but also the initiation into a life as the true center of someone's universe. Our sisters and priestesses hold us through this transformation.

The early years are overwhelming and isolating; mothers juggle so much at once: breastfeeding, nap schedules, feedings, diaper changes, fevers, and the ever-changing demands as they grow from infants to toddlers. As my own children approach their teen years, I look back with awe at how traumatic it was to be thrust into parenting, while still trying to work and find time for the most basic self-care, without family support and a partner who worked long hours.

We've set mothers up to fail. We're increasingly isolated, asked to mother in a vacuum rather than in a community, without the sisters, aunts, and women who, before modernization, would have formed the village that helped carry the work of care.

From the moment my children came into this world, a part of my awareness reorganized itself around them. I move through my life with a constant sense of orientation, like a satellite that never fully loses its signal. It is a quiet, persistent knowing of where they are in relation to me, a background awareness that never turns off.

That tether matters. It informs how I move through the world and the choices I am willing to make. I am no longer deciding only for myself. I am responsible for another human life, and my actions ripple outward in ways they did not before. Risk feels different. What might feel like a clean leap for someone without children carries a different gravity when you know your choices will shape the emotional landscape your children grow up in.

And desire? Well, mothers aren't allowed to feel that, are they?

Motherhood changed me in ways I could never have prepared for. It asked me to be both mirror and nurturer, to hold my children close while allowing them their own reflection. Every day, I face the choice between repeating what I learned and creating something new.

In many ways, parenting IS about putting someone else's needs ahead of your own. Especially when children are young, their survival, safety, and regulation depend on us. We can't always place our own desires first, nor should we. The first few years require the depths of us, leaving our freedoms to orbit the world of a child. It's a huge shift in identity, and many of us grieve our former lives when we are thrust into the full-time care of an infant.

Maybe if we acknowledged that grieving more honestly, we could avoid the trap of undue self-sacrifice, which becomes damaging when we silence our desires and postpone them indefinitely. When we repeatedly swallow our desires, something essential begins to wither. Through healing and the work of self-discovery, the aim is not to abandon responsibility, but to restore balance. We learn how to meet our children's needs without disappearing from our own lives and model care that includes, rather than excludes, us.

This is how the cycle shifts. Not through perfection or rigid ideology, but through conscious choice. Through showing our children that love does not require self-abandonment, and that devotion can coexist with truth, desire, and presence.

As someone re-patterning this cycle in their mid-forties, it can feel messy and clunky. But I trust myself now and I trust that even when I falter or fumble, I'll find my way back.

My daughter is fifteen now. One evening as we drove home from a softball game, she opened up about a boy she had been talking to for a few weeks. He was more serious than she was, and she could feel herself losing interest.

We were winding through the San Gabriel Mountains, the road opening out into a vast and beautiful landscape when she said, almost to herself, "You know, the more I try not to hurt him, the more I hurt myself."

She was absolutely right. Something in me cracked open, and I could have cried right then and there. But I played it cool and reached for her hand. As a smile nudged at my cheeks I said, "You're a wise young woman."

Later that night as I tucked her into bed, I reminded her how wise I thought she was. It had taken me—and many women—years to learn that simple, devastating truth. Protecting someone else's feelings at the cost of your own doesn't make you kind. It makes you disappear. She listened, nodded, and rolled onto her side, already at ease with something that had taken me decades to name.

That moment felt like evidence that something had shifted. Without needing to do everything right or falling back on old patterns, the cycle loosened its grip. She was listening to her body. She trusted her knowing. She understood, instinctively, that self-abandonment was not love.

I mother differently than I was mothered. I will never be perfect, but my commitment to understanding what gets passed down edges me closer to the mother I want to be and the mother I wish I had. For years I have traced patterns I inherited, asking where they came from, and even more importantly, whether they still belong. My mother's love was generous but weighted by duty and longing. Through healing, I've learned that love does not have to mean self-sacrifice. It can mean honesty, presence, and repair. When I lose my patience, I apologize. When my children cry, I don't rush to stop them. I let them see my humanness because I want them to know that love can hold imperfection.

We are the bridge between what was and what can be. Every time we pause before reacting, every time we soften instead of seeking control, every time we choose awareness over repetition, we shift our lineage.

This is the work of generational healing—to mother not only our children, but ourselves. And that is where the mother wound begins to reveal itself.

Not as an accusation.

But as an invitation.

WHAT IS THE MOTHER WOUND?

The mother wound is the ache beneath the ache; the quiet, inherited grief of every daughter who learned love through sacrifice or self-betrayal. It's the place where we swallowed our words to stay good, where we dimmed our light to stay loved, many times because we watched our mothers do the same. It lives in the body as vigilance and over-care, in the way we mother everyone but ourselves. The mother wound teaches us to earn worth through doing, to find safety in being needed, and to mistrust the stillness where our own needs whisper back. It's the stain of patriarchy, of women surviving a world where they were told their needs came last, generations of women whose lives depended on being silent and obedient. Those imprints are passed down, and they may fade over generations, with more liberties, but unless we go in and heal the wounds that sit below the surface, we find new ways to pass them on.

When I work with women, the mother wound resurfaces, coming up for air in our psyches because it exists inside us, not around us. Women come to me carrying stories as broad as abandonment to love being rescinded as they reach maturity, suddenly a threat and a mirror to their families. It's clear that these wounds are not individual failures, but the result of a system that consistently asks too much and offers too little.

My mother carried wounds of her own; I understood that only in hindsight. What I knew as a child was the shape of what she couldn't give me, and the outline of what she had survived. She survived war and immigrated to Canada with my grandparents. The courage, the resolve, the willingness to board a ship that would carry her across an ocean into an unknown life. That act offers me the faintest glimpse into my grandmother's inner world. She was formidable. Unbreakable in the ways women often had to be.

My grandmother was a woman who could fill a kitchen with warmth. She was a wonderful cook and had a sharp sense of humor, but her tongue could be biting, especially toward her daughters. Praise was inconsistent, criticism quick, and affection often laced with judgment. Love was present, but so was the sense that they were always being measured.

My grandfather was stern and loving, but from a distance. Everyone around him seemed acutely attuned to any rise in anger and my mother was fiercely protective of me in those moments. Safety meant vigilance. It meant reading the room, staying quiet, and learning how to prevent an explosion before it happened. I learned that from her body before I learned it from any words.

Like all of us, she was determined to mother differently, to live differently.

She had dreams she was never allowed to follow; I knew that much, but many details of her life remain shrouded by her unwillingness to revisit them.

In a moment of openness, she told me that on her wedding night she knew she had made a mistake. She stayed anyway. She had a child—my half-brother—worked as a nurse, and made the best of what she had.

They finally divorced, sharing custody of my brother when I was conceived.

While working as a nurse, she met my father at the hospital. What followed between them exists in fragments, details I would only come to understand much later in my life. What mattered was simple. They had an affair; she got pregnant with me. He didn't stay.

I know very little because she has not told me much of that time. There are shards of truth: her closeness to her female friends, the spark of the feminist movement, her advocacy for women's autonomy during birth.

It all sounded like a rare fire in her that burned beneath so much suppression.

I can only imagine how difficult those years must have been. A single working mother, the logistics of care, and the ideological courage it took to stand inside a new wave of feminism.

Eventually, her parents offered to help, but the support came with conditions. She had to move back to Canada, leave the life she had begun, and also be far away from her son.

When I was three, she made that sacrifice.

That detail stayed with me—that generosity was transactional. It required a trade. Belonging came with terms. The promise of safety came with shrinking her dreams. It demanded that she fold herself into something smaller, safer, more acceptable.

It was another quiet lesson in the inheritance of the mother wound: Care is often conditional, and a woman's needs are negotiable.

This is where the reclamation begins.

To turn toward the mother wound is to touch the lineage of women who forgot their own softness, or were forced to surrender it, and to decide it ends with you. It's a holy unraveling—*the moment you stop trying to be the daughter she needed you to be and start becoming the woman you were born to be.* Healing the mother wound isn't about blaming her; it's about freeing both of you. It's the slow, sacred act of mothering yourself back into wholeness— nourishing the places she couldn't reach, and remembering that you are, and always have been, your own source of love.

Mothering is complex and meant to be done in community. Most of us are thrown into full-time, twenty-four-hour care with little support. We set out to be 'good mothers', to give our kids what we didn't have, to set right the wrongs of the past with our good intentions, and many of us achieve it to some degree. Women of our generation have more choices about birth, post-partum care, and at varying degrees a division of labor and work choices with their partner. We are living out the dreams of our grandmothers, for whom these choices were not possible. And still the insidious weight of patriarchy carries through our DNA into the generations to come, and unless we actively seek a more conscious existence, and do the difficult and messy 'work' of healing, we pass on more than just eye color and genetics to our children; we pass on the beliefs, fears, and limitations of our parents, too.

My clients come to me with dreams of leaving their jobs, their marriages, blowing it all up to follow an indescribable, and sometimes irrational desire. Their biggest weight? The opinion and approval of their mothers. And many of these mothers did not themselves have the chance, the means, the courage, the opportunity to live a different kind of life. Some have cultural norms and rules to follow, and some didn't have the support or encouragement of other women, and so they stayed, living a life they had outgrown but nowhere to go.

I bow with gratitude to the women who've been by my side through this season. The access to resources and support we have is better than it's ever been, yet many of us find ourselves isolated, afraid, and trying not to listen to the unsolicited advice of a mother who is well-meaning but telling us not to blow anything up, because of her fears about what happened to women who did.

My mother believed I had everything I could ever want, and when my life started to fracture, she made it known that I should be prioritizing my family. What I wanted was her support, her faith in me. What I got was her fear.

How many well-meaning and well-intentioned people in your life will tell you to play it safe, to keep your blessings counted and not rock the boat? Plenty.

When you blow up your life, you will lose people.

You will also find the courageous and outspoken people who see through that fear, who have lived and risked it all for a life that feels *authentic* and *true* to their soul. And they will stand by you; they will talk to you on the late nights when you want to cry and wonder what the F you've done. Not everyone, and dare to say especially not our mothers, can see past their own fears and projections, to hold their truth to the light. It exposes the cracks in their own façade; it requires them to look in the mirror and ask, "Am I living in my authentic aliveness?" And when that truth is too uncomfortable, they will share that fear and make it your problem.

Sometimes you have to limit your proximity to these people. Even if it's your mother.

A Meditation on Mothering

Take a moment and bring your own mother to mind. Take some deep breaths into your belly and feel your womb. What's your earliest memory of being mothered? Do you remember being a baby, held in your mother's arms? Can you feel the safety and love of being mothered?

If you feel your body tense or tighten, take another deep breath and ask, what does this tension want me to know?

Imagine yourself as an egg inside your mother when she was in your grandmother's womb. Can you remember your grandmother? What's your memory of her? Was she kind and caring, loving and gentle? Strict or withdrawn? Sometimes the clues of our mothers are found in the grandmothers.

A WIFE. A MOTHER. A DAUGHTER. A FRIEND.

My husband and I met in New York, courting each other through a snowy January. What started as a dalliance evolved into more, and eventually, we were traveling back and forth from Chicago to New York to spend weekends together. We fell fast and hard for each other, and despite circumstances that kept us apart, we were determined to make it work.

In a kind of preemptive self-protection, I found myself a therapist right away—a quiet promise to the part of me that didn't want to repeat my mother's mistakes. I thought therapy could save me from falling into her patterns of self-abandonment, as if awareness alone could rewrite my instincts. It helped, in small ways, but I can see now that I was already rewriting my dreams to fit into a life that wasn't fully mine.

When the long-distance strain reached its limit, I moved. I told myself Chicago was a stepping stone, a place to land before Los Angeles. But we had unspoken, mismatched assumptions about what was temporary and what was forever. I wanted a partner. Stability. Date nights and movies on the couch. Someone to wake up beside.

So, I made a trade. Loneliness for the promise that something would fill it—only to discover a different kind of loneliness waiting for me.

The winter that followed was brutal. There were snowdrifts taller than me, days that dissolved into reruns, yoga classes where I pondered if I had made the right choice, leaving behind the vibrance and independence of my old life. I told myself it wasn't just for him, that I was tired of the grind of New York, the nomadic quality of subletting life and never settling into my own space for four years. There was a kind of grief in the stillness—for the woman I'd been in New York, for the ambition I'd folded away like a costume that no longer fit.

But I was good at starting over. Reinvention was my native language.

Eventually, life opened again. Acting classes. Friends. A rhythm that felt like progress.

By the time we moved into a one-bedroom, life had found its rhythm. I was teaching yoga, auditioning, and bartending to fill the gaps. He was managing a restaurant an hour away. We met in the middle most nights, both exhausted but committed to building something together.

He proposed one evening in our living room in a casual, al-most offhand way. It was not the sweeping moment I'd imagined. I'd been pressing for forward motion, needing to feel like all I'd given up had led somewhere. It wasn't romantic, but it was something to hold onto. I said yes and got to work planning a wedding. I was twenty-eight when we married. We'd been together for two years when he asked me, and by then I was already impatient—craving the next step, the confirmation that my life was on track. There was a quiet urgency beneath it, a belief that time was slipping through my fingers. I needed to know if this man—the one I'd crossed the country for—was going to be my forever.

Looking back, I see it clearly: I was afraid of the void. Afraid of stillness, of not knowing. If I'd trusted that pause, I might have saved myself a great deal of pain. Our first home together was a one-bedroom apartment—oddly shaped, crooked corners, not a single square room—but it felt luxurious after his tiny 600-square-foot studio where I'd spent the first six months perched between a bed, a table, and a tiny kitchen. Privacy meant sitting in the bathroom to make a phone call. Still, it didn't matter. We were in love, or at least inside that intoxicating beginning where the world feels small enough to hold in your hands.

I had wanted a beach wedding in Mexico, barefoot in the sand, but my father wouldn't travel, and it mattered to me that he would be there. We chose a venue just outside Chicago, where a friend had recently married. I wore a dress bought by my father in Ireland, an important piece of family that I wanted so much to create. We hired a shaman to officiate, and his one condition was counseling—"marriage prep," he called it. Family, money, and sex—the three things that undo most couples.

We dove in. His family: large, orderly, Midwestern; mine: fractured and frayed. His extended family gathered regularly, mine hadn't spoken to one another in years. My mother, twice divorced and estranged from her siblings, was always at war with her family.

The day of the wedding was beautiful and full of chances to pivot with grace. Just as I was about to walk down the aisle, the sky split open, and rain poured down. Guests scattered, dresses soaked, music halted. I stood inside, devastated, feeling like even the weather was testing my resolve. But then the storm passed. We started again. The ceremony began with us circling each other, placing garlands around each other's necks—an infinity loop, a promise without end.

And then, thunder. Rain again, wild and unrelenting. We ran for shelter, our guests crowding into a small wooden structure, laughter echoing off the walls. There, drenched and breathless, surrounded by everyone we loved, we exchanged our vows. It was imperfect and raw and, in its own way, magical.

Our honeymoon was a dream—a private island in the Grenadines, a trip our guests had paid for instead of pots and pans. We promised we'd return someday, with children in tow.

And then, the morning after our first-year anniversary, he had the cardiac arrest. He was on the treadmill at the gym. His heart stopped beating, an electrical misfire, random and without warning. Not illness or a sign, just fate. He was rushed to the ER. He spent five days in the ICU. It was an inflection moment.

The night before, we had gone to dinner and smoked a joint afterward in our apartment. He wanted to make love when we got home. I didn't. I laid in bed awake that night wondering if I had made a mistake. He was working long hours, I was alone in a city I didn't love, with a mortgage, my career not moving forward, nothing seemed to be working.

Had I made a mistake?

The next morning as I got coffee, the phone rang and I heard a woman's voice telling me that my husband was in a coma and that I should find a ride to the hospital. She wanted to call his family, telling me that I should prepare for the worst.

In a moment, the world seemed to shift off its axis. I spent the next week in crisis, facing the possibility that I would be a widow. I begged God, the Universe, to keep him here. I promised I would be a better wife and partner. I walked around the hospital, coordinating family in the waiting room, listening to the doctors giving me updates. I moved through crisis mode, managing the moment-to-moment decisions that could keep him alive. Suddenly, all my doubts felt trivial. I hadn't wanted him to die, and I found myself bargaining with the universe to go back to the way things were.

Miraculously, he survived, and with only a few complications. He didn't have the brain or heart damage typical of an out-of-hospital cardiac arrest. We were told that only 2% of those heart attacks survive.

He woke up and his first words were "I have to get to work." He had no memory of the accident or the week in a coma, and his last memory and first instinct was to go to work.

Filled with relief, I pushed aside the doubt I'd felt the night of our anniversary and spent months nursing him back to health after surgery and complications.

Survivors of near-death experiences often radically change their lives, leave relationships, in other words they have a "wake up call."

But my husband wanted to go back to normal, wanted the attention of the accident to quiet down. We had very different experiences of the week he almost died. I spent a lot of time thinking about what might change, how he could work less, how we could find our way back to love that had brought us together in the first place.

What about the spouse of the survivor?

We moved so fast from crisis to after care, relief pouring in from all corners of the world, that surely, I wasn't leaving now. I wonder what a circle of sisters might have asked in a ceremony, or what questions a therapist might have led me to if I'd had the support of one.

Instead of mining that doubt for insight, I doubled down and stayed. I dove into being the wife and partner I promised I'd be. A year later we had our daughter. Three years later, our son. We sold our condo, moved to a duplex closer to the city, juggling pregnancy, toddlers, and debt. Life had sped so fast that it blurred. I remember very little beyond exhaustion—feeding, working, surviving.

Only later would I learn that during those same years, he was having an affair. The revelation reframed everything: the quiet nights on the deck, the TV flickering in the basement, the laughter of our children upstairs. I heard the echo of two parallel lives unfolding—mine filled with diapers, dishes, and deadlines; his with secrets and escape.

How did we drift so far from the couple standing in the rain, vowing to be each other's safe place? Maybe it was inevitable—the impossible expectation that two people could be each other's entire village. We were both so tired. Passing the baton each night: Your turn, my turn, goodnight.

"Try not to fall asleep, love."

"You're snoring, dear."

"Oh, never mind."

We rolled over and went to sleep, not realizing how far apart we already were.

IT'S TIME TO WAKE UP

What is a wake-up call, really?

It's the moment life shakes us from our patterns, from comfort or monotony, and invites us to pay attention. Sometimes it's a health scare, a crisis, a move, or the sudden ending of something we thought would last forever. For many, the Covid-19 pandemic created that moment. The noise stopped long enough for us to hear what we'd been running from.

My first wake-up call came as a move.

It was the moment I finally claimed my desire—no matter the cost. I was willing to disturb the stability of my family, to risk being misunderstood, to choose something that only made sense to me.

COVID prompted our first fateful, but temporary, move to Florida. In the process, it shook up our routine. When the world told us to stay in one place, we mobilized, and it freed something inside me. My kids were fine. I was thriving. Something had shifted. I dreaded going back to the cold, grey winters of Chicago, but mostly it was the thought of going back to a life that felt smaller than my longing. Beneath the fear, a knowing began to rise— quiet, but unshakable. It was time.

We spend a lot of time in our minds, weighing logic and safety, making choices that look good on paper but cost us our aliveness. I recognize the privilege it took to move my family, but I also know I could have done it years earlier with fewer resources—if I'd had more courage.

If I had trusted my longing.

On one hand I thought of myself as wildly brave, moving to NYC and leaving my life behind, but now, with kids and this life, I also felt stuck.

What I longed for, for nearly my entire marriage, was to move to California, but it was never the right time. My husband never had the right job and beneath that practical resistance was an unspoken refusal to shift our life around for the unknown, for a dream. What did I want there? Was it worth uprooting our lives for an intangible longing I couldn't explain?

Eventually, I stopped bringing it up. I convinced myself to be grateful for what I had: healthy children, a good man, a beautiful home. I made my choice. I told myself stability was enough.

But what parts of you suffer when your desire lies silent for too long?

Not all wake-up calls are dramatic, but most come with a reckoning. Sooner or later, something cracks open—a loss, a betrayal, a crisis—that forces us to ask, *What do I really want?*

That wanting is the seed of desire, our inner compass, guiding us to a life that is uniquely ours, but most of us have been taught to ignore it. We get swept into the current of the life we've built, and with each passing year, the changing course feels less possible.

I was called to California by an inexplicable pull that defied logic. I had moved to Chicago for love, the promise of stability, partnership, and belonging—to be chosen. In my twenties, it was what seemed important above all else: my dreams, my desires, my autonomy.

But my dream of California couldn't help but resurface at every turn. It was my soul's siren calling.

Something about California—Los Angeles specifically—represented a dream that refused to die. During our divorce, my husband finally said what I'd always felt but never admitted: *"The only reason we moved was because you wanted to. I never did."*

His words pierced through the illusion I'd been holding together. He never wanted to move. It wasn't our shared dream—it was mine and mine alone. The truth stung but also liberated me. In a single moment, I realized how long I had been betraying myself for harmony, for safety, for love. We don't abandon our dreams all at once. It happens quietly, little by little, until one day we can't remember the last time we said yes to ourselves.

Women tell me: *"I've just lowered my expectations,"* or *"I've learned to be grateful for what I have."* But underneath those words, I hear the echo of self-abandonment. The way we shrink to fit inside a life that no longer fits.

We are raised to believe marriage and motherhood will fulfill us completely, only to discover how easily those same roles can smother our individuality and desire.

Self-abandonment is learned early. Most girls are taught they are too dramatic, too loud, too much from the time they are little. They learn to please, to perform, to keep the peace. We shrink to survive.

For two decades, I suppressed my desires to fit inside the life I had built. I told myself I couldn't ask my husband or children to sacrifice for me. I put myself last, and all that did was build quiet resentment. Eventually, that resentment became another wake-up call. The process of choosing myself was not graceful. It was messy, painful, and filled with grief. But it was the only way. It was the moment I began the long journey back to my own truth.

Healing changed me. Not only in the obvious ways, but in how I inhabit my body and move through the world. My therapist tells me my energy is different now, softer and more grounded. I still feel like me, but lighter. More spacious. I fill up the room of my body.

Through healing, my capacity for grief has also grown. I am no longer afraid of being alone.

I am finally willing to advocate for my desire because I know that taking up space is not selfish. It's sacred. This is the awakening I see in so many women: the moment we realize that our longing isn't a flaw to be managed but a compass pointing us home. When we stop apologizing for wanting more pleasure, more rest, more truth, life reorganizes around that truth. Desire becomes a form of devotion. It's how the feminine re-enters the body after years of exile. The ache is a holy summons, inviting us to remember what we were made for.

Taking up space is honoring the divine design of your being. It says, *I belong here. My voice, my body, my rhythm are part of the sacred order of things.* The work of reclamation is not about becoming louder or harder; it's about becoming truer. When we root into that truth, our presence becomes medicine for our children, our partners, our communities. A woman in her fullness doesn't steal oxygen from the room. She breathes life into it.

This work, this dedication to the unwinding of family codes, the soft dismantling of the patterns that kept us small, is nothing short of revolutionary. To stand in sovereignty as a woman is to defy generations of conditioning that taught us to shrink, to serve, and to stay quiet. It asks us to meet discomfort, to lose versions of ourselves that keep others comfortable, and to risk being misunderstood.

This is what it means to want more. Not in greed, but in grace. To claim desire as sacred, to honor grief as teacher, and to live as the embodied proof that freedom is worth the cost.

THE SACRIFICES OF MOTHERHOOD

Some nights, after the house settles and her bedroom light clicks off, I pause in the hallway outside her door. I don't linger the way I did when she was small (she'd roll her eyes if she caught me), but I still feel that same tug in my chest. Through the thin crack of light, I can see her sprawled across her bed, headphones on, lost in her own world. The same girl who once reached for my hand at every crossing now barely tolerates my reminders. Her hair, once a tangle of light beneath my palm, now falls over her face as she scrolls or journals or dreams about a life that's already pulling her forward.

In these moments, I feel the ache of both love and lineage again—not as nostalgia now, but as a reckoning. The unbearable tenderness of watching her become a woman while knowing how much the world will ask her to forget herself. The quiet terror that no matter how consciously I've parented, I might still pass along the very codes I've spent a lifetime trying to rewrite.

There's a sacred distance growing between us. The natural one that forms when a daughter begins to claim her autonomy, her edge, her power. And while every instinct in me wants to hold on, the wiser part knows my work is to let go. To trust that the ground I've spent years tilling—of truth-telling, of self-trust, of permission to desire—will root somewhere deep inside her.

Motherhood asks everything of us. Not always in dramatic gestures, but in the quietest ways imaginable. It's the invisible labor of emotional management, the constant response to requests, the anticipation of needs, the ones that don't rest until everyone is tucked away in bed. It's in the way we bite our tongue when we want to scream, how we smile through exhaustion, how we hold space for everyone's storms while quietly drowning in our own.

For those of us parenting *consciously*, forging new patterns, breaking feminine silence, and refusing self-abandonment and duty as the highest form of love, this sacrifice takes on another layer. We are raising our children while reparenting ourselves. We are learning to offer what we never received, to stay present where our own mothers disappeared, to soften in the places where we were hardened by necessity.

This is not the kind of presence that earns praise or gold stars. It's the one that happens internally and quietly, in the pause before reacting, in the choice to breathe instead of lash out, in the apology when we yell and wish we hadn't. It's in the sleepless nights staring at the ceiling, wondering if we are doing it *right*, wondering if love is enough to heal what lineage has left behind.

Our mothers did what they knew. Their mothers before them did the same. They survived within systems that demanded endurance over expression, and compliance over authenticity. So much of what we carry isn't personal—it's ancestral. The mother wound is not one woman's failure, but the echo of centuries of suppression and self-sacrifice.

When we choose differently, the world reorders. When we choose to rest, to tell the truth, to prioritize pleasure, solitude, or creative expression, something radical happens. We interrupt the inheritance. We show our children that love can coexist with boundaries. Care can include the self. A woman's radiance is not something to fear, but something to be revered. That's what motherhood and healing the mother wound has given me: the knowing that presence is more powerful than perfection. That my wholeness is the medicine.

I choose what I give, and I give it fully, with an open heart and a grounded root. I am writing a new code where motherhood is not martyrdom, but a reclamation of lineage, love, and life itself.

THE GOOD MOTHER

For years, I believed that being a good mother meant self-sacrifice. That the measure of my worth was how much of myself I could give away. I was proud of my ability to multitask, to anticipate everyone's needs, manage other people's moods, and hold the harmony of our home as my unspoken responsibility.

But somewhere in my devotion to others, I lost the thread that led to myself.

Good mothers are meant to hold it all, but no one tells you what to do when your hands are already full, and your soul is starving. In my unraveling, I realized I didn't need to stop mothering; I needed to learn how to mother differently. I needed to bring myself into the equation to care for the woman who was doing the caring.

That's what self-mothering became for me: the radical act of tending to the woman inside the mother, the one who still dreams, aches, and wants.

California was my big leap. The dream that had waited patiently for me to remember it. Moving broke open parts of me that had been frozen in time. It was both terrifying and exhilarating, a full body yes that arrived after years of silencing that very instinct.

I spent a long time talking myself out of it: the timing, the money, the logistics, the children. Every excuse was fear in disguise. When I finally made the leap, I understood what people meant by "divine timing." I don't regret waiting, but sometimes I wonder who I might have become if I had trusted myself sooner.

The pandemic gave many of us that same window of reckoning. It stripped away distractions and forced us to see our lives for what they were. The patterns. The comforts. The quiet compromises we'd built entire identities around. It interrupted the momentum of "business as usual" and left us face to face with truth.

Whether your dream is to move across the country, change careers, leave a marriage, or finally feel fully alive in your body, the truth is the same. No one can blow up your life for you. Only you can choose to believe that your desire is reason enough.

Desire, when it's pure, doesn't need to be justified.

But when we have others who rely on us, that choice becomes layered. We begin negotiating between our own needs and the needs of those we love. The work is to learn to hold both—to see our desires not as threats to the whole, but as vital parts of the ecosystem that sustains it.

Blowing up my life was reclamation. It was the moment I realized I could want something, survive the rupture it caused, and live in the transformation that followed.

If you're reading this thinking, *I can't*— move, leave, change, begin again—you're right. Our thinking creates our reality. You'll have to change your thinking, but even more than that, you'll have to embody the version of you that can. It's not easy work mining the stories that are keeping you from your greatness, confronting them, but it's brave.

You are brave.

As you bring new narratives into your mind, they must also come into your body. Affirmations only got me so far, but when I attuned to my body as the oracle, as the keeper of wisdom, I learned how to trust her. Things shifted rapidly. I felt my way to a new truth.

If fear wasn't your guide, if you trusted life to rise to meet you, what would you ask for? Believe in? What do you desire that you are afraid you don't deserve? What would you create for yourself if *I can't* was followed by *not believe in myself*?

DEVOTION OVER DISCIPLINE

For most of my life, I thought discipline was the one thing that could save me. It kept me in control, the chaos at bay, and made sure I was always striving: to achieve, to be good, to prove my worth. It was how I survived, which means it wasn't how I healed.

When everything began to fall apart—my marriage, my identity, the version of myself that could no longer perform—I reached for what I knew: structure, routine, productivity. None of it worked. My body refused to be managed.

Discipline couldn't hold me anymore. Something new was emerging.

Devotion was poking its tendrils from the soil.

Devotion isn't about perfection or punishment; it's about presence. It's about showing up for yourself every day, even when you're tired, scared, or unsure. In the early days, my devotion looked like sitting in meditation, even when my mind raced. It looked like journaling every morning, writing prayers and questions to a God I wasn't even sure I believed in anymore. It looked like long walks and salt baths, tears and cacao, breathwork and stillness. Eventually, devotion became pleasure.

Pleasure was the softest kind of prayer. The kind that reminded me my body was holy and my joy was allowed. Devotion over discipline became my mantra. My way of building a life not from control, but from care.

Discipline asks: *How can I improve myself?* Devotion asks: *How can I love myself more deeply?*

It's a subtle shift, but it changes everything. Now, when I wake up each morning, I don't force myself into a routine. I listen. Most days devotion is meditation.

It's ten minutes where I practice mindfulness and stretch time through silent observation. Some days it's movement, music, or writing. Most of the time, it's all of them, the length of each activity dependent, but not deterred, by the demands of the day.

Other times, it's simply placing a hand on my heart and whispering, *Here I am. Sometimes it's all I have, but I still choose to give it to myself.*

This practice became the bridge between the woman I was and the woman I'm becoming: the mother, the lover, the Priestess, the human. Because healing, at its core, is a daily devotion to your own becoming.

Motherhood didn't become easier when I chose devotion, but it became honest. I stopped trying to mother from obligation or fear and began mothering from presence. Devotion didn't ask me to be perfect; it asked me to be here.

Which is a relief, because some days "being here" looks like forgetting school spirit week, getting take-out (again), or realizing at nine o'clock in the evening that the following day is early dismissal. I can laugh at it now. I don't spiral or apologize for being human. I ask for help. I text other parents. I trade carpools and sleepovers.

Things that once felt like admissions of failure now feel like participation.

A few years ago, that kind of asking would have shattered my pride. I told myself it was necessity that changed me, but it's deeper than that. Devotion softened me enough to let myself be supported. It allowed motherhood to be shared. I let myself be seen—unfinished, imperfect, and still deeply trustworthy.

These days, I say I'm tired when I am. I don't hide it. I take space when I need it. I retreat to my room and nap without making excuses or turning it into a lesson. And instead of pulling away, my children lean closer. There's less tension in the air, fewer sharp edges, and more room for all of us to breathe.

For years, I compartmentalized rest, pleasure, grief, desire—tucking them away so motherhood could appear seamless. But at a certain age, children can feel the difference between what's said and what's lived. They don't need explanations; they need coherence. As I've begun to integrate all the parts of myself, our home has softened. Honesty has replaced performance.

Motherhood, I'm learning, is not about holding it all together. It's about letting all of me to be here: the mother, the woman, the one who needs rest, and the one who feels joy. This devotion to truth has become the bridge between who I was and who I am becoming. And my children feel it, even before they have words for it.

✦ Temple Practice: The Art of Self-Mothering

Every woman carries an inner child. The tender, unguarded part of her that once believed she had to shrink to be loved, to care for others before herself.

When we begin to awaken, that part of us also wakes.

She doesn't need fixing.

She needs mothering—gentle, unconditional presence.

This ritual is a homecoming.

It's an invitation to reparent yourself with the softness and devotion you may have always longed for.

✦ STEP ONE: CREATE THE NEST

Find a quiet space where you feel safe.

Light a candle or dim the lights.

Gather something soft—a blanket, a scarf, a pillow—and let it symbolize the comfort you once sought outside yourself.

If it helps, play gentle music or place a hand over your heart to begin arriving in your body.

Take a slow breath in through your nose, and exhale through your mouth.

Feel your body supported beneath you.

You are safe here.

✦ STEP TWO: CALL HER FORWARD

Close your eyes and imagine the younger version of you—maybe a child, maybe a teenage girl, maybe the woman you were just a few years ago when everything began to shift.

See her clearly.

Notice her face, her posture, her energy.

Now, invite her to sit with you.

Let her know you're here, not to correct her, but to listen.

Ask her gently: *What do you need? What have you been carrying alone? What do you wish someone had told you?*

Listen without rushing to answer.

Let her speak in images, sensations, or emotions.

✦ STEP THREE: OFFER THE MOTHERING YOU NEEDED

Place one hand on your heart and one on your belly.

Say softly:

I am here for you now.

You are safe with me.

You never have to be quiet, small, or perfect to be loved.

Let these words travel through your body as truth.

Let them land where once there was absence.

You might want to wrap the blanket around yourself or hold your own shoulders. A physical reminder that you are both the mother and the child, the nurturer and the nurtured.

✦ STEP FOUR: ANCHOR THE NEW STORY

Take three deep breaths.
On each exhale, release an old story—
"I must earn love."
"My needs are a burden."
"Sacrifice is the price of belonging."
On each inhale, invite in the truth—
"I am worthy of love as I am."
"My needs make me human."
"Living is the bedrock of belonging."

✦ STEP FIVE: BLESSING

When you feel complete, whisper a simple blessing over yourself:
I am my own safe place.
I re-mother myself with tenderness, patience, and love.
I am whole, and I am home.
Let this practice become a touchstone—something you can
return to whenever you feel untethered, overwhelmed, or alone.
Because this is what healing the mother wound truly means:
learning to hold yourself with the same devotion you once
sought from someone else.

CHAPTER THREE

Father Code

I spent most of my twenties trying to reverse engineer my mother's mistakes. I wanted to choose differently, love differently, *live* differently. I wanted to find the man who would prove that the story could change: that a father could stay, that love could be safe, that I wouldn't have to do everything alone. But the unconscious mind is a brilliant trickster. It doesn't rewrite the story; it casts the same characters in different costumes, until you finally break the script.

For years, this repetition felt like one failure after another. I wasn't trying hard enough, healing deeply enough, or choosing wisely enough. I mistook negative recurrences for personal deficiencies rather than seeing them for what they truly were—transformation seeds.

Patterns don't repeat because we are broken. They repeat because something essential is still asking to be seen.

Most of my work has been devoted to understanding desire, the body, and the feminine. It took me longer to name the other half of the equation: the masculine. Not men themselves, but the imprint of masculinity I carried inside me. The expectations, longings, and protective strategies that were shaped by what was present, missing, or never repaired.

We often talk about the mother wound because it is intimate, embodied, and close to the surface. But there is another imprint running just as quietly beneath our lives, shaping how we choose partners, how we trust, how we receive support, and how safe we feel to let go.

The masculine, at its healthiest, is pure presence. It's dominance without control. It's protection without possession. It's the steady force that creates safety, allowing life, creativity, and vulnerability to unfold.

The masculine provides structure, not rigidity. It holds the edges so that the feminine can move freely within them. When it is embodied well, it offers direction, permission, and trust. It says, *You are safe to explore, to feel, to become.* It is the force that meets the world on our behalf and makes room for the feminine to grow.

For children, the masculine is often their first experience of the world responding to them. It teaches us what to expect when we reach outward. Whether we will be met, protected, ignored, or abandoned. Whether our needs will be held with steadiness or left unanswered. Long before we have language for it, our bodies learn what love feels like when it comes from outside ourselves. When masculine presence is inconsistent, unavailable, or absent, something foundational shifts. We learn to brace for impact rather than trust.

To self-contain instead of reach. To become hyper-independent or chronically in longing. The father wound is not just about a person. It is the rupture of safety, direction, and belonging that shapes how we relate to the world, intimacy, and our own sense of worth.

The mother teaches us how to receive love. The masculine teaches us how we will be supported when we step into the world. One shapes our sense of belonging and emotional safety, the other shapes our trust as we take risks, ask for more, or finally stop carrying everything alone.

When the masculine is absent, inconsistent, or unreliable, we don't just grieve what wasn't there. We adapt. We brace instead of lean, manage instead of trust, survive without asking.

That adaptation becomes its own mask: the Father Code.

The *Father Code* is the wound written in invisible ink. It's the way a girl learns to take care of herself when no one else does. In the absence of the masculine, it's the voice that whispers *Don't need too much, don't ask too loudly*. It's the habit of swallowing connection because desire feels dangerous when no one shows up to meet it. Without the masculine, we become fluent in independence—the kind that looks admirable on the outside but is forged in loneliness.

For years, I walked through the world with a phantom limb where the masculine should have grown. I didn't have a father who taught me what protection felt like, or what it meant to be cherished without condition. I learned how to rescue myself and to hold my own heart when it cracked open. I wore my competence like a crown, never allowing it to tip, but beneath it pulsed an ache, one that still wanted to be held.

When I say that most men have disappointed me, I say it factually, without bitterness. I have not met masculine energy that matches their sacred potential. And yet, I remain a romantic. I still believe in the alchemy of two souls meeting in wholeness. I still believe in love, and in finding someone who has done their own work, faced their shadows, and chosen partnership with intention.

But until that day, I am husbanding myself. I am rebuilding the temple masculinity chose not to tend.

Blowing up my life was the initiation.

It taught me the difference between being protected and being possessed. Between loyalty and self-abandonment. Between the fantasy of safety and the reality of sovereignty.

The Father Code shaped me. The rupture freed me.

I am no longer the daughter waiting by the door for someone to come home. I am the woman who built her own house, lit her own fire, and learned to stay.

THE ARCHITECT

The Father Code is written in the nervous system long before we have words for it. It's not just the story of a man who left, it's the subtle pattern the body learns when masculine energy is inconsistent, unreachable, or unsafe.

Author and trauma expert Gabor Maté writes that *trauma is not what happens to us, but what happens inside of us as a result of what happens.* When a father is absent—emotionally or physically—the child's developing system makes an adaptation: *I'll take care of myself.* It's brilliant, really. The psyche closes the loop by deciding, *I don't need you. I'll be the strong one. I'll be safe by being in control.*

But that adaptation becomes the architectural structure of our adulthood.

We grow into women who can hold everything: career, home, motherhood, heartbreak. Then we struggle to let ourselves be held. We equate independence with worthiness, control with safety. Our bodies hum at a higher frequency, vigilant in their search for the next rupture, while our hearts quietly ache for rest.

Maté's research shows that this kind of early, subtle disconnection is one of the most common roots of later anxiety, perfectionism, and addiction to doing. The external father may be long gone, but the *internalized wounding* still whispers: *Don't need too much. Keep earning your right to belong.*

In my own healing, I began to see how this wounding ran everything. It was the rudder as I steered headfirst into hyper-independence. I felt safer when I was the one managing, fixing, and anticipating issues. It was the reason intimacy felt suffocating at times, because to receive meant risking renewed dependence. My nervous system equated closeness with danger. When I finally understood I was experiencing trauma, not failure, everything changed.

There was nothing wrong with me for wanting to be met and held. My body was simply protecting me from a familiar absence. The Father Code lives in the gap between what the child needed and what they got. Healing is the art of reparenting that space. It's becoming the steady, sovereign masculine within—the part of me that shows up, not with control, but with devotion. The part that says, *I will not leave you again.*

THE LONGING

I met my father in my twenties. I sent him a letter—typed, printed, sealed—and mailed it into the great unknown, like releasing a prayer. I had no idea if he would write back. As I wrote him, *I hope maybe we will have the chance to meet in person, and I can see where I get my eyes from. If not, then it will be enough for me to have reached out and said hello.*

A few weeks later, he called. His Irish brogue was thick and unmistakable. He had lots of questions, and so did I. That call changed my life. A few weeks later, I flew to Florida.

We built a relationship slowly, awkwardly. I was young and optimistic, still forming who I was. He was in the sunset of his life when my letter arrived, a man who had chosen work over fatherhood, and now someone was knocking on his door asking to connect.

I didn't realize it then, but I was still hoping he could fill something in me that had never been filled.

When he died twenty years later, he left me what he had—an inheritance tied to a legacy—the thing he had devoted himself to instead of me. After he passed, I cleaned out his home, and among his belongings I found the letters I had written to him over those first few years. I could hear longing in my voice.

The ache of a girl who wanted her father to see her, to return, to stay.

That longing became my pattern. It played out again and again, through the men I loved, through the ones who couldn't meet me, through the ones I tried to save. My twenties were full of them. Men who would touch my body but never claim my heart. Men who needed my light but couldn't hold it. Each one was a mirror of the same unhealed ache.

When I finally left Toronto for New York, a toxic relationship behind me, I thought I was breaking free. I was building a new life, but my wiring hadn't caught up. My nervous system was still tuned for confusion and longing. Even years later, through marriage and motherhood, I could see how those old circuits still ran the show.

It became especially clear in my divorce, when I watched myself trying to find safety in the familiar pattern—choosing men who looked different on the outside but carried the same unavailable frequency on the inside. I realized I had to rewrite myself if I wanted something new. I couldn't keep mistaking breadcrumbs for a feast.

The lessons kept circling, appearing in new forms. A romantic connection that awakened deep desire but lacked alignment. A business deal with a charming man who promised to take care of everything, only to collapse into chaos and demand more from me than he gave.

Each experience tested my trust, my boundaries, and my capacity to hold myself through uncertainty.

When business, as well as intimacy, began to unravel, the stress became overwhelming. My body carried it like a current of dread. Every morning, anxiety gripped my chest. My mind spun stories of failure and loss, how I was the one to blame.

One morning, as I sobbed on the phone with my best friend, Sophia, she asked, "Whose voice is that? Because it doesn't sound like you."

I closed my eyes and saw them—my father, my stepfather, the chorus of men who had pointed fingers, saying, "You're wrong. You're bad. You'll end up just like your mother."

Their voices had crescendoed into mine.

Sophia encouraged me to call my Angels. To ask them to clear away any energy that wasn't mine and clear any projections or distortions from my field.

I sat in meditation, my face wet with tears, and said, "Please take this away and leave me only with Divine Truth."

Almost immediately, I felt relief. The fog lifted. My chest softened. The same circumstances surrounded me, but they no longer defined me. I could breathe again. It's a powerful practice to ask for help from the Divine, to remember we are not alone.

The longing itself had always been my teacher. It showed me where I had abandoned myself. Now, when that ache rises—especially around the masculine—I meet it with curiosity instead of fear. I ask, "What part of me needs tending?"

This is what the longing truly is: a signal from the soul, calling us home to the parts still waiting to be loved.

THE HUNGER BENEATH THE CODE

There comes a moment when the body stops numbing and begins to feel the hunger it has been protecting us from. Suddenly, we feel it all: the years of quiet ache, the tenderness we learned to live without, the needs we tucked away so we could keep going.

In childhood, when our need for attunement, affection, or safety goes unmet, we adapt. A child can't survive without attachment; she learns to suppress her authenticity. She hides the parts of herself that were "too much," "too sensitive," or "too demanding," to preserve the relationship that ensures her survival. As children, we made an impossible choice. We learned that staying connected required staying small, that belonging meant tucking parts of ourselves away. We chose attachment over authenticity, not out of weakness, but because we are built to survive; however, those suppressed needs don't vanish. They go underground, stored in the nervous system, woven into our breath, our muscles, our relational patterns. We internalize "fine," as we master the art of self-abandonment.

Then, years after inner work, heartbreak, or finally finding a semblance of safety, the body begins to loosen its grip—the armor cracks.

Life rises to the surface and you begin to move again. The ache to be held, the craving for tenderness, the tears that come out of nowhere—these are the suppressed needs returning home. It can feel destabilizing.

We may interpret it as regression: *Why am I suddenly so needy? So emotional? So tender?*

It's not regression, it's repair. The nervous system is reopening to the possibility of connection.

The return of suppressed needs, in truth, is the reawakening of our capacity for intimacy. It's the body saying, *I'm ready now to receive what I once had to live without.*

This is the Sacred Feminine remembering her right to be held. It's the daughter putting down her sword and letting herself cry. It's the woman who has carried it all finally realizing that longing is not a flaw—it's the evidence that she's still connected to her heart.

To meet that need consciously—to feel it without shame and without turning it into a story about what is wrong with us—is to become both the Mother and the Father of ourselves. It is the capacity to soothe and to protect, to tend and anchor. This is sovereignty, the grounded knowing that we will not abandon ourselves when we are open to being met.

In my work, I invite women to meet this longing as a holy signal. The ache is not evidence of a deficiency or failure. It is proof of aliveness.

It is the body remembering what it was designed for: connection, co-regulation, communion.

THE SACRED MASCULINE

Much of my work regards the feminine. It's about remembering how to receive, how to attune to the rhythms of nature, and the pulse of pleasure. But the feminine can only truly rest when she trusts the masculine to hold her.

My astrologer once said, "The cosmos has their own masculine energy. Think of it as Sky Daddy, the one who holds the container that the feminine fills."

When I began to pour myself into this energy, I became hyper-aware of all the wounded versions of the masculine that had shaped me. The ones who puffed out their chests and said, "Don't worry, I've got you," and then let you fall. My circuitry, still shaped by the story of a missing father, wanted to believe them. I wanted to be held. I let the exploitative energy of the wounded masculine cloud my reality.

I embraced the cliché. I stepped into autonomy—romantically, emotionally, financially. "Choosing myself" became real when I stopped participating in dynamics that kept me small. When the promise of safety in someone else's arms became less interesting than the safety in my own body, I began to protect and provide for my feminine self in a way no partner ever could.

A year after our divorce, as I navigated the world of dating again, I felt the shift. The foundation had altered. The old wiring had been replaced with something truer. I was no longer performing or pretending; I was rooted in harmony between my inner feminine and masculine.

One morning, on an early date over coffee, I listened to a man talk about his daily devotion to the stock market. I felt the echo of an old pattern and wondered if I'd magnetized another version of my father to me.

I told him gently, but clearly, "I'd rather be adored in the morning before you check your stocks."

These days, I prefer my dopamine in the form of an orgasm. He didn't get a second date.

This is what integration looks like: messy, imperfect, human. I still catch myself softening too quickly, skipping conversations about boundaries, saying yes when I mean no. But now, I notice it. I name it. I course-correct in minutes, not months.

When I say to a man, "Any hint of you calling me 'too much' is a dealbreaker," I am protecting the little girl who once believed she was. When I say, "Don't ever make that turn again while I'm in the car," I am honoring the woman who values her safety above someone else's comfort. When I tell a man, "I deserve to be adored," I am standing in my wholeness, no longer bargaining for crumbs.

Through therapy, ceremony, pleasure, and thousands of micro choices, I rewired my own system to be the protector I never had. I am my own sacred masculine. I will soften for a man who meets me with clarity and sovereignty, but I am no longer waiting to be chosen or rescued. I am already held by the Great Mother's abundance and the Great Father's steadiness. Together, they form the field I walk within.

Suspended in that balance, I am whole.

THE PAIN OF OUR PARENTHOOD

As I write this, I am shepherding my children through the loss of their father as a part of their daily lives. When our divorce was finalized, he chose to move out of state, which had a strange, meta quality to it.

Watching the very wound I'd spent years trying to understand take shape in my children's lives, allowed me to feel the scope of it in real time. His absence will quietly shape them in ways neither of us can fully predict or protect.

I know my steady presence is what is within my power to give them a happy and healthy life. I know it is the best of me.

But still, they are experiencing the very thing I wanted to spare them from.

That truth lives alongside me. The grief of what couldn't be avoided, the humility of knowing that love does not grant immunity from loss, the resolve to stay present, to name what is happening without dramatizing it, to trust that repair does not come from perfection but from honesty, steadiness, and care over time.

I cannot rewrite their story for them. But I can walk beside them as it unfolds.

No matter how much healing work we do, the stories of our parents and our own parenting live inside us. They are the first codes we receive, the ones that shape how we love, how we protect, and how we show up for life. For years, I tried to rewrite those stories by erasing them. I wanted to build a new life, untouched by the pain that came before. But healing doesn't come from denying our lineage. It comes from reclaiming it.

To reclaim the pain of our parenthood stories is to see them as sacred initiations. The places that once hurt us most often contain the keys to our becoming. The mother who couldn't hold us guides us toward holding ourselves. The father who disappeared awakens our longing for safety and ignites the strength to create it. The loss, the absence, the ache—all of it carries medicine.

Healing is never about erasing what happened. It is about transforming its energy. We meet the wound with compassion, with breath, with presence, until the grief softens and something new emerges. The same energy that once created pain becomes the energy that births wisdom.

When we begin to feel it all, when we allow the emotions that were once forbidden to move through us, we stop carrying the weight of what was never ours to hold. Our parents, like us, were shaped by their own unhealed stories. Many of them never had the tools or the permission to look at their pain, so they passed it along unconsciously. Compassion is not about excusing what hurt us. It is about ending the repetition.

To reclaim is to return. It is to gather all the pieces of ourselves that were scattered across years of surviving. The child who learned to stay small. The teenager who rebelled out of self-protection. The adult who tried to hold it all together.

We invite them back, one by one, into the wholeness of who we are now.

When we integrate these parts, we stop trying to heal through others. We stop looking for our parents or our partners to give us what they never could. We begin to mother and father ourselves. We create safety from within. We become the divine parent we have been waiting for. Parenthood, whether literal or symbolic, calls us into a higher form of love. It asks us to choose presence over performance. It asks us to forgive without forgetting, because in forgiveness we find true freedom. It asks us to stay open when it would be easier to shut down, and to stand in the fire of our emotions without losing ourselves to them. When we practice this kind of conscious love, the lineage begins to shift. The patterns lose their power.

The story changes.

We are the bridge between what was and what can be. Every choice of ours to pause, to breathe, to feel, to repair sends ripples through time. It heals our children and strengthens the roots of what will come after us. It untangles the energetic threads that kept us bound to old stories, and in doing so, offers us peace. When we reclaim what was once lost, we free not only ourselves, but the next generations.

To reclaim the pain is to hold the wound as sacred, to honor the lessons inside it, and to choose to live from wholeness rather than from defense. It is to stand in the knowing that the story does not end in pain. It begins again in love.

✦ Meditation Practice: Held by the Divine

Close your eyes.

Take a long breath in through your nose and let it spill softly from your lips.

Feel your body begin to settle.

Bring your awareness to your shoulders.

Behind your right shoulder, feel the presence of the Divine Mother—warm, nurturing, steady. She wraps you in the energy of unconditional love.

She whispers, "You are safe to soften."

Behind your left shoulder, feel the presence of the Divine Father—clear, grounded, protective. He is the mountain that holds your ocean.

He whispers, "You are safe to trust."

Breathe both presences into your heart.

The Mother and Father.

The Earth and the Sky.

The softness that receives, and the strength that sustains.

Let your body lean back into their embrace.

Let yourself be held by what is both beyond you and within you.

You do not need to hold it all together.

You do not need to figure it out.

You are guided. You are loved. You are safe.

Rest here for a moment, breathing in the balance.

When you are ready, open your eyes and remember:

The Divine Mother and Father walk with you.

Always.

✦ Inner Child Practice: Letter to Our Nine-Year-Old Self

Sweet girl,

You came into this world already longing to be held, to be loved, to belong. And you were. Your mother loved you, even when she didn't know how to show it all the way. She was scared and doing her best. That longing you feel in your bones, you got that from her; it was already there before you took your first breath.

She wanted a man who would stay. A man who would choose love over fear. When he didn't, she told herself stories to survive. That's how she kept going. You'll do that, too, for a while—tell stories to make the pain make sense. But you'll learn that the truth doesn't hurt as much as pretending does.

You'll have a dad, but he won't feel like yours. He'll come and go, and it will make you wonder what's wrong with you. Nothing is wrong with you. You are good. You are love itself. His leaving says nothing about your worth.

When you're with the horses, you'll remember. The way they meet you without words, the way your heartbeat slows to match theirs. That's home. That's God. That's you, unbroken.

I know you think you have to do everything alone—hide the

truth, hold everyone else up—but you don't. You can lay it down. There are people who will help you carry it. Let them.

There will be heartbreak and beauty, loss and beginning. You'll become a mother and understand things your own mother could never say out loud. You'll find your way back to softness.

If you forget, close your eyes and I'll be there, wrapping my arms around you. And somewhere far ahead, she's holding us, too—the older one, the one who already knows—whispering, *It's all going to be more than okay.*

Your Turn

Take a quiet moment, somewhere you feel safe—maybe with a candle, a cup of tea, or your bare feet on the earth. Close your eyes and picture your younger self. The one who still believed in magic before she learned to hide it. The one who carried so much without the language to name it. If you have a photo of yourself as a child, place it by your candle or a crystal that supports your healing, creating an altar as you begin to journey back in time to when you were small.

When you're ready, write her a letter.
Let it come from your heart, not your head.
Begin with:

- *Dear little me...*
- *Sweet girl, I remember you...*

Tell her what she didn't understand then. Tell her what you now know to be true about love, safety, worthiness, and desire. Remind her that she was never too much or not enough. If you're a mother, it may be helpful to think about your own children and the softness you desire to share with them.

This isn't about fixing her, it's about *remembering her.*

When you finish, place a hand on your heart and whisper: "I've got you now."

Part Two

The Anchor: Reclaim Your Freedom

✦ The Anchor Ritual

Let's take a moment together to drop in.

To find the energy of anchoring, and to awaken the current of desire that lives within you.

Close your eyes.

Feel your body and the weight of your hips, your feet on the floor, the rise and fall of your chest as you breathe.

Let your posture stay tall but soft, like a flower stretching toward light.

Now imagine a golden cord extending from the soles of your feet, moving down into the earth.

Watch as it travels deep into the soil, wrapping gently around a luminous crystal at the earth's core.

Feel the pulse of that crystal, steady and alive.

It draws up through the cord, through your feet, through your legs, the wisdom of the Mother, the heartbeat of creation itself.

Let this golden light move through you.

It clears what no longer serves the fear, the hiding, the doubt, the shame.

They dissolve like morning fog under the warmth of the sun.

Keep breathing as the light rises through your belly, softening the space that receives.

Let it travel to your heart.

Feel your shoulders release, your throat open, your voice awaken.

The light continues upward, through the space between your eyes, and out through the crown of your head.

A radiant lotus unfurling, pouring golden light all around you.

You are bathed now in this light.

Floating in the glow of the earth and the angels, held between heaven and ground.

Listen for the whisper that lives inside your heart, The truth that wants to guide you.

What is the knowing that you can no longer ignore?

The one you are ready to honor fully?

Bring your hands to your heart—left hand first, then right, cupping softly as if holding something precious.

Imagine the essence of this truth gathering between your palms, a seed of light born from your own heart.

It might take the shape of a color, an image, or a word.

Hold it gently.

Only you need to see it.

Only you need to know it.

Trust that it lives within you now, always.

If it feels right, place that light back in your heart.

Or release it into the golden field around you, knowing it will return when called.

Now see the lotus above your head begin to close, drawing all that golden light inward.

Feel every cell, every atom in your body glowing with this energy.

Let the golden cords beneath your feet loosen and return to the

body.
Bring the grounding energy of the earth back home within you.
Rest here for a few breaths.
Full of light.
Rooted.
Sovereign.
You carry a deep knowing now—
the truth of what is alive in you, the light that guides you
through even the darkest nights.
Let your hands fall softly to your lap, holding this sacred secret
close.
It doesn't need to be shared yet.
For now, it is yours alone—your awakening, your
transformation, your beauty.
Take three slow breaths.
With each exhale, return more fully to the space around you.
When you are ready, open your eyes and come back to
yourself—
anchored, alive, and awake.
What truth revealed itself in the stillness?

CHAPTER FOUR

Pulling the String

I was laying on the floor of a Manhattan yoga studio, sobbing and screaming, "I don't want to be quiet anymore."

For a moment, the room went still. Then, slowly, the sounds of others returned—sighs, wails, low murmurs—as though the collective field exhaled with me. I was in a somatic therapy lab; we were a group of twenty that had gathered over the last six months to study the body's memory. We are learning how our characters were formed, the survival strategies that once kept us safe but morphed to keep us small. In that space, we moved energy. We let the body speak what the mind had long silenced.

In the exercise, we were partnered, laying on yoga mats, we took turns moving our hips in slow, rhythmic thrusts while our partner watched. It was uncomfortable at first, vulnerable even. Then came the twist. Our partner turned away, withdrew their attention, mirroring the way a caregiver turned away from us in the depths of childhood anytime we expressed need, aliveness, or desire. My partner turned away, and my breath caught in my throat. I kept moving, but I couldn't stop the tears.

My body recognized the withdrawal, the familiar ache of disconnection.

Then, something unexpected happened. She turned back toward me, placed her hand on my arm, and whispered, "I'll protect you."

Her words reached something tender. My whole body began to shake as I discharged energy from my body. I felt loss and anger for not being protected. My hips unwound years of stored energy, releasing what was held in silence. The grief, the longing, the shame—all of it moved through me, clearing out the stored energy of the past.

The facilitator knelt beside me, voice low and steady, reminding me that I didn't need to stay quiet anymore. I was forty-seven years old and I was, and still am, learning to give voice to the parts of me that were told to stay small. I am not a quiet person. I've been on stages, led programs, hosted a podcast, spoken boldly about pleasure and liberation. But somewhere deep inside, there is a nine-year-old girl who learned that safety meant being agreeable, easy, undemanding, and most of all silent.

I was the "good girl." The one who never cried, never caused trouble. My mother used to say how grateful she was that I was so easy, so self-sufficient, so quiet. And I'm sure I was. Children are wise to replicate what gets them love and attention. They learn early on what keeps the system stable, what keeps love intact.

Years later, as a mother myself, I saw what mine couldn't. Every child cries. Every child needs. Every child demands attention, sometimes loudly and inconveniently. And when those needs go unmet, they live in the body, waiting for the moment when they are strong enough to feel them. This is the work of reclamation: to invite the parts of ourselves that went quiet back to life. We need to let the body do what it has always known how to do—release, tremble, open, express. To reparent ourselves from a place of love until the little girl inside knows she is safe to move, make noise, and be fully seen.

HOW DARE SHE

Fall of 2022: I went to my first writer's retreat in California. It was led by a woman whose book I had devoured, one that cracked me open with its rawness and honesty. I was in awe of her voice and secretly longed for that kind of permission—to be both vulnerable and powerful on the page. This was the first time I had claimed the title *writer*, and I arrived hungry to create. Healing wasn't on my mind.

But life doesn't always separate the two.

Days before the retreat, the teacher had made the decision to leave her marriage. She had met someone new, and the ground beneath her life shifted. She stood before us, not as the composed leader I expected, but as a woman in the middle of her own unraveling. Her honesty was electric, but it also stirred something in me that I could not name.

I felt an irritation that I mistook for moral superiority. A whisper had risen up: *How dare she?*

How dare she taunt us with this fantasy of freedom—the easy escape, the new lover, the reinvention. How dare she give voice to the thing so many of us buried.

It took me time to understand that my judgment was not about her. It was about me.

Her courage forced me to face the places where I had settled, the ways I had compartmentalized my longing. I felt the tug of something deep and ancient, the quiet ache that grows when a woman forgets what she wants. We like to think that disapproval keeps us safe, but all it does is keep us separate.

When we judge other women for wanting more, we protect the illusion that we are content. We call it stability, loyalty, duty. But underneath, there is often envy, the quiet wondering: *What if I could choose differently, too?*

That weekend cracked something within me. I began to see how my own righteousness was a shield against desire. I had built a careful life, a family, a rhythm that looked fine from the outside. And yet there, in that retreat room, I could feel the first tremors of unrest, the early rumblings of a truth that would one day rearrange everything.

Disapproval is a clever disguise for longing.

We turn away from women who live freely because they remind us of the parts of ourselves still locked away.

How dare she? we say. *I wish I could,* we mean.

UNRAVELING THE TRUTH

By the time I stood in that retreat house in California, I had already begun to meet the quiet fears that had ruled my life: the fear of wanting too much, of being too much, of breaking the unspoken rules that kept everything tidy. For years, I had silenced my desires until they were a low rumble in the background of life. The only one loud enough to hear was my dream of living in California, and even that had been rationalized away a hundred times.

One night, sitting outside beneath a wide Florida sky, I finally said it aloud. "I'm out of excuses. I want to live in California."

That moment changed something in me. It wasn't only about geography; it was about permission. My longing no longer needed to make sense to anyone else. I was reason enough.

We tell ourselves stories that keep us from our destiny. We build elaborate narratives about timing, loyalty, logistics, anything that keeps the edges of our discomfort from splitting open. I had become fluent in the language of justification. The house, the kids, his job, the schools; it all made sense on paper. *Hold on*, that life begged. But my ache grew louder with every compromise, so loud that it cracked the foundation.

I tried not to disturb my life, but my silence, my desire to keep the peace for others while I shriveled away, was too great a threat to me, to who I am.

I pulled the thread. I noticed all the places my life started to fray. The retreat in California planted something small, but irrepressible, like a seed of truth I couldn't un-know. The trip that took us in different directions revealed the vast canyon between us that no amount of "fine" could bridge. The quiet moments became unbearable, not because of what was happening, but because of what wasn't.

There's a particular kind of loneliness that blooms in a marriage, when you're still setting the table, doing the dance, but you're miles apart in the same room.

That Thanksgiving, my uncle, who is in his nineties now, told the story of how he met his wife. They were both married at the time, the two of them willing to risk everything for the aliveness they found in each other.

He looked at me and said, "No one leaves a happy marriage."

The words landed somewhere deep in my body, humming like a tuning fork against the places I had been afraid to touch. I smiled and passed the mashed potatoes, but inside, something went still. Later that night, as I washed the dishes, those words continued to echo—an invitation and a warning.

As I began to dismantle the life I'd built, it felt like death. After almost fifteen years together, how did I stand there ready to smash the whole thing apart? How did one year become two, then five, then two decades of your life? It didn't unravel all at once. It was slow, invisible decay, made up of tiny moments and silent withdrawals.

I remember typing a message to the estate attorney, asking what would happen if we divorced. My stomach twisted as I hit send, guilt flooding me. Two opposing forces stood inside the same body: one asking the question, one terrified to know the answer.

People like to ask when I knew it was over. It didn't happen in a moment, but the accumulation of small ones. The thousands of micro-choices that added up to the unbearable loneliness of a marriage that had stopped breathing.

In March 2023, I stood in the living room of our California home, a place I had dreamed of for decades. Then, I looked at the man in front of me. A stranger. We hugged with the gentle affection of old friends. I knew it was over.

A month earlier, he had looked up from his laptop and asked, "Are we ever going to have sex again?"

Just like that. Between emails and sips of coffee.

Normally I would have deflected, changed the subject, made it light. But something in me had changed. I had been sober for over a month, microdosing, and I had recently met a man who reminded me what it felt like to be truly alive in my body. On Valentine's Day, I went and got a tattoo instead of planning dinner. I told the kids we'd celebrate another night. I wanted that day to belong to me— to mark my body with a symbol of my own power and the sacred current of life that had begun to move through me again.

In those weeks, I felt that my body was waking up from decades of dormancy. So, when he asked, I turned from the sink, hands dripping with water and strawberries, and said, "I think we need to talk. I don't want to do this anymore."

What followed were quiet, uneven conversations, squeezed between moments when the kids weren't in the room. We floated ideas about an open marriage. I had been reading *The Ethical Slut* and left it on his nightstand, a breadcrumb of possibility.

We could create space to breathe, if we wanted to.

But he was leaving for Milwaukee to open a restaurant, and I was preparing for a trip to Costa Rica to sit with Ayahuasca. The timing felt divinely cruel and perfect. Standing at the counter, my palms pressed into the cool marble, I hovered at the edge I knew I had reached. I could keep the beautiful illusion, or I could speak the truth and watch it burn.

We lived parallel lives for several weeks—same house, different worlds. He wanted to try, stay for the kids, wait until they went to college. But I knew that if I stayed, I would wither. Something inside me would rot from the inside out.

Even the numbers reflected it. After four years of marriage, only 48% of married women want regular sex. Married men thrive and are happier; the same goes for single women. The math speaks for itself.

Still, this wasn't about statistics. It was about the quiet, private ache of disconnection. I remember watching another couple at dinner, the way he touched her arm as she spoke. They had children, too. It was ordinary affection, but it pierced me. I missed that.

By then, even my preteen daughter asked questions about me and her father. "Why doesn't Dad ever hug you?"

It didn't happen overnight. Motherhood consumes you, exhaustion becomes normal, and somewhere amongst that survival, we stopped turning toward each other. The distance quietly built between us until it became irreversible.

BURNING DOWN THE HOUSE

The truth can set you free, but it can also burn your life down. Sobriety and microdosing had sharpened my knowing. When I met a man who reflected that aliveness back to me, I stepped willingly into the fire.

I did what I thought I would never do, what I had judged others for, what I had categorized as unimaginable. I let myself be swept into desire, into lust, into life. Every cell in my body awakened and said, *Yes. This is living.*

It wasn't about him. But he was the spark that lit the fire. The kindle was already inside me, waiting to burn.

For months, I lived between two worlds: the one I had built and the one that was breaking me open. My body was alive in a way it hadn't been in years. Every nerve ending felt electric. I couldn't eat, couldn't sleep, couldn't focus on anything practical. I had been dormant for so long that the awakening itself felt like an emergency, a surge too powerful to contain.

Desire can do that. It moves through the body like a truth that refuses to be quiet. At first, I tried to frame it as exploration, a season, an exception. We agreed to keep it contained, to stay under the radar, to pretend we were not destroying anything. But the truth was that something was already gone long before I crossed any line. The real betrayal had happened years earlier, when I began betraying myself.

For the first time, I understood how women ended up in the arms of someone who was not their husband. It wasn't just lust or rebellion. It was the body's attempt to remember what it felt like to be fully alive. It was the soul clawing its way out of the cage of "should."

Still, the freedom came with consequences. I would wake in the middle of the night with anxiety pulsing in my chest, my heart pounding, breath shallow. The guilt came in waves. The fear of being found out, the fear of hurting my children, the fear that maybe I had misread everything. But beneath the fear was something even stronger—clarity.

I was experiencing the raw reality of truth.

The affair was the culmination of every moment I had abandoned myself. And like any fire, it burned through what could not last. When you start living from truth, you can no longer live from obligation. When you start listening to the body, you stop negotiating with what numbs it. When you start touching your own aliveness, you realize how long you've been half-dead.

The fire consumed what was false. It burned away the identities I had been holding onto: the good wife, the reliable mother, the woman who could hold it all together. What remained was something raw and real—a woman who wanted to live in full color, who wanted to feel everything, who was willing to lose her life as she knew it to find herself again. A woman who became unrecognizable to herself because she refused to go back into a life that felt suffocating.

That's what they don't tell you about liberation. It isn't graceful. It's messy and painful and full of contradiction. It doesn't come in a single epiphany. It comes in waves of burning and rebuilding, of choosing yourself when it hurts, even when it feels like it may cost you everything you love. There were nights I wanted to turn back, to retreat into the safety of the familiar. But every time I tried, my body refused. She had tasted freedom, and she would not be silenced again.

This was the beginning of my awakening—the moment I began to understand that desire was never the problem. The problem was the way I had learned to cage it, to mistrust the wild intelligence of my own body. The affair, the awakening, the fire—none of it was random. It was a reckoning. My body had reached her threshold. She could no longer live inside a system that treated her aliveness as dangerous.

When I began to work somatically, I understood what had been happening all along. The body stores what the mind cannot hold. Every flinch, every apology, every time I crossed my own boundaries to keep the peace, the energy didn't disappear. It buried itself deeper. And when I began to listen to my body, to let her move and breathe again, what rose first was not pleasure but pain.

That pain was sacred. It was grief from all the women before me, the inheritance of centuries of silenced longing. The feminine doesn't awaken in a straight line. She descends, she unravels, she remembers. The Priestess path returns us to our bodies, the earth, the pulse of life that patriarchy taught us to fear. We are taught that pleasure is sinful, that desire is dangerous, that a good woman is one who wants less. Even for those of us raised outside the church, purity culture still shapes the air we breathe. My Irish Catholic roots run deep with a kind of moral restraint—unspoken but absolute. Women carry guilt like a second skin. Pleasure is something to be earned, not embodied.

I learned to minimize, manage, and survive. I learned that being "good" meant being small. And I see that same quiet suffering reflected in so many women now. I watch them, bright and capable, caught in webs of their own making. They are partnered with men who feel distant, intimacy eroded by the weight of routine. Their children's lives overflow with activities and demands. Some have kept their careers; others have paused them to care for their families full-time. In the business of marriage, everyone has their role: one brings in money, the other keeps the machine running.

Even women with engaged, loving partners feel the weight of invisible labor that never ends. They hold the mental load of motherhood: remembering appointments, forms, birthdays, and grocery lists. They track every small detail required to hold a family together.

So, when these women contemplate happiness, when they quietly ask themselves, *Is this all there is?* They're not only facing desire, but they're also facing the near impossibility of holding it all alone. The fear doesn't just come from leaving a man. It comes from leaving the entire structure of life as we know it.

So, we stay.

We stay loyal to the harbor. We stay faithful to the dock. We stay unfulfilled but intact. We excuse mediocrity in ourselves and in them, telling ourselves that comfort is enough. But the truth is, it never was.

And that's where awakening begins.

The crack doesn't come from selfishness; it comes from the soul's refusal to stay numb. It's the moment a woman starts to remember that her pleasure, her power, and her freedom are not luxuries. They are the path home to herself.

This is the Priestess path—the descent into what was once forbidden, the return to the sacred within the body. A remembering that what is dangerous is divine.

THERE ARE MANY DIFFERENT ENDINGS HERE

The moment came when I stood in the living room with my husband and knew it was over. I didn't feel passion or grief or even loss; I felt nothing at all. Only emptiness.

Within days of returning from a plant medicine ceremony, I was preparing for surgery to remove an ovary. The grief that came with it was overwhelming. In the jungle, I had already begun to ask myself *Why?* Why was this loss the one that broke me open? Why wasn't I grieving the marriage that was already dissolving, or the man who had ignited my body with one illicit text? Why was the pain lodged here, in my womb?

One afternoon, sitting in a palapa with one of the facilitators, I sobbed about the surgery, about my life, about the ache I carried for my children and for all the parts of myself I had abandoned.

He listened quietly, then said, "The ovaries are the seat of creativity. They are how you create life physically, but also energetically." He paused and asked, "What if the cyst formed out of all the creative energy you suppressed? What if it was the body's way of holding everything you didn't express?"

The doctors told me the cyst had been growing slowly for years, maybe as long as eight, but lately it had accelerated. That landed on me like a truth I already knew. When I arrived home, I felt disoriented, like a stranger in my own life. My husband and I were already sleeping in separate rooms. I wandered the house listening to the songs from the ceremony, still carrying the heartbeat of the jungle inside me. The medicine of Ayahuasca opens the heart, and without time to integrate, it felt brutal to drop back into ordinary life.

I had debated canceling the retreat when I learned the surgery was scheduled for June 1, but it was meant to be a birthday trip. I asked my surgeon how close to surgery I could safely drink Ayahuasca.

She thought for a moment before answering, "We tell you to stop Advil seven days before, so probably the same."

Perfect, I thought. The final ceremony would be exactly seven days before the operation. Four days after returning home, I would be under anesthesia. Not ideal but somehow fitting.

Before leaving for Costa Rica, I had booked a boudoir photo shoot. It was an impulse. I had followed the photographer for months, quietly fascinated by the women she captured, and something in me wanted to see myself that way, too. I wanted a physical memory of my body before the surgery, before anything changed.

Miraculously, she had an opening two days after my return and the day before my operation. She came to the house, and for four hours we moved through every room—bedroom, living room, hall-way—finding the light, the angles, the pulse of aliveness. We played music, laughed, and created art together.

I wore the closest thing I owned to lingerie. One lace bra, a pair of animal print panties, a few pieces that still felt like me. The rest had been bought with my husband. I couldn't bear to wear them.

It was one of the most liberating experiences of my life. I felt sexy, alive, powerful. My body felt like mine again. After nearly two years of strength training, sobriety, and microdosing, I had shed twenty pounds and arrived in my strongest, most radiant form. I sensed it might never feel quite like this again. The camera caught all of it: the wild hair, the hungry eyes, the arch of my back, the spark of a woman on the verge of burning her life down to save her soul.

The next day, I had the ovary removed.

When I told my husband about the photos, he asked, "Why?"

That one word said everything. It revealed more about our disconnection than any argument could. It said more than his repeated insistence that I had changed, that he didn't like who I was becoming, that he didn't want to follow me into this new terrain.

I never told him what the ovary meant to me. How much grief I carried. How I understood the cyst as a physical manifestation of years of repressed creativity and life force. I didn't tell him how the surgery felt like a death and a rebirth.

And he never asked.

Or saw the photos.

But I still have them. And even if no one else ever sees them, I know what they captured. A woman in full bloom. A woman standing on the threshold between endings and beginnings. A woman free, finally, to be herself.

FREEDOM ISN'T FREE

After the surgery, something in me quieted, and something else began to stir. The physical release made space for truth to surface. I had spent fifteen years living with the volume turned low on my creativity, my passion, my voice. I was deeply contained. My joy had been rationed to fit inside the edges of what was acceptable.

For years, I had carried chronic headaches that no doctor could explain. They began in Chicago and followed me to California, flaring with stress and fading when I felt free. As my marriage dissolved, the headaches began to disappear. When he came home from a trip, they would return. My body had always known what my mind refused to see.

It was teaching me to trust it, to let it lead.

In July, just weeks after the surgery, I flew to New York for a creative project that would become another initiation. I was working with a former TV producer to film my founder's story, speaking openly about trauma and the cost of silence. It was the first time I had said the words out loud in front of a camera. The first time I had been fully visible in my truth.

The morning of the shoot, I woke in the hotel room in Brooklyn and couldn't bend my right knee. The pain was sharp, and I couldn't put any weight on it. I sat on the edge of the hotel bed, laughing and crying at once. Why today? I had invested so much to be here, standing in my truth. Perhaps my body, loyal as ever, was trying to protect me from being seen. I googled Louise Hay's interpretation of knee pain: *Fear. Feeling unsupported. Resistance to moving forward.*

I took two painkillers, whispered a prayer, and did it anyway. Limping through a Brooklyn park, I told my story, letting my words land in the world at last. I surrendered to their ripples, no matter what. I was done keeping secrets, done being the one holding on to the story for who it might hurt. I was ready to let the chips fall.

Days later, I was back in Minnesota, at my husband's parents' fiftieth wedding anniversary. The timing was poetic—a celebration of endurance while my own marriage collapsed in silence. His parents, devout and kind, had no idea. We smiled for photos and toasted to forever, pretending we were still intact. Inside, I felt like I was suffocating.

It was only a few weeks earlier that I had found out about his affair, as well as his new relationship in Milwaukee. It was both devastating and clarifying. The marriage had already ended; we were performing the afterlife.

The pastor spoke about commitment, sacrifice, and the holiness of staying the course. Everyone applauded. I could barely breathe. The idea of lifelong endurance no longer felt noble to me; it felt like spiritual amputation. I had spent enough years mistaking suppression for devotion.

That night, I lay awake in the Airbnb. We had separate rooms, separate lives. I knew there was no going back. The next morning, I opened my phone and saw a Facebook message from my stepbrother. My stepfather had died. I hadn't spoken to him in twenty years. I noticed a folder of unread messages and saw that my cousin had followed up with more questions.

I opened his profile, but what I found was an obituary. He had died two years earlier, shortly after writing to me.

Two men, gone.

They were both threads in the tangled web of my story. One, the man my mother had chosen, the reason she was gone so often, the figure who taught me early that love could cost you safety. The other, the boy who crossed a line he didn't yet understand, who carried his own broken childhood and passed that pain on to me.

News of their deaths arrived on the same day, and I couldn't ignore the symmetry. Was it chance? Poetic justice? Divine timing? I don't know. But something inside me shifted. The air felt lighter, the space inside me wider. In a matter of days, I told my story out loud, felt the injustice of a life built on pretending, and saw two important men pass away. My system was registering it all moment to moment. I wouldn't integrate the real impact of those events falling like dominos, until months later.

For years, I had carried their stories in my body—the fear, the confusion, the unspoken shame. I made sense of myself through their secrets, even as I tried to outrun them. And now, in one swift moment, they were gone.

I got a feeling that this was what freedom truly meant. Not through erasure, forgiveness, or condemnation, but allowing their stories to end where mine continued, and it freed me. The masculine, in all its fractured forms, began to loosen its grip on me that day. The father I lost, the man I married, the lover who awakened me, the men who wounded me—each of them had shaped my journey back to myself. And now, their roles were complete.

It felt like a closing ceremony. A clearing. A reclamation.

I didn't know how life was going to look without those stories defining me, but I knew I was finally free to find out.

By the time we returned to California from the anniversary celebration, I was ready. The separation was no longer theoretical. It was alive and inevitable. Freedom was coming. It was raw, holy, and real.

It cost me everything I thought I was and gave me everything I was afraid to claim.

Pulling the string changes everything. It dismantles the entire foundation of who you thought you were allowed to be. The secrets I'd carried were blueprints for a life built on other people's rules about safety, goodness, and worth. When those blueprints burn, you lose more than your husband. You lose your identity as the good wife, the perfect mother, the woman who doesn't complain and never asks for too much.

In that space between breaking apart and becoming whole, something wild can finally breathe: the woman you are when the performance ends. For me, the pull had begun. And there was no going back.

Freedom is not a destination. It's a daily practice of choosing yourself over everyone else's comfort. It's terrifying in the same way standing at the edge of a cliff is—not because you're going to fall, but because you might fly. When you blow up your life, when you stop living according to other people's scripts, everything becomes uncertain. The safety net of predictability disappears. You wake up each morning not knowing exactly who you'll be by evening. Your friends might not recognize you. Your family might not approve. The woman in the mirror might be a stranger for a while. But here's what they don't tell you about blowing up your life: the terror is matched, breath for breath, by an electricity you forgot was possible. By mornings when you wake up curious rather than resigned. By the wild realization that you can trust yourself to navigate the unknown. By the slow recognition that the woman you're becoming was always there, waiting for you to be brave enough to leap.

✦ Embodiment Practice

This practice asks nothing of your mind. It asks everything of your body.

Start with your song. Choose it the way you choose anything that matters—with your gut, not your head. Something with a charge. Something you've maybe turned up too loud in the car when no one was watching. Something that holds what you've been holding.

Find your space. Floor, mat, bed—anywhere you can move, stomp, flail, and fall without catching yourself. Bare feet if you can.

Stand still. Both hands on your lower belly. Three slow breaths.

Then ask yourself honestly: *What am I shaking loose today?*

Is it rage that never got a voice? The years of being quiet, of accommodating, of making yourself smaller than you are? Is it grief for the life you didn't live, the things you said yes to when every cell in your body was screaming no?

What are you done being quiet about?

Sit with that. Let the body answer.

Before you press *play*, find her. The version of you who already knows how to do this. She might be younger, wilder, less managed. She doesn't watch herself. She doesn't apologize for the sound she makes. She just moves.

Let her lead.

Press *play*.

Follow whatever comes—a sway, a stomp, shoulders shaking, arms pushing something away, the whole-body flailing on the mattress. When the pressure builds in your chest or throat, grab the pillow. Press it to your face and let the sound out. A groan. A wail. A *NO*. A *FUCK THIS*. Your body already knows what it's been waiting to say.

Let it come more than once if it needs to.

When the wave passes, be still. Hands back on the belly. Feel what has moved.

What do you know now that you didn't know before you started?

Reach for your journal. Write for five minutes. No editing. No explaining. Just let what shook loose find the page.

The string has been pulled. Trust the unraveling.

CHAPTER FIVE

Unmarried

It was dinner time and the house was buzzing with evening chaos. Kids were running in different directions, dogs were barking, and my mom chatted in the kitchen while the nanny tried to get dinner on the table.

I was leaving for Panama in the morning, another trip in a month full of them. A year before, the idea of packing my suitcase every week would have felt impossible, but now it felt like freedom. Or at least, movement. For the previous four months, I'd been trying to refinance my mortgage. It had been grueling, not just because of the paperwork, but because the process itself was a mirror of everything I'd been disentangling—removing my ex-husband from accounts and assets, proving that I could afford this life on my own.

If you've ever applied for a loan, you know the feeling. It's like inviting a stranger to rummage through your underwear drawer. There's something invasive about it, and it takes real effort not to collapse into scarcity or shame while someone in a cubicle decides your worthiness. Staying rooted in my feminine energy has been a daily practice throughout this.

At six pm, the notary arrived. She stepped into the whirlwind of dinner, children, dogs, and conversation, and I thought, *How perfect.* What better moment to sign my mortgage than in the middle of this beautiful chaos I've rebuilt?

She was young, polite, and efficient. She spread out her papers on the counter and handed me the pen. I signed my name—still my married name—page after page until we reached the final one. The title transfer. The house was technically mine, but now it would be legally, fully mine. I glanced at the page and stopped. Next to my name, it read: *An unmarried woman.*

I laughed out loud. "Really? Do we still need to say that?"

The notary looked up, mildly confused. "It's just how the forms are written."

She was tired. She had a whole life I couldn't see, maybe she was going home to her boyfriend, hoping he'd propose soon. She shrugged and said, "Yeah, it's kind of strange."

"Kind of?" I mutter, half amused, half outraged.

I kept signing. *An unmarried woman.* The words were heavy and electric all at once. I looked around at the beautiful chaos of my new life. The one I created with my children, the one I fought for with my tears and heartache. And in that moment, something inside me clicked into place.

Unmarried. Untethered. Unhooked from the system of ownership and expectation that has defined women for centuries. Spinster. Cat lady. All those old, tired archetypes swirl through my mind, and

I grin. Let them. If this is what unmarried looks like—standing in my kitchen, surrounded by love, chaos, and freedom—I'll take it.

It felt less like a label and more like a declaration of independence.

There's power in that word now. *Unmarried.* Whole. Reclaimed.

It's one more thread untangled in the web of marriage, one more knot undone. They really should print a warning on the marriage license: *Easy to enter, hard to unravel.* No one tells you that you'll have to separate belongings, dreams, bank accounts, even your Netflix profile. Every detail unbraided, strand by strand, until you find yourself again. And here I am.

A woman who signed her name to her own freedom in the middle of dinner, with the dogs barking and the pasta boiling over.

DIVORCED

It was a gloomy, sleepy day at home in the suburbs. For two years I had been moving back and forth from my apartment to my house, something called nesting, where the kids stay and the adults move. I felt like a satellite, always in orbit. This week I was home, in my house, with the kids, fresh off a trip to Costa Rica—a big, expansive exploration of my sensuality and erotic energy. The contraction afterward was familiar, expected even, but it still felt heavy. I was tired, unmotivated, distracted by the gray rain and the weight of a long to-do list, business calls, refinancing paperwork, emails.

Around three in the afternoon, I opened my inbox to an unfamiliar name. The subject line was simple, clinical. I scanned it quickly, and then my brain caught up with the text:

The parties are divorced as of today: March 6.

It was from the judge. My attorney was copied.

I read it once, twice, again. Then the tears came. Full body-shaking cries. It wasn't grief for the ending, but grief for all the living that came before it. The young bride with garlands around her neck, the mother juggling babies and building dreams, the woman who kept showing up long after she stopped being seen.

I filmed a short clip of myself crying, as I once did after leaving my first lover post-marriage. Not for anyone else, but as a record. Evidence of feeling. A reminder of the strength that comes from meeting the dark instead of running from it.

Then I napped. Life continued. There was dinner to make, kids to pick up, dogs to walk. The rhythm of our new reality. I never planned to be a single mother. The stories I grew up with painted it as failure or punishment: women alone, overworked, quietly suffering. I didn't want to repeat my mother's story of loving the wrong men and paying the price. And yet, there I was. It didn't feel like failure. It felt like freedom.

The air in the house was different now, lighter somehow. There was no one to calibrate my moods around, no one to perform for, no one to manage. Just us. Our family, redefined.

Of course, freedom had its cost. The bills didn't get smaller because the marriage ended. There were nights I lay awake wondering if I'd be able to hold it all: the parenting, the work, the money, the longing. But even in that fear, there was something deeply alive about it. I would rather navigate uncertainty than numbness.

That night, my daughter and I curled up on the couch to watch a movie about two teenagers having sex for the first time. Afterward, we talked about intimacy, boundaries, and how to know when you're ready. She told me her fears and her hopes, and I felt such gratitude that we could have that conversation at all.

I told her that I was learning at forty-seven what I hoped she could know at fourteen: that intimacy begins with yourself. That safety and pleasure belong together. That your body is not something to earn love with, but something to honor as sacred.

After she went to bed, I sat in the quiet and thought about how different that moment might have been if I hadn't been willing to burn it all down. The generational silence had been broken. The next morning, I woke early and felt the peace I'd been waiting for. I worked out, dressed up, and met a friend for lunch by the ocean. It felt surreal to be clear of a two-decade chapter, to be free of the contracts, spoken and unspoken, that had bound me.

Endings require courage. They ask us to go all the way down, to face the grief, the stories, the identities that no longer fit, and then rise. When we allow ourselves to reach the bottom, we find not emptiness, but clarity.

And from that clarity comes something unshakable: the knowing that we can hold it all—the fear, the freedom, the beauty, the cost—and still choose ourselves.

That's the real liberation. Not being chosen. Choosing ourselves.

The term *single mother* used to make my stomach tighten. It brought to mind struggle and survival, women weighed down by exhaustion or loneliness, quietly carrying it all. It was never a title I wanted, and yet there I was.

At first, I carried the old stories with me. The whispers that single mothers were either broken or brave, but never both. The ones who were told they worked too hard, wanted too much, or should be grateful for what they had. Over time, something shifted. The label started to dissolve, and what replaced it was agency.

There was fear, and there still is. The bills, the logistics, the endless decisions. But there was also a new kind of safety that came from self-trust. My home was quieter now, but it was peaceful. The air itself felt different, charged with possibility.

Motherhood, it turned out, did not get smaller when I was on my own. It expanded. It became less about performance and more about presence. Some nights I fell asleep worrying about money or the future, but other nights I sat on the floor surrounded by laughter, knowing that this, in all its mess and imperfection, was enough.

Becoming a single mother has been one of my greatest initiations. It stripped away the illusion that I needed to be rescued or completed. It showed me that freedom and devotion can live side by side, that strength can coexist with softness, and that leadership can feel sensual when it rises from love.

But inside me, there still lived a wanting.

A wanting for a partner who could meet me fully as I am. Not as someone to save, but as someone already whole. A partner who honored both my sovereignty and my softness, who could stand beside me in the sacred balance of motherhood, power, and pleasure.

The wild art of wanting more has become my devotion. I have learned to believe that I can have both: love and freedom, motherhood and sensuality, sovereignty and surrender.

This is where the real work began. I had to trust that life was reorganizing itself even when it felt uncertain. I had to remember that when everything seemed to fall apart, it was often falling into alignment. I had to learn to surrender again and again to the Goddess, to the intelligence that built something sacred from whatever had burned away.

This is not the end of my story. It is the sacred middle. The place between destruction and creation, between the woman I was and the woman I am becoming.

AN OLD CEREMONY FOR NEW SKIN

The urge for a new tattoo arrived quietly, like the idea of brunch that lingers until it becomes a plan. At first, it was just a thought—maybe something on my arm. Then, one day on Instagram, I saw a woman I'd met at a retreat. She had posted a new tattoo on her forearm and described it as a sacred-geometry ceremony. I followed the tag, found the artist, and forgot about it.

Months later, in the middle of what I call the *holy fuck* phase, when I could feel my life cracking open, I sent an inquiry. The only date available was February 14. Valentine's Day. *Why not? I* thought. My kids would be fine, and it seemed like a poetic declaration: self-love as the theme of the day.

I paid the deposit and received the address. Eagle Rock. The morning of the appointment, I dressed in black pants and a white T-shirt that read *Let Love In*. I parked on the street, feeling both nervous and sure. The door opened to reveal a young man with a shaved head and piercing blue eyes wearing all white, with tattoos covering his arms and neck. The house was small and full of symbols: incense burning, spiritual artwork on the walls, a Buddha in the corner. He offered me tea and asked what had brought me here.

We started talking about my move to LA, my awakening, my healing, the reclamation of pleasure after trauma. I told him more than he needed to know, but the words kept coming. I was done with silence.

We talked about placement and intention. I told him I had been considering my arm, but lately the solar plexus had been calling.

He nodded. "That is a powerful chakra, the center of your sovereignty and power."

"Yes," I said. "That's exactly what I need."

We moved into another room, with two chairs and a rainbow prism of light streaming across the floor. We sat across from each other to meditate. Feet flat, palms open, I could feel my heart racing. I closed my eyes and dropped into the stillness, letting the ceremony take me.

He took time to draw the design while I walked down the street for lunch. When I returned, he led me into a back room lined with sacred artwork and religious icons. He placed the stencil on my chest, between my breasts, a sacred geometry symbol, called a Yantra, pointing downward toward my sacral center.

"I love it," I said.

He gathered his tools, long sticks and fine needles, tying them together with a red string. The room filled with the sound of Krishna Das.

The first puncture startled me. The pain was sharp and direct. He asked if I was all right, and I nodded. It was a hand poke tattoo, each mark made by hand, one deliberate poke at a time. The rhythm was hypnotic: poke, poke, poke. *Om Namah Shivaya. He chanted and I breathed through the pain.*

The sensation became its own meditation. Some areas were tender, almost unbearable, but I stayed with my breath through the waves, through the sharpness that made me want to run. The longer I sat, the more I could feel something ancient releasing.

After a few hours, he stood me up and guided me to an altar covered in statues and candles. He placed gold leaf on my tongue and at the edges of the tattoo. Then he tied the red string from the needle around my wrist.

"Do not remove it for sixty-six days," he said. "The skin will heal quickly, but the energy takes longer."

He covered the tattoo with clear plastic and gave me instructions. No sauna. No workouts. Reflect. Meditate. Integrate.

When we returned to the front room, his young son was sitting on the couch playing video games. The holy and the ordinary coexisting. "The ecstasy and the laundry," as Jack Kornfield says. I smiled at the reminder that the spiritual and the mundane are never separate.

I drove home feeling both raw and renewed. My kids were still awake when I arrived. They wanted to see the new tattoo, and I showed them.

Over the next few days, I felt something shifting. My chest ached and pulsed with energy. I cried in the shower for no reason, felt waves of emotion rise and fall. The activation had worked.

The tattoo marked a threshold—an initiation into a deeper version of myself.

A new beginning, etched into my skin.

LOVE'S LIBERATION

Over the next year, I returned to the ceremony five more times. Each tattoo became its own portal—an initiation, an imprint, a prayer. Six months after that first one, I walked back into the same bungalow, a little more certain, a little more undone. I told him, for the first time out loud, that I was leaving my husband.

I was blowing up my life.

"I've set out on a journey across a dark sea of change," I said. "I know there will be days when I can't see the shore or remember why I started."

This time the design was for my arm. A visual reminder of strength and courage, something to hold onto when the darkness closed in. He poured the tea, we talked about the chaos and beauty of transformation, and then he began to draw. A snake, wrapping around the yantra. The snake, symbol of the Divine Feminine. The awakening of the Goddess within me.

Each time I returned, I was further along in the unraveling. Another chapter of the story inked into skin. Another threshold crossed. These ceremonies became mile markers in my initiation like the plant medicine journeys that had guided me before, each one offered its own transmission, its own medicine. Every tattoo held a story, a promise, a vow to remember who I was becoming.

They formed a map across my body, a constellation of symbols marking the moments I chose truth over comfort, awakening over illusion. Each piece a reminder of my devotion to life, to pleasure, to my becoming.

And somewhere between the ink and the intention, I realized that this was not about art. It was alchemy.

A SHORT STORY OF LOVE ON THE ROCKS

That summer, I danced barefoot in the living room of an Airbnb in Venice Beach with my writing coach, this book—*the one in your hands*—calling to me even then. So many chapters unformed, so many pieces of me still rearranging.

My lover showed up just as everything was crashing down, the waves of my old life colliding into each other. My tears ricocheted to the rhythm of breaking glass, my marriage dissolving, his infidelity still hot in my veins. We met in hotels. I wore lingerie that made me feel like fire and texted him photos between therapy sessions where I smashed foam boxes and screamed until I could breathe again.

I played it cool, but I wondered when he would disappear. The fear lived under my skin, the same old story. He texted hearts and sweet hellos, but there was always a wall. I kept offering more, a quiet whisper pleading: *Pick me.* He offered what he could, which wasn't much, but to me, the breadcrumbs were a feast.

He drove me to the airport the next week. I was flying out, and he kept going deeper. I let him because it felt so good to be wanted. But he couldn't stay. He was still tangled in his old life, and I told myself it was fine. We were just lovers. I was fine.

Until I wasn't.

He vanished into his own chaos one day, and I learned what *ghosted* really meant. My life was already built on scaffolding, and when he pulled away, it was like someone had yanked out the final piece. I spent the weeks before Christmas in agony, walking around my beautiful home with my kids, feeling gutted by grief. My marriage, my home, my first Christmas alone. And his absence felt like a kick in the ribs.

The rain that week was relentless. Gray skies, wild wind—it all mirrored my inner storm. I felt like I was drowning in sadness but still had to make dinner and watch *Grey's Anatomy* with my daughter. I was grateful for the tragic storylines so I could cry freely.

Between the suburbs and the city, between motherhood and solitude, I blasted "crash out" songs, wanting to roar and rage. I was still submerged in grief, swept under by the storm.

And then he came back, promising to do better. He told me he didn't want it to be over. My mother was in the hospital that month; I was too tired to say no. We met in the city for mid-afternoon delights, and he called every day. His affection carried me through the fear, the hospital visits, the exhaustion. He was my only bright spot.

But the roller coaster didn't stop. Another reunion, another crash. Taylor Swift and Billie Eilish were the soundtrack of my heartbreak as I drove back and forth between my two worlds—kids, city, tears by the pool, tears at the gym.

Why can't I quit this? I asked myself. My nervous system was hijacked by the highs and lows.

When it was good, it was intoxicating. When it wasn't, it was chaos. By summer, we tried traveling together. My gut told me not to go, but I did anyway.

You're not out of the woods, a voice whispered.

He needed space. Another dagger in the soft tissue of my intimacy wound. Every inconsistency jabbed at my system. By fall, I finally I ended it. I was crushed, but I knew I was gasping for air and reaching for my dignity. I cried my way up Runyon Canyon, tears blurring my vision.

That was my final recoding.

The little girl and the teenager in me screamed to go back, but something deeper had shifted. I stepped into the woman I had been becoming: the mother, the caretaker, the sovereign one.

"No more breadcrumbs of love," I said out loud. "I am enough, alone."

In the tenderness that followed, I saw it clearly: the wound playing out all over again. Who was I, really? And what would I tell my daughter if it were her? This is soul contract work. It loops until you decide to break it. I was exhausted, but beneath the ache, a small flicker of conviction appeared. I remembered the long road to this moment. The loss and heartbreak. The surgery. I will not sacrifice any more of myself.

And then, time did what time does. A day passed, then two, then a week. I thought about him less. I started to smile again.

One morning, I lay in bed and placed my hands over my belly, whispering to all the parts of me that still longed to be loved, held, and chosen.

"I love you. You are doing great," I said softly.

And I was.

PARTNERSHIP IS A MIRROR

The theme of the weekend was *Relationships, Attachment, and Repetition Compulsion.*

Naturally, I brought my situationship with me.

I laugh about it now. The irony felt cinematic, but at the time it felt perfectly reasonable. Returning to New York always brought me face to face with my former selves, the versions of me that still lives in those streets. I was excited to share that world with him, to let him see the city that had shaped me, to deepen our connection in a new environment. It didn't quite unfold that way.

When people asked what this program was, I shrugged and jokingly call it a *trauma camp*, half deflecting. What it really was, was a year-long study in embodiment, a living laboratory for transformation. We gathered five times over the course of a year, spending long days and nights in a yoga studio, shedding layers of story and protection. The group was its own ecosystem, each person an organ in a shared body, responding and adjusting to one another's healing. There was an alchemy in the room that is impossible to describe without diminishing it.

That weekend in July, New York was a furnace. The air was thick; the kind of heat that pressed your patience and made you want to duck inside cold cafes and shops just for the relief. The smell of garbage and the crowds of tourists in the hot summer made July in New York my least favorite time, and yet I'm swayed by the nostalgia and idealization of the city, even in its harshest conditions. It was clear my guest didn't feel the same forgiveness of it's packed streets and oppressive heat.

Inside the studio, we began with attachment theory, the study of how we learn to give and receive love. We had been asked to bring a photo of ourselves as a child. I chose one of me at five or six, standing beside a bicycle in a green terrycloth jumpsuit and red leather slip-ons, bowl cut and wide-eyed. One by one, we introduced these children. We spoke of their homes, their caretakers, their longings. The work was to trace the patterns, to see how the ways we attached as children mirrored the ways we sought connection now.

And meanwhile, in the margins of all this, was him.

Travel reveals people. Dosed with heat and hunger, it reveals even more. He spent his days wandering the city, visiting galleries, texting me when he was downstairs waiting. I would come down on breaks, flushed from hours of emotional excavation, to find him leaning against the wall with an easy smile and a cool detachment that both comforted and left me wanting more.

Eighty percent of the time, it was beautiful. There was the way he touched my back and made me laugh over iced coffee. But there was also the other twenty percent, the subtle corrections. *Don't slouch. You walk too fast. Why can't you respond to my text?* Our meals were tense, and when I shared how emotional the day had been, instead of curiosity, I was met with criticism. I bought tickets to a musical, managing his mood with distraction, an invisible pattern as old as time.

When I introduced him to my teacher, he hung back, cool and detached. What had been so attractive about him now felt alienating and at odds with the intimacy and vulnerability I was experiencing in the room.

All weekend, I oscillated between two worlds: the deep intimacy of the somatic space, where people were unraveling lifetimes of pain, and the tension of keeping peace with a man who didn't quite believe in what I was doing.

Inside the studio, I confronted my abandonment wounds and anxious attachment. Outside, I reenacted them in real time. He was avoidant, and I was anxious, a perfect polarity for repetition. Even when his criticism stung or his detachment triggered me, I worked harder to be lovable, to be chosen. I rationalized his behavior, mistaking crumbs for connection.

On our last night, we walked through SoHo while he spent nearly an hour on the phone, comforting the wife of a friend of his who'd died suddenly. I walked beside him, convincing myself he'd hang up any moment and return to my side, but the farther we walked, the angrier I got. And yet, I stayed quiet. I simmered in silence. He was doing something honorable, but at the expense of us.

It wasn't until much later that I saw it clearly. His avoidance wasn't personal; it was familiar. My body recognized it as home. His distance triggered the same longing I had carried since childhood, the ache to be seen and to be worth staying for.

This is repetition compulsion. We return to the scene of the original wound, hoping this time it will end differently. A month later, I broke it off. Something had shifted inside me, and I could finally see myself shrinking, despite everything I said and projected externally, a woman of independence, authority, and grace, and yet in this one area of life, I was playing out an old wound.

The antidote to the wounds, the masks, the characters we create is self-love. Truly accepting and loving ourselves and all our flaws and shortcomings. I had to love myself through this, falter on new legs through a recalibration, until I could finally say: *Enough.*

The work had worked.

I was shifting from a child's wiring of anxious love to the woman's truth of sovereignty.

BREAKING FREE FROM THE PATTERN

"You're my Barbie," he had said as we walked through the heat of a New York summer; a compliment—tall, beautiful, blonde.

But something in me recoiled. I smiled, but inside I felt that old familiar contraction, the one that whispers, *Don't make a scene, don't be too much, just let it go.*

Later, I realized that moment wasn't about him at all. It was my body remembering. I had spent a lifetime learning how to stay small enough to be loved—quiet enough, pretty enough, agreeable enough. My nervous system was calibrated to survive in the presence of those who needed me to shine but not outshine them.

He wasn't the first man to adore me and diminish me in the same breath. He was simply the last one I was willing to confuse for love.

For a long time, I couldn't see the link between my mother and the men I chose.

It's easy to name the absent father as the source of longing, but harder to see how our mothers, even the loving ones, write the first code of attachment into our cells. My mother loved me fiercely, but her love was braided with control, dependency, and unspoken expectation. She needed me close, compliant, shining just enough to reflect her light back to her.

That is what my body learned to call *connection*.

In her world, feelings were liabilities. Sadness, anger, longing, were indulgences that threatened the family image. I learned to manage myself, to become the well-behaved daughter who didn't make messes or waves. Her approval was steady only when I was pleasant, accomplished, supportive.

My nervous system had been shaped to feel approval, admiration, and safety as love.

When a man looked at me with that same proud ownership, calling me his Barbie, my body recognized the signal. It wasn't safety I felt, it was familiarity.

To be adored but unseen was the only love my system knew how to metabolize.

These men, these lovers, were never random. They arrived as mirrors, each one reflecting the lineage of conditional love that raised me. The pattern was always the same. Be beautiful. Stay bright. Don't need too much. My worth was measured in how well I reflected someone else's light.

When I began the somatic work, the pattern started to fray.

It was subtle at first, a small pulse of awareness that I could barely catch. A faint tightening in my stomach, a whisper somewhere inside that said, *This doesn't feel right.* I couldn't name it yet, but my body could sense it. The early work was just to notice, call attention to it, like, "I want to come back to this."

It showed up as a twinge, a glitch in the field, a moment when time seemed to slow. While standing on the familiar streets of the city I once called home, I could feel that inner signal rise, the quiet insistence of truth pushing through the noise. But habit was louder. I had spent a lifetime ignoring that voice. The armor I had built to survive still told me to smile, to smooth things over, to stay quiet.

The nervous system clings to what it knows.

It's like riding the same trail again and again, until the grooves are so deep, they feel like the only way. To choose differently is to veer off the familiar path and into the unknown. It feels strange at first, almost dangerous. But that is what healing really is: learning to pause at the first flicker of discomfort and listen before the old pattern takes hold. Each time I caught the signal, each time I slowed down long enough to notice it, something rewired inside me. The old grooves began to soften, and a new rhythm began to take shape. It was slow at first, but it was real. It was the sound of truth returning to my body.

It was the feeling of coming home.

Somatic work gave me a test ground to understand that what I mistook for passion was my body re-enacting survival. I began to understand this circuitry of response. He wasn't just a person; he was a pattern, the embodied echo of my earliest attachments. Every time I tolerated the silent treatment, the criticism, the subtle undermining, I was reliving the invisible bargains I'd made as a daughter: *I'll be good. I'll stay close. I'll make you proud. Just don't leave me.*

It detangled me from my mother's story, too—her silence, her righteousness, the ways her unmet pain had spilled into me without either of us fully knowing it. I can hold compassion for her now. She was shaped by what she inherited, just as I was shaped by her.

This is how trauma works: the body seeks familiarity, not safety. The child who learned to regulate through a parent's approval grows into a woman who confuses anxiety with chemistry. But compassion doesn't mean continuation. My healing came the moment I stopped trying to prove my worth to people who fed off my light. When I stopped mistaking intensity for intimacy. When I stopped being the mirror.

Now, I can love without abandoning myself. I can be radiant without apologizing.

In the midst of my divorce, my mother could sense that the perfect-daughter story was beginning to crack. My choices seemed to confront something in her she wasn't ready to look at. Instead of support, I got long, anxious text messages that arrived like sermons.

One evening, before I had even spoken the word *divorce* aloud, I asked her to watch the kids so I could meet a friend. I hesitated when I asked; her help was never without cost. Once inside my home, she slipped easily into commentary—what my children were reading, how much screen time they had, how often I was out. It was the familiar blend of care and control that defined our dynamic.

Later that night, my phone buzzed. Her message was gentle on the surface but sharp underneath. I should be cautious. I should protect my family at all costs. None of what I had built would mean anything without it.

It landed like a verdict, a judgment disguised as love.

Hours passed before I found my words. I told her, as calmly as I could, that her fears were her own, and that what I needed from her was not guidance, but support.

I even offered her the script: *What you meant to say was, "I have your back, no matter what."*

She never replied. Silence—the language she used when faced with a truth she couldn't hold.

Her silence said everything.

It was the same silence that had followed me through childhood, the withholding that trained me to fill the air with a quiet apology, to make things right without repair. As a child, I was well-behaved because our strongest survival instincts adapt in subtle and intelligent ways. This time, as an adult woman, I didn't bend myself back into the daughter she preferred. I let the quiet stand. For the first time, I could feel the tectonic plates shifting inside me, the old contract dissolving.

It's possible she experienced this as defiance, but for me it was the first pulse of trust—for myself.

My mother still tries to protect the image of perfection for safety. As if it could insulate us from the world.

She warns me that my work, my expression, my truth is unsafe, too revealing.

She means well, I suppose, but what she's really saying is: *Your authenticity threatens the story that keeps me safe.* For her, survival depended on containment. But my liberation depended on breaking it. This isn't blame, it's clarity. I can love the woman who taught me how to perform and refuse the next performance. I hold compassion for her suffering and still insist on a life that makes room for mine.

Breaking free of narcissism wasn't about rejecting men. It was about reclaiming the parts of me that were trained to sparkle but never spill. It was about letting myself be fully human—angry, tender, desirous, messy, alive.

This was my moment of real liberation. It wasn't vengeful, it was peaceful. We can't change someone else, but we can stop participating in the patterns that keep us stuck and triggered.

I've noticed something subtle but unmistakable: my tolerance has changed. I catch myself when I start to overexplain. I practice saying, "No" as a full sentence. I stop saying yes, when I mean no. I pull back from conversations that no longer feel aligned, and I'm learning to trust myself before my mind rationalizes. These are the small, daily acts that build a new nervous system. Boundaries, as I've learned, are not walls, they're muscles. And like any muscle, they strengthen through use.

Breaking free of the pattern didn't require confrontation or collapse. It required discernment and self-trust. Through this process I learned how to say no to anyone who wasn't safe for intimacy, to attention that left my body feeling confused or anxious, or love that asked me to stay quiet or small. It sounds so simple, and common sense, but rewiring my patterns took awareness, time, and practice. And with that practice, intimacy stopped being something I chased and became something I chose.

✦ Healing Practice: Disentangling from Narcissism

A PRIESTESS PATH TO RECLAIMING POWER, PLEASURE, AND PEACE

1. **The Seeing—Awaken from the Spell**

Theme: Truth as initiation.
Body focus: The eyes, the heart, the gut.
The first step is the awakening: seeing the dynamic for what it truly is, not what you hoped it could be. Narcissistic relationships thrive on illusion, projection, and intermittent reinforcement—the hot/cold pattern that mimics love but feeds addiction.

Your work begins in the body: *Can I feel what's true, even if it breaks the fantasy?*

This is the moment you stop explaining, justifying, or self-abandoning, and begin witnessing reality as it is. Seeing clearly is sacred. It pierces the spell of confusion and opens the first portal to sovereignty.

"The truth doesn't hurt, it frees. The pain comes from holding onto the lie."

2. **The Untangling—Reclaim the Body**

Theme: Somatic sovereignty.
Body focus: The nervous system, breath, and boundaries. Narcissistic entanglement isn't just emotional, it's physiological. The nervous system becomes addicted to the push-pull cycle of validation and withdrawal. Untangling begins when you learn to regulate from within rather than chase regulation through their attention. This is where your pleasure practices and somatic rituals are essential: breathwork, movement, sound, sensual ritual—each one rewires the body toward *safety inside self.*

Boundaries become more than words—they're energetic, cellular, ancestral.

"The body doesn't lie. It knows who feels safe and who drains your life force. Listen to it."

3. **The Repatterning—Heal the Lineage**

Theme: Reparenting the mother wound.
Body focus: The inner child, the womb, the ancestral line.
Disentangling from narcissism means meeting the pattern that made their love feel familiar. The work here isn't about them, it's about the early imprint. It's the moment you recognize that your nervous system was conditioned to equate approval with love, and you decide to rewire that truth. This is where forgiveness becomes liberation, not the condoning of harm, but the reclaiming of agency.

You begin to mother yourself the way no one could. You learn that your worth is not conditional, and your needs are not inconvenient.

"Every time you choose peace over performance, you rewire an entire bloodline."

4. The Returning: Embody the Sovereign Self

Theme: Pleasure as proof of freedom.
Body focus: The heart, the pelvis, the voice.
The final step is embodiment. It's when you can walk through the world unhooked from their energy, no longer performing or defending, but simply *being.* Your radiance is no longer something they can take credit for. It's yours, sovereign and self-sustained. Here, pleasure becomes your compass again. You can feel joy without guilt, desire without fear, power without apology.

You've moved from survival to creation.

"Freedom is when you no longer need them to be the villain in order to be the heroine."

Stage	Portal	Practice	Embodied Shift
1. The Seeing	Truth	Journaling, mirroring, naming reality	From illusion → clarity
2. The Untangling	Nervous system	Breathwork, movement, sensual ritual	From dysregulation → safety
3. The Repatterning	Lineage	Inner child work, boundary repair, forgiveness rituals	From inherited pain → autonomy
4. The Returning	Sovereignty	Pleasure practice, creativity, voice activation	From survival → creation

CHAPTER SIX

Bodily Autonomy

My body had been whispering for years, but I had forgotten how to listen. At first, it spoke softly through exhaustion, tension, minor discomforts, which I brushed off as normal. Then, when I ignored those, it began to shout.

The day I found out I needed surgery to remove my left ovary, something in me went still. It wasn't the diagnosis itself that shook me, but the recognition of what my body was trying to say. I knew, even before the doctor did, that this was more than a medical event. It was a message.

The ovary is the creative center—the wellspring of feminine life force!—the seat of desire and creation. And mine had been holding what I had refused to feel. Every unspoken truth, every swallowed need, every "I'm fine" when I was anything but. All of it had gathered there, dense and unexpressed.

When the cyst was removed, I grieved its sacred loss. But deep down, I knew it was my body's way of releasing what my spirit had carried for far too long. It was the physical manifestation of all I had suppressed: the artist, the lover, the woman who had learned to make herself small to stay loved.

For years, I had lived from the neck up: rational, polished, in control. It was safer that way. Feeling too much had always been dangerous. Desire was dangerous. Need was dangerous. Even joy was dangerous if it drew too much attention. But during that season of my surgery, in the stillness, the recovery, my body reintroduced herself to me. She said: *I am not your enemy. I am your oracle.*

Every sensation became information.

The ache in my pelvis wasn't just pain, it was the residue of all the times I had overridden my knowing. The tightness in my chest was every unspoken truth I had ever buried under "keep the peace." The flutter in my heart when I allowed myself to imagine something more, that was my aliveness, waking up again.

What I had once called illness, I began to understand as initiation. The cyst was not punishment. It was an invitation. An invitation to come back into my body, to reclaim the sacred conversation between flesh and soul, to no longer outsource my wisdom to others—not doctors, not men, not the collective voice of what a "good woman" should be.

Healing my body required surrender. It required grief and pleasure, and rage and tenderness to coexist, to stop editing the full expression of being alive. It was another moment of true liberation. Leaving my marriage and burning my life down brought me back to the home that had always been mine: my body.

BACK IN MY BODY

Two weeks after breaking free from my toxic situationship, I went back to New York.

Tender, but steady. Confident that I'd pulled myself back from somewhere I had wandered. It harnessed a well of empathy within me, one I have been able to dip into again and again. I believe it was placed on my path so that I could meet the women in my circle, those who chose lovers, boyfriends, and husbands who hurt them, with compassion and knowing. I had been there—we could ask the question together: *Why do I return to a love that hurts me?*

Together, we excavated, repatterned, and took an honest look at how we got here in the first place.

It was September, and the air in New York was crisp and cool. I could feel something shifting. I was weaning myself off the addictive high of attachment, learning how to live without the hit of being chosen. I walked the streets of the East Village, breathing in the freedom of anonymity, grateful for this space away from Los Angeles, my kids, the intensity of my half-life in Hollywood.

Somatic therapy had become my scaffolding. If pleasure is my medicine—the alchemy of all that calcified anger and grief—then somatic therapy has been the scaffolding that holds me steady while I crack the foundation and rebuild. In this work, I let the energy move through me like an earthquake, trusting that the reality of destruction is release. Sisterhood, pleasure, and compassion have been the hands that pulled me from the rubble and guided me into a new season of becoming.

This weekend's module was about character—the archetypes we build at each stage of development to keep ourselves safe. From infancy to adolescence, each of us learns to adapt to the places love didn't fully reach us. When our sense of being lovable is challenged, we create masks, armor, and performances to protect the vulnerable truth beneath.

What surprised me most in my first year of somatic work wasn't the father wound; that ache had always been familiar, almost expected. What I hadn't yet faced was the wound I carried from my mother. Somewhere in her orbit, I learned to mistake endurance for love. To hold space for narcissists long past the point of health. To tend to the emotional needs of others before my own, as though that was the price of being loved.

HEALING FOR ALL

The deeper I went, the more my body revealed. Each session peeled back another layer of protection until I could no longer hide behind words. That was when the work with Sherri deepened. In her space, healing was not something that happened to me; it was something that happened through me.

Decades ago, the psychiatrist **John Bowlby** and psychologist **Mary Ainsworth** gave language to what my body already knew. They called it **attachment theory**—the idea that the way we bond with our caregivers in early life shapes how we love, relate, and regulate as adults.

In those first years of life, safety is not an idea; it is a felt experience. The infant learns trust through attunement, through the steady presence of a caregiver who meets their needs. When that presence is inconsistent or self-referential, the child's nervous system adapts. It learns to over-function, to perform, to please, to anticipate, to earn love.

We call it anxious attachment or avoidance or disorganization, but beneath every label is the same truth: the body's longing for safety.

We grow up believing those adaptations are our personality, when in truth they are our body's attempts to belong. What we were doing in this therapeutic space was giving the body a second chance at attachment—a chance to be held, seen, and mirrored without condition. Each reenactment, each breath, each tear was a way of rewriting the story my nervous system had carried since childhood.

This is the real alchemy of healing: We don't think our way into safety; we feel it.

I spent years focusing on the storyline of my biological father, an almost mythological story in my home about his absence, the setup of a legendary man who might appear one day. His absence was the most visible wound, but the deeper truth revealed itself slowly through my work with somatic therapy. My greatest wounding was not from the father who left, but from the mother who stayed. Her lack of boundaries, her inability to meet her own needs, and her unconscious reliance on me to fill that void had shaped everything about how I learned to love.

It is a hard truth to face. To look into the mirror of our most formative relationships and see how they live on through us—not as memory, but as pattern. It can shatter everything we thought we knew about love. But it is also the only road to real forgiveness, the kind that begins in the body.

In the world of coaching and therapy, there's a seduction in the idea of breaking people open, of shattering the old story to birth the new. Without mastery and care, that kind of work becomes performance. It can retraumatize rather than liberate. True transformation requires reverence. It is not about breaking someone down; it is about holding them as they reassemble. The real skill lies in rebuilding and repatterning safety after the storm.

This room was one of those rare spaces. The integrity of the facilitators was unquestionable. Each of us held healing as our responsibility. We were not there to save one another, but to stand as mirrors and witnesses—sovereign yet united in the sacred contract of transformation.

Shadow work required humility. It demanded we move slowly and remember that the human heart is not a performance art piece but a living organism. It's resilient and unbreakable, but also tender and delicate. We began with role play. Partnered, one of us as the adult, one as the child.

My partner placed a book on my head and instructed me to be quiet, polite, pretty. "Be seen, not heard," he said. "Smile. Be good."

He told me to be the prize on his arm—to be pleasing, effortless, composed. My body contracted.

In a flash, past and present collided. I was no longer in that studio; I was back in my childhood home. My unconscious adaptation to stay small and quiet, and safe, to protect my mother. Her pride in me was a weight that I carried, striving to be good enough and not cause her more emotional stress. I saw her fragility and distress and took on the role of caretaker and protector.

I learned that being admired and praised for being easy and good was equal to love. In a turbulent household, safety required smallness and appeasement. The exercise deepened into "process work," a kind of embodied reenactment of our original family system. We used the room itself as a map of our early relationships. Each participant drew a stick-figure diagram of their childhood home: the mother, the father, the siblings, the unspoken hierarchies. Then we placed people in the room to stand in for those figures. It was astonishing how quickly the field came alive, how our bodies remembered what our minds had long suppressed.

When it was my turn, I placed my "mother" on one side and my "children" on the other. A foam block separated us: the symbolic wall that had always existed between us. My mother's proxy began to speak, repeating phrases of superiority, judgment, and disappointment. I felt the child in me surface. I kicked and screamed and begged her to stop. The sounds were primitive, guttural.

Then the energy shifted. It was as though every version of me—the three-year-old, the nine-year-old, the teenager—came surging to the surface. My body became a conduit for generations of silenced rage. I screamed until I lost my bearings, until space and time dissolved.

Time collapsed and Sherri was beside me.

"Do you know where you are?" she asked softly. "Do you know my name?"

I had to find my way back. My body was trembling, my chest was heaving, my face was wet with tears. I felt the hush in the room, saw that others were moving through their own emotions. I was submerged in the beauty of group work—even when you are not the one in process, you are still healing. The resonance travels through the field. My story might be personal, but the pattern is universal.

It took several minutes to catch my breath. It felt less like release and more like completion. Something ancient had moved. I had touched a rage so deep it was almost holy—the rage of every silenced daughter who learned to perform love to survive. It was as if my soul had gone back through time and gathered up every piece of me that had ever been lost.

When I finally began to reorient, I could feel Sherri was beside me, her voice calm, her presence grounding. This is what happens when the body crosses a threshold it hasn't known how to integrate before. In somatic work, it's called **flooding**. The moment when the nervous system becomes overwhelmed by the surge of energy, emotion, or memory moving through it. It's not something to fear. It's the body doing what it has always done to survive—shutting down what feels too big, too fast, too much. In a safe and contained environment, flooding becomes part of the healing process rather than a repetition of harm. The body learns that it can come back, that intensity does not have to equal danger.

When Sherri asked, "Do you know where you are?" she was inviting my system back into safety. Naming, orienting, breathing, feeling the texture beneath my hands—these were the small, somatic, grounding acts that told my body the threat had passed.

I was repairing.

Attachment theory calls this the rewiring of safety. In that room, we were repatterning attachment in real time. Through embodiment, through witnessing, through the nervous system's return to safety, we were creating a new imprint—one where love did not mean performing, and connection did not require collapse. Each breath, each movement, each tear was a new signal to the body that it could be fully alive and still be safe.

For me, that moment was the beginning of real autonomy—not the independence I had fought for all my life, but the deeper sovereignty of being able to stay present with myself, even in intensity. That is the art behind this work. Teaching people they can survive their own aliveness.

THE DESCENT INTO THE BODY

Once I began to listen, I realized how loud my body had been all along. The whispers were not new; I had just been trained to tune them out. For most of my life, I had lived as a performer in my own body. I knew how to make it look good, how to make it desirable, how to make it productive. But I didn't know how to let it feel or how to listen to its wisdom. I had mastered control, but I had forgotten presence.

My work with Sherri was the beginning of my descent into sensation. It was raw, primal, and holy. In those early sessions, I learned that the body carried the vibration of our memories. It remembers everything we have lived through, even the things our minds have long decided to forget. Every time I said, "I'm fine," my muscles took the weight of that lie. Every truth I swallowed settled somewhere inside me, waiting for permission to move.

When I talked about something painful, Sherri would ask, "Where do you feel it?" and I would pause, surprised that there was always an answer. Sometimes it was a pressure in my chest, a knot in my throat, or a trembling in my hands. She would guide me to breathe into that place, to allow the sensation to exist without trying to fix it.

At first, it felt like reading in a new language. I was used to solving things, to finding a plan, to rationalizing my way through pain. But this was different. It was about surrender. I needed to trust that my body had its own timing and wisdom. There were sessions when I shook uncontrollably, waves of energy moving through me.

Sherri would say, "That is you, your essence, the truest blueprint of your soul in that energy. Let it move."

These practices became my compass. Somatic tools—breath, shaking, sound, and grounded movement—taught me how to come home to myself when words or logic could not. There were days when I wept for hours without knowing exactly why. My body was finally metabolizing what it had been holding for decades.

This could not have been done through intellect. The healing came through embodiment, through remembering the language of breath, movement, and sound. I learned that safety is not the absence of pain, but the presence of self. My body could be both witness and healer.

Liberation is not about transcending the body but inhabiting it fully. Each time I allowed myself to stay with the discomfort, I reclaimed another piece of myself. I began to trust the tremor, to welcome the tears, to recognize the sacred intelligence within sensation. The body that had once been silenced was finding her voice again. And she had so much to say.

In the weeks that followed, I felt an unfamiliar stillness move through me. My foundation had shifted; I had touched and moved something ancient and generational, but also very personal. I could feel my cells rearranging. It was not the silence of suppression, but the silence that comes after the storm; the body reorganizing itself around truth. Every cell felt softer, wider, and something inside me unclenched.

Healing is not the return to who we were before the wound. It is the slow remembering of who we were before we learned to leave ourselves.

For the first time, my body wasn't waiting for the next impact. She was resting in her own rhythm, in her own pulse, in the knowing that she could hold it all. Rage and tenderness. Grief and grace. She no longer needed to choose. This is what integration feels like. Not the high of a breakthrough, but the grounded hum of belonging to yourself.

It is from this place—this sacred stillness—that desire rises naturally like breath.

No more chasing, no more performing.

Awake, it says: *I am home now. I am ready to feel again.*

MONEY

When my father died, he left me an expected tool: money.

In the twenty years that followed our first meeting, I saw him only a handful of times. He was quiet, self-contained, and the least generous person I have ever met. He was from the generation that survived the Great Depression, and he was in constant fear of losing everything. He never sent a plane ticket, never offered to help, never eased the financial strain of my life in any way. But the distance wasn't just financial. Emotionally, we never grew close. So, when I learned that he had saved quietly for decades and left it all to me, with no plan and no instructions, it felt surreal. Poetic, even. The man who had given me nothing in life left me the one thing that could change it.

I was named executor, and it became a full-time job. There were bank accounts to untangle, taxes to file, lawyers to meet. The bureaucracy behind his death consumed me, and with it ran a river of irony and grief. This was the first time my father had ever provided for me, and he wasn't here to witness it.

But also, the money revealed everything unspoken in my marriage: the power dynamics we had ignored, the silent scorekeeping of who earned what, the resentment that came from ease arriving in my name. We fought because we didn't have money, and then because I had it and he didn't.

I made mistakes. I let money become a way to keep the peace, to avoid hard conversations between my husband and me, as well as with my mother. I gave freely, believing generosity would equal harmony. It didn't. It blurred boundaries that were already fragile.

The inheritance gave me a privilege that I am eternally grateful for. But there was a complexity to the sudden responsibility of stewarding money without preparation or support. I carried the weight alone, afraid to misstep—to squander—but I was also determined to release the energetic pattern my father had created.

People imagine that coming into money is freedom; for me, it involved another initiation—a test of capacity, discernment, and self-trust.

Over time, I began to see the deeper lesson. I was being invited to heal my relationship with the masculine through responsibility rather than resentment. To learn that abundance without boundaries can be just as destabilizing as scarcity. Safety is not something money can buy; it was something I had to build inside my body. It took years to find balance—to carry both gift and burden without guilt. Recognizing my privilege was its own battle, I was in constant judgement of myself through others' eyes. But what I've learned is that privilege doesn't make you immune to pain; it simply gives you a different curriculum.

This was mine.

Money became my next teacher, showing me that true wealth is not held in the bank, but what you hold in your nervous system.

Money became my embodiment practice. It asked me to ground myself in the same way pleasure did. To breathe when the numbers scared me. To expand, rather than contract, when I spent, received, or invested. I began to understand that wealth, like desire, was a current of energy moving through the body. If my nervous system couldn't hold it, it leaked.

This is the work I have learned to teach—to build capacity for both pleasure and prosperity. To let life flow through you without gripping or numbing. The more I anchored into my body, the more I held: grief, joy, money, love. As it turned out, abundance was not the reward for being good or productive. It was the natural overflow of a woman who trusted herself enough to receive.

LOVE / INTIMACY

For a long time, love was the one place my intelligence appeared to hinder me.

I was capable, confident, successful. I knew how to build a life, run a business, mother my children, and hold responsibility. And yet, when it came to intimacy, I kept finding myself looped into dynamics that drained me—relationships that asked me to be flexible, easy, undemanding, while quietly eroding my center.

This is the quiet ache so many women know. We are conscious and competent everywhere but in love and intimacy.

We've done the work. And then, somehow, we hand the steering wheel of our nervous system to men who can't meet us, hoping this time it will be different.

Before my marriage, I wouldn't have called my dating intentional. If anything, I perfected the art of being the cool, available girl—the one who could be picked up at a bar, taken home, kept light and unattached. I told myself I was free. But beneath that performance lived a longing for depth, devotion, and real intimacy that was never named, let alone honored.

So, it never arrived.

Then came twenty years with one person. A life built. And when that ended, when I blew up my life, I ran straight into a grown-up version of the same relationship pattern. This time it sounded like *I can keep it casual. I can be spacious. I don't need much.*

But the truth is, I'm not built for casual relationships. I never was. What I've learned is that short relationships and pleasure partnerships do not have to be casual. They can be intentional. Devotional. Respectful. When entered consciously, they can be incredibly rewarding.

After my awakening, love felt different in my body. Desire stopped feeling like a command I had to obey and became something I could tune into, adjusting the frequency depending on my needs. I stopped moving toward intimacy as a way to regulate my nervous system and started meeting it from a steady place. From there, I could finally choose.

I had a relationship enter my life during this season of profound transition. It was clearly time-bound from the beginning, shaped by circumstances that made partnership impossible. And still, there was immediate recognition—a deep, embodied knowing that didn't rely on fantasy or projection. I chose to enter it anyway, not because

I hoped it would become something else, but because I knew what I wanted from the experience itself.

It felt like calibration.

Like my nervous system chiming in tune.

What we shared was passionate and reverent. Slow. Curious. Present. Pleasure that didn't pull me away from my life; it anchored me more fully inside it. Even as I navigated grief and uncertainty in other areas of my life, my body stayed open, and pleasure became the sweetener that softened the edges. I was learning that turn-ons and sorrow could coexist—that intimacy didn't require me to abandon myself or numb what was real.

We experienced rupture, as real intimacy does. In the past, that would have sent me into retreat or performance. This time, I stayed. I felt anger without collapsing or disappearing. I named what was true. He listened. He took responsibility. Repair happened cleanly.

With that clarity, I could see the edges. His humanity, his journey, and the limits of what we were meant to be.

When the relationship ended, it did so with tenderness and truth. It hurt, and I let myself grieve it fully. I missed the connection, the devotion, the way my full erotic expression had been welcomed and celebrated. And I did not regret it. The experience showed me something essential: intimacy could be *that* good. Each lover, I realized, hadn't healed me, but had refined my capacity to know myself.

Later, he wrote to me and told me he had decided to return to a former partner, and something in me closed. Not in jealousy, but in discernment. His choice revealed a divergence I could feel instantly in my body. He hoped we could stay connected and eventually be friends. But my system already answered. I felt the subtle contraction that signals misalignment—by choosing his past he chose safety over expansion.

In both the beginning and the ending of this love affair, I did something new. I attuned to my nervous system, to my desire, both my physical desire for intimacy and my desire for greater connection and partnership and I made my choices from my own inner alignment.

I am not just responding to what my partner, or potential lover, desires, I am leading from my own desire, and from a place of sovereignty.

That means knowing what I want before I enter. Knowing my intimacy recipe. Naming the agreements, the boundaries, the limitations, and the desires up front—not as demands, but as devotion to my own nervous system. From that place, intimacy becomes sovereign. Chosen. Clean.

This is what bodily autonomy looks like in love.

I can love without performing. I can desire without bargaining. I can choose intimacy that meets me where I am, rather than where I once learned to survive. Love is no longer the place I go to be chosen. It is something I enter consciously, from wholeness, already at home in myself.

JOY

Joy was the last place my nervous system learned to trust.

I noticed it one afternoon in the somatic lab, during a season when I felt unusually lit up. I was open, optimistic, alive in my body because of the way romance was unfolding. I remember feeling its brightness and, almost immediately, questioning whether I could hold it. Not whether I deserved it, but whether it would last.

In the exercise we were practicing, we were asked to stand with a partner and voice a fear. When it was my turn, the words surprised me as they left my mouth. I wasn't afraid of loss or abandonment in a way that once dominated me. I was afraid of tasting this much joy—this much passion, connection, aliveness—and having it disappear.

It was a scarcity story, but this time on the opposite end of the spectrum. I was afraid I'd finally get what I wanted. It seems an odd thing to admit and yet I recognize it in my clients, too, as if it could be too good to be true and so we brace for the loss instead of relaxing into the flow of life. I have years of mindfulness and meditation training under my belt, and I still have to remind myself (and my clients) to remember the feeling of trust in the inevitable give and take of life, of the expansion and contraction that we can learn to ride like a wave instead of resisting.

There is a beauty in this kind of awareness, almost like lucid dreaming—being fully present while also watching yourself be present. Awake to the sweetness and the impermanence at the same time.

I felt it acutely when I was ending a journey with a lover, and as the ending approached, I could feel myself race ahead to the sadness. In a few days, he would move back overseas, to his life, and I would go back to mine. We had a beautiful, sensual journey together, but we were not meant to be more than a season. One night, lying next to him I shared this and we both embraced the poignancy of our choice, the depth of our love, and the ending in sight. We didn't regret our time together, and we were both going to feel the loss and heartbreak.

It was worth it.

There is a relief in being able to stop bracing and lean into life; trusting that loss will not crush us, and joy will arrive again, the way we trust the waves to keep washing up on a shore. We begin to accept all of life, not just the joy and the highs but also the losses and the grief, as part of the beauty of our humanity.

GRIEF

Grief is as nuanced as joy, showing up unexpectedly sometimes, and bringing with it a heavy blanket that can feel suffocating. You don't blow up your life without moving through deep valleys of grief. No matter how clear or determined or supported you are, to walk away from a life you created and start over requires a deep and meaningful relationship with grief.

For most of my life, I tried to process grief through story. I let it in as much as I could tolerate without losing myself in the current. I found outlets like acting and writing to be a way to feel, but it wasn't until somatic therapy and pleasure that I let myself go into the depths of grief, because I trusted I would not get lost there.

Grief isn't just experienced in our minds, it's felt in the body, and it demands our full presence. It feels like driving through a storm, when the rain feels relentless and it takes your whole presence just to stay in your lane. When the rain finally subsides, there is a wave of relief, and even though you knew it couldn't last forever, it feels miraculous that it didn't. That's how grief felt in my body, as though it would consume and lay me bare, but when I fully surrendered to it, when I bowed and gave over to the dark Goddess of Death, I was liberated. After my divorce, I spent days lying in bed, weeping, I would pull over in parking lots and cry and scream, I had sessions with my therapist where I said repeatedly, "I can't stop crying." Each time it felt like a tsunami of emotion could drown me, but when I stopped resisting, it passed. It was not the end, and if we are willing to feel it, to fully embrace the depths of our grief, it serves as a passageway. **Pleasure is a way to ride through the rough waters. The intensity of grief and rage isn't a problem to fix—they're bodily** experiences that need enough safety and capacity to move through us, and pleasure is their regulator. Pleasure, and specifically erotic energy, is a way to metabolize grief, whether it's an orgasm that brings you to tears, or embodied movement that alchemizes expressed energy and returns you to your power.

Liberation doesn't eliminate struggle or perfect balance, it builds *capacity*.

The capacity to feel without collapsing, receive without gripping, want without apologizing. To grieve without losing yourself. To love without disappearing. To hold joy without bracing for its loss. To keep stretching your capacity to hold more of the good and the bad, the highs and the lows to stay coherent in your heart, mind, and soul through the ride.

Money, love, grief, and joy are all training grounds for the same truth: Your body has wisdom to share, data that was easily overridden, but as you learn to stay present with intensity, to trust the only way out is through, there is freedom on the other side.

You might find yourself fixing the symptoms: the money story, the relationship patterns, the grief that once felt impossible to move past. We keep trying to put a bandage over the pain, but the body doesn't work in compartments. It's built—slowly, imperfectly, devotionally—as is your capacity to stay with sensation, to stay with yourself.

Women quietly yearn for this reclamation. No amount of achievement or better coping strategies will fill this desire. But the felt sense that we can meet life fully without shutting down, numbing out, or over-functioning will hold us. Because when the body learns safety, everything reorganizes. Money stops being a source of shame or control and becomes a current you can steward. Love stops being a performance and becomes a place you can stand. Grief stops being something to survive and becomes something with legs.

Joy stops feeling dangerous and becomes something you can inhabit.

We do not need mastery alone, we need intimacy. Intimacy with our own inner weather, our desires, our limits, our capacity.

Pleasure isn't the opposite of responsibility or depth, it's what helps us handle life. It's how the body processes everything we're asked to hold. It's our birthright. Why else would we have been born with the ability to experience so much pleasure? It's only through cultural conditioning that we have been taught to suppress our natural state.

Pleasure doesn't make us reckless; it moves us through making sense of who we are. By attuning to pleasure, you attune to your natural state of being.

That's why pleasure isn't a luxury. It's a skill. And like any skill, it can be practiced.

What becomes possible when a woman trusts her body to let life move through her? When she stops bracing against joy or tightening around desire? When she knows, in her bones, that she can survive her own aliveness?

This is the threshold we're standing at now. Once you can hold yourself through money, love, grief, and joy—once you can stay present inside intensity—something else wakes up.

Pleasure.

Power.

The kind that changes you.

✦ Temple Practice:
Descent into the Body

Find a quiet place where you can rest without interruption. Sit or lie down comfortably, allowing your body to be supported by the ground beneath you. Take a few slow breaths in through your nose and out through your mouth, each one a little deeper than the last. With every exhale, feel yourself arriving.

Let your awareness sink down from the mind into the body like a pebble dropping gently through still water. Feel the pull of gravity holding you. The earth beneath you. The rhythm of your own breath. There is nothing to fix, nothing to change. Simply notice what is here.

Let the breath widen through your ribs. Feel the subtle expansion and release with each inhale and exhale. If you can, let the out-breath be just a little longer than the in-breath. That lengthening tells your body it is safe to soften.

Now bring your awareness to the places that call your attention: your chest, your belly, your hips, or the space behind your heart. Ask softly, *What's here right now?*

You don't need to label or understand. Just listen. You may feel warmth, tightness, tingling, or even numbness. All of it belongs. If emotion begins to move, let it move. Sigh. Hum. Let a quiet sound leave your lips.

Shake your hands, roll your shoulders, sway your hips, whatever helps the energy shift and flow. This is the language of the feminine body—gentle, cyclical, sensing. She doesn't rush toward meaning; she listens for what wants to be felt.

If your mind wanders, return to the rhythm of your breath.

Inhale softness.

Exhale surrender.

Stay with the quiet invitation of the moment. When you are ready, place a hand on your heart and whisper to yourself, *I am home here.* Let that truth land. Let your body know that she has been seen, felt, and heard. You can stay here as long as you need.

The practice is not to arrive somewhere new, but to return to the body, to the present moment, and to the quiet pulse of life moving through you.

An Invitation: Reclaim Your Desire

CHAPTER SEVEN

Pleasure Is Liberation

I walked into a room in upstate New York among strangers and walked out three days later as a different person. Or maybe more accurately, as myself.

I had no idea what I'd said yes to. Only that I wanted to make sense of the mess of my life, to trust my body again, and to find my way home to myself. All the therapy, the mindset work, the self-help—it had pointed me in a direction, but I was beginning to understand that none of it could take me all the way home.

The body is where the compass actually lives.

We each wrote about coming home to ourselves. About our longings and desires to be seen, to be known, to be freed from the constant self-judgment.

I wrote:

Home to her desire, her pleasure, her wildness, her raw-ness. Anchored into herself. No more abandoning herself to please others, to keep peace, to be loved. She only has space for love that is freely given.

I was in the midst of the reckoning of my two lives. Following my desire had led me here, but now I was walking through vast darkness trying to create a life that felt like me and I didn't yet know who that was. Who was I when I stripped away the good mother, wife, daughter, friend that had buoyed me for so long? What did I want, and did it matter? Could I have it?

These are the questions that fell out of my body, breath by breath, lying on a mat on the floor.

Breathing rhythmically and continuously, hips thrusting, arms reaching for the sky—it felt like an exorcism of stagnation, every-thing stale and stuck moving up and out through the breath. And then a voice told us to reach for someone. To reach for what we need.

There was no one there.

My body knew this feeling. Recognized the loss, the abandon-ment, the endless grasping. Breath by breath I felt it—the relentless ache of a truth I had known as a little girl. And somewhere beneath the breath a part of me gave up because what's the point of reach-ing when no one is coming? Better to manage. To retreat. To never admit you needed it in the first place.

I was out of breath, tears and moans racking my body, curled on my side on the floor, the sound of others around me doing the same work in their own darkness.

But there was more than just breaking open.

I wrapped my arms around myself and felt the weight of my own hands. The softness of my own skin. It is possible to feel both childlike and maternal in the same moment; to be the child who needed holding and the mother doing the holding. That's what it felt like. I was both. I held the girl who had believed she was unlovable, not enough, too much. And I held her with tenderness rather than judgment, maybe for the first time.

I am a woman who no longer needs to be saved.

I let that settle. Then slowly, I moved from curled and fetal to hands and knees, running my palms over my legs, swaying my hips to music only I could hear. My fingertips found my neck, my chest. Slowly, deliberately, I traced the soft outline of my breast with one hand as the other drifted from my cheek to my lips, catching the soft wetness of my mouth.

There I am.

From the wreckage of my brokenness, I pulled out my aliveness. My eros. The ancient wisdom of a sensual, erotic body—alive now in the room, in me, finally allowed.

This was my homecoming.

DESIRE OPENS THE DOOR

When my desire returned, it did not knock politely.

It arrived inconvenient and a little rude, completely uninterested in the life I had arranged around its absence. It didn't care that I had a schedule or a reputation or a very sensible plan. It just arrived, and it wanted more.

More of what, exactly?

Everything.

More aliveness. More honesty. More of the feeling I'd had on that mat in upstate New York when I pulled myself up off the floor and felt my own skin, recognizing something ancient and ungovernable was moving through me. I wanted to live inside that frequency rather than visit it once on a retreat and then go back to managing.

I wanted to integrate that wildness into my motherhood, my life, my work.

The part that frightens women most is not desire itself, but what desire sees. Because she's honest in a way that's almost rude. She will walk through the rooms of your life and tell you plainly what is working and what is dead and what you've been calling contentment when really, you've just been tired. She doesn't do this to blow up your life. *She just loves you and she's been trying to get your attention for a long time.*

But she was never the disruption.

She was the thing that was true the whole time.

The intelligence I was learning to trust wasn't in my head. It was in my body—in what I felt when I finally stopped scanning everyone else and turned the attention back to myself.

What felt alive?

What felt dead?

What was I sustaining out of habit?

What was I choosing out of fear?

The answers were not abstract. They lived in my body. In the way my breath shortened in certain rooms. In the way my shoulders tensed at the sound of a familiar footstep. In the way my chest opened when I allowed myself to imagine something different.

I began to pay attention.

We have been taught to meet our longing with skepticism and restraint. To weigh the needs of everyone else, and dismiss our desires, so habitually we almost don't notice. Instead of tracing our desires and following the threads with curiosity, we negotiate with it instead. *I'll feel this later. I'll want that someday. This isn't practical right now.* But desire does not want to be tampered with reason, it wants to be met with truth.

When we listen—through sensation, through pleasure, through the subtle intelligence of the body—something remarkable happens. Life starts to move again. Desire becomes a compass back to our essential, individual soul path. The compass may show us we're wildly off course, but if we have the courage to listen, desire becomes the map back to center.

Pleasure, resourced from our own body, from connection with our own pussy and her wisdom, is what returns our power. Despite social, family, and cultural conditioning, when we move toward the wisdom of her pulse, we find the fuel, the inspiration to create a life that feels vibrant, free, and authentic.

Pleasure doesn't have to be something we chase or earn. It can be a way of living, a devotion to being fully alive in the body we have, in the life we are living, now. It becomes a daily practice, a returning to our own pulse, again and again, as the source of everything.

Most of us learned desire relationally. We figured out what we liked by reading what our partner responded to. We shaped our wants around what was acceptable, what kept the peace, what made us easy to love. Not dramatically. Just gradually, the way a river reroutes so slowly you don't notice until you look up and have no idea where you are.

And then someone asks what you want, and the first thing you do is scan their face before you answer.

That reflex—I see it everywhere. We read the room before we read ourselves. We run the calculation—what's practical, what's likely to land well, what does he prefer—before we've even arrived at the only question that actually matters.

What do I actually want?

Claiming it privately first feels selfish. It isn't. It's just first.

You can't ask for what you want if you've never let yourself know what it is. And the bedroom and the rest of life are running on the same channel. The woman who goes quiet about what she wants sexually is generally the same woman who defers on where to go for dinner, who absorbs her partner's mood like it's her job, who hasn't ordered what she wanted at a restaurant in years. When you start getting clear in the small daily places, something starts to loosen in the more intimate ones. It's the same body. The same frequency.

So, this is where we start. Reading ourselves before we read the room.

CLARITY

Clarity began as the faintest flicker.

A lover would shift his tone. Dismiss something lightly. Change a plan without care. Pull away in a way that felt small enough to question and large enough to register. The sensation moved through me quickly, almost imperceptible. A tightening in my throat. A slight retreat in my body. It happened so fast I often missed it.

At first, it would take me days to understand what had happened. I would replay the moment, trying to decipher why I felt unsettled. I had been trained to override the signal, to smooth the room, to assume I was being sensitive.

So, I began with something simple. I gave myself permission to name it.

"Ouch."

"Something pinged in me and I need to come back to this."

I didn't always know what it meant. I only knew it was there.

Noticing became the work.

Gradually the space between the inciting moment and my response began to shorten. From a week to days. From days to hours. Until eventually, more often than not, I could say it in real time.

"That feels like a no."

My voice might shake, and my hands might tremble, but I was listening for the whisper of my truth and holding her until she steadies.

Women are taught to read the room before they read themselves. To anticipate tone shifts. To smooth discomfort. To preserve harmony. We call it empathy. We call it being easy. We call it love.

It's just overriding ourselves so many times it becomes normal.

Clarity is trusting the flicker of desire as much as the current of no. You build it the same way, one noticed moment at a time.

For me, voice was the integration point. The body could whisper, but liberation required that I speak.

I sat next to a woman on an airplane who told me, still visibly shocked, that her best friend had just admitted to faking orgasms with her husband for twenty years.

Twenty years.

I've thought about that woman a lot since. Not with judgment, with recognition. Because that's not a story about sex. That's a story about a woman who ran the numbers and decided her own experience was the acceptable loss. The cost of speaking up, of navigating the complexity of differing needs, of first having to admit she wasn't really enjoying it and then having to figure out what she actually would. Somewhere along the way, she calculated all of that and quietly removed herself from the equation.

And once you've done it that many times, in that many moments, across that many years, pleasure stops feeling like something that belongs to you. It becomes a nuisance. More work than it's worth. Something that complicates things rather than nourishes them.

I met a girlfriend for lunch on the roof of the Four Seasons on a bright January afternoon. We had known each other since kindergarten. Our mothers were friends before we were, our lives braided together across countries and decades. We ordered champagne and guacamole and let the sun warm our shoulders while we compared notes on life after marriage.

There was something tender in those conversations. Dating stories. Awkward first kisses. The strange recalibration of desire after years of being someone's wife.

At one point she started laughing. "You know," she said, "you were always wild."

She reminded me of the time I got in trouble for dancing on my desk in first grade. I had stood on top of it in the middle of class, spinning and swaying to music only I could hear, completely unconcerned with whether anyone approved.

"You've always danced to your own rhythm," she said.

I could see her then. That little girl. Balanced on a school desk, grinning, unbothered.

I am the woman who dances on the desk.

For a long time, I forgot that.

I wasn't faking orgasms. But my omissions were just as costly. I was something quieter and harder to name. A woman who had made a calculation so gradually I didn't notice I was making it— trading my aliveness for stability, for partnership, for a steadiness for my kids that I didn't have and desperately wanted for them. I took leaving off the table. I had tucked parts of myself away so completely I forgot they existed. I just wasn't there. Not really. Not to myself.

She faked it for twenty years. I disappeared for about the same.

She lied to him. I lied to myself.

The loss was the same.

And I wasn't the only one.

This is what living without clarity looks like from the inside. Not dramatic. Not a crisis you can point to. Just a slow, incremental substitution of his experience for yours until you can't find the seam anymore. Until you're not even a variable.

It is tragic. It is also so familiar it's epidemic. Women in midlife quietly estranged from their own desire, not because something broke, but because they kept choosing the path of least disruption until the path became the only thing they knew.

Clarity begins the moment you put yourself back into the equation.

Not with a revolution. Just with a question asked honestly, maybe for the first time:

What do I actually want?

DISCERNMENT

Clarity taught me to hear my body.

Discernment taught me not to betray it.

Most women were never taught to want for themselves. We were taught to be wanted. To be chosen. To be good enough, available enough, accommodating enough that desire would be directed at us rather than sourced from within us. Pleasure was something that happened in relationship to someone else's appetite—his timing, his initiation, his satisfaction as the measure of our own.

This is not an accident. It is a system.

We raise girls to be responsive rather than initiating. To be agreeable rather than specific about what they need. To read the room, manage the mood, keep the peace. By the time most women arrive at adulthood, they have been so thoroughly trained in the art of adaptation that their own desire feels foreign, even suspicious. Wanting too much, wanting too specifically, wanting at all feels like a risk. Like ingratitude. Like too much.

And then we become mothers.

Motherhood is the place where self-erasure gets its highest cultural endorsement. A good mother puts her children first—their needs, their schedules, their emotional worlds—and she does it without complaint and without apparent cost to herself. The cost is invisible because we have agreed not to look at it. We call it love. We call it sacrifice. We call it what mothers do.

What it actually does, over years, is teach a woman that her desire is the last item on the list. And eventually she stops putting it on the list at all.

I know this from my own life. And I know it from sitting across from women who arrive exhausted and bewildered, unable to articulate what they want because they genuinely don't know anymore. They over function in almost every area of their life but have no capacity or relationship to intimacy. They've been so responsive to everyone else's needs for so long—his moods, his appetite, his vision for the relationship, the children's endless requirements—that the question, *What do I want?* lands like it's in a foreign language.

I spent years in a marriage like that. Not a bad marriage. A managed one. I handled the finances, the schedules, the school decisions, the birthdays, the vacations. I smoothed tension before it escalated. And in the managing, we lost any magnetism. I lost my path of desire. Somewhere inside that devotion, I went slightly dim.

For a long time, I told myself this was maturity. That passion settles. That love evolves into something quieter.

But quiet is not the same as dead.

There is a particular loneliness that comes from lying beside someone and feeling a thousand miles of distance inside your own skin. And the insidious thing about that loneliness is how normalized it becomes. Women sit across from each other at dinner tables and admit, casually, that they're not really having sex anymore. And everyone laughs and tops off the wine and nobody says what they're actually feeling—which is that they can't quite remember what it felt like to want something and simply go after it.

This is what pleasure repression actually looks like. Not a dramatic suppression. Not a moment you can point to. Just the slow, accumulated weight of always coming last in your own life, in your own body, in your own bed.

Discernment is how you reverse it.

Not dramatically. Not all at once. But in the small, repeated choice to notice what you feel before you accommodate what someone else needs. To register the "no" before you perform the "yes." To ask yourself—honestly, maybe uncomfortably—where you are still choosing the path of least disruption over the path that is actually true.

Where are you going along with something that stopped working for you a long time ago?

Where are you calling it *fine* when you mean something closer to defeated?

Where are you still choosing his comfort over your own clarity?

These are not easy questions. They have real consequences. Discernment is not a soft practice, it is the moment the inner work meets the outer life and demands something of you. It asks you to value your own experience enough to let it be visible. To stop editing yourself before you've even spoken.

Discernment is self-respect in motion. It's saying *no thanks* to the ex who pops into your DMs three months later with *I miss you* as though longing were enough to make up for his silent exit. It is declining the man who wants to "go with the flow" when you know that flow, for you, requires care and direction.

You are a Priestess. To be invited into your intimacy requires attunement, follow-through, reverence for what is being offered. Not every man who wants access has earned it.

Discernment allows you to distinguish between words and actions. You see clearly who is simply captivated by the idea of you and who is willing to meet you in presence and maturity. Chemistry is easy, but alignment is rare.

The body will tell you where you've been going along. It always does.

A tightening in the chest when the answer is no. A flatness in the presence of something that once felt alive. A relief so sudden and physical when you finally say what you mean that you wonder why you waited so long.

That's your discernment. It was never gone. It was just waiting for you to trust it more than you trust the habit of accommodation.

Clarity taught you to hear it.

Now you learn not to betray it.

TRUST

Pleasure as liberation is not a single act. It is a series of choices that return you to your own body. One breath. One boundary. One permission at a time. It's choosing to move through life with ease and pleasure rather than white knuckling and grasping. It's a moment-to-moment pivot away from holding, resisting, gripping—and into softness, opening, and receiving. It's trusting your strength and resilience can be harmonized with your curiosity and playful, pleasure hunting.

Desire is not the opposite of safety. It is the signal that safety has returned.

I sit in quiet ceremony by a fire, calling in the spring equinox with candles and cards. I write love notes to my future self and whisper prayers into the dark, marking the first return of light.

Among those prayers is a simple wish. That my daughter will feel the impulse of desire in her body and trust it. Not second-guess it. Not negotiate it away.

She has watched me wrestle with my past, my choices, my failings. She has watched me break apart and rebuild slowly, piece by piece. She has seen steadiness and self-containment. She has seen rupture.

There is something that shifts when a woman begins to inhabit herself again. It is subtle. The way she breathes differently. The way she laughs without checking the room. The way she reaches for what feels good without bracing for consequence.

That shift does not stay contained to one body.

Every time I listen to my body, something shifts a little more.

Neuroscientists studying interoception—the brain's ability to sense and trust the internal condition of the body—have found that the women who experience the most sexual satisfaction aren't necessarily the ones with the most willing partners or the most experience. They are the ones most attuned to their own body's signals. A 2024 study found that body trusting—the capacity to listen to and believe what your body is telling you—was the strongest predictor of sexual satisfaction in women across both solo and partnered experiences.

I trust the no. I say the thing. I ask for what I want. I risk being too much, too loud, too opinionated, too sexy, too slutty. And every time I do it anyway—every time I feel the fear and speak through it rather than around it—I am building a track record with myself. With my body. With my nervous system.

And that trust is physiological, not just emotional. Research consistently shows that when women are in chronic stress—cortisol elevated, nervous system scanning for threat—desire chemically exits. The body will not open what it doesn't believe is safe. Which means every boundary honored, every time you chose your own signal over someone else's comfort, you were not just doing emotional work. You were changing your body's chemistry, creating the internal conditions for desire to return. Every time you chose yourself, you were writing a different message to your own nervous system. Over time, it started to believe you.

That's what trust is. Not a feeling that arrives and stays. A record. Proof, built slowly, that you keep your word to yourself.

And something else happens in the process. I'm not just building trust, I'm building capacity. Every time I choose pleasure, I expand what I can hold. Not just in bed. In life. Because life will stretch you. It will bring friction and loss and moments that ask everything of you. When my pleasure reservoir is full, when I have been devoted to softness and surrender as much as strength, I meet those moments differently.

Not without fear. Fear still shows up. It always does.

But it doesn't drive anymore.

What if you became so dedicated and devoted to your pleasure, as a daily practice, to meet your body where it is, and invite yourself into the sacred dance of the erotic?

I am a woman in devotion to her own becoming. To pleasure as practice. To the daily choice—ordinary, ongoing, never quite finished—to trust what I feel before I manage it into something safer.

That is the track record I am building.

That is the trust.

REVERENCE

Somewhere along the way I stopped waiting for permission to feel good in my body.

It starts like this.

The kids are downstairs. The dishwasher is already running. I draw a bath in the other room—candles lit, rose petals floating, the water just hot enough. And then before I get in, I set up my phone on the tripod, angle it just so, and I put on the pink lights.

I open my playlist. I choose carefully. The song matters.

Then I go to my drawer and I dress—intentionally, deliberately—in lacy layers. A delicate top, something that moves. A robe over everything. Because I am going to undress, and the undressing deserves something worth removing.

I tell my clients to be their own best lover. To bring to themselves the quality of attention, the slowness, the genuine curiosity they would want from someone who truly adored them. It sounds simple until you try it, until you notice how quickly the critical voice arrives, how automatically you rush, how strange it feels to linger in your own body without an agenda.

The striptease is where I learned what that actually means. Not as a metaphor. Literally—the slow reveal, the unhurried hands, the camera that doesn't flinch. You become both. The lover and the woman being loved. Sometimes for the first time.

When the music starts, I let it find me. My hips before my hands. I don't rush toward the removing. I live inside the song first, let the wanting build, let my body remember it knows how to do this. And then slowly, one layer at a time, I begin. The robe first. Then whatever is underneath. An arch of the back caught in the frame. A shoulder. The curve of a hip. Thirty seconds of something true.

Sometimes I send it. Thirty second bites to a lover, arriving in his afternoon like a small deliberate fire. But the sending was never the point. What happens before that—the way I feel in my own skin when I stop rushing through it, the way desire starts in me, for me, before it touches anyone else—that is the point.

I watch them back sometimes. The videos. And what strikes me every time is the artistry of it—the creativity, the playfulness, the woman in the pink light who is so clearly having fun. She is not performing. She is not trying to be anything other than exactly what she is. Just alive in her body and unashamed of it.

You're not just undressing. You're dressing to undress. Choreographing your own pleasure in advance, arranging the conditions for your own delight, and then giving yourself the experience of being seen and finding it beautiful. Your own appreciative audience. Your own witness. Your own best lover.

I do this before big meetings. Before I need to write something that requires me to be fully present on the page. I put on the music, I dim the lights, and I come back to myself through the body the way some women come back to themselves through prayer. Because for me it is prayer. The most honest conversation I know how to have with myself.

I encouraged a client to try it. She came back the following week and told me that halfway through, she had caught herself thinking *Oh, what's the point?*

I asked her, "Whose voice is that?"

She went quiet.

"How old is she?"

She laughed, but not easily. Because she knew immediately. It was the voice of a girl who had learned somewhere between twelve and fifteen that this kind of expression—unguarded, sensual, just for herself—was silly. Embarrassing. Too much. That voice had been sitting in her body for twenty years waiting to veto exactly this moment.

That voice is not yours. It was never yours. It was handed to you by a world that has a very long history of deciding that a woman's pleasure, sourced purely from herself, for herself, is dangerous.

It is not dangerous.

It is devotional.

And it is not always graceful.

This is the part nobody tells you. Reverence does not require composure. It does not require candles or ceremony or the perfect playlist or a body that cooperates elegantly with your intentions. Sometimes it's laughing so hard at yourself in the camera that you have to start over. Sometimes it's desire arriving inconveniently, loudly, in a form that is wet and wild and slightly ridiculous and nothing at all like the curated version of female sexuality you were handed growing up.

That version—soft lit, tasteful, always somewhat contained—was never the whole truth of it.

The whole truth is messier. More animal. More surprising. Your body has its own ideas, and they are not always dignified, and they are not always timed well. And sometimes desire shows up looking nothing like desire is supposed to look, and you have the choice in that moment to manage it back into something acceptable or to just follow it. Into the mess. Into the laughter. Into the raw, unfiltered, slightly feral aliveness of a woman who has stopped editing herself in real time.

Play is where shame loses its grip.

You cannot be fully playful and fully ashamed in the same body at the same time. They cannot coexist. So, when a woman starts to play—really play, the kind that is unselfconscious and a little ridiculous and completely unconcerned with how it looks—something in the shame architecture starts to crack. Not dramatically. Just a hairline fracture. Enough to let some light in.

The mess is part of it. The wet and the wild and the wonderful inconvenient juiciness of a body that is actually alive, that is not something to be cleaned up or apologized for or hidden away until you've managed it into something more presentable. That is the thing itself. That is what you've been negotiating away, one careful managed moment at a time, for years.

Reverence says all of it. Even this. Especially this.

And sometimes I call another goddess.

There is something that happens when women do this together—strip slowly, praise each other openly, refuse to look away from one another's bodies with anything less than full attention. We have been trained to compete, to compare, to find in another woman's beauty a quiet measurement of our own lack. What happens instead when you look at your sister and say, *You are so beautiful* and mean it so completely it lands in her like medicine?

It lands because most of us have been starving for it.

I have sat in a circle of four women, each of us in lingerie, one woman at a time receiving the slow deliberate stroke of a rose along her skin while the rest of us witnessed her and spoke her beauty back to her. Soft music. Candlelight. The rose moving from her shoulder to her collarbone to the inside of her wrist, unhurried, as though her body were something worth taking time over.

Which it is.

Which yours is.

The woman receiving would sometimes cry—not from sadness—from the shock of being tended to without agenda.

I watch it happen every time. The rose touches her shoulder and something in her goes still. Not relaxed. Still. The kind of stillness that precedes a decision. You can see her working something out, running some internal calculation about whether this is allowed, whether she is allowed, whether receiving this quality of attention without immediately reciprocating or deflecting or making a joke about it somehow breaks a rule she didn't know she'd agreed to.

Most women have an entire architecture of unspoken rules about intimacy. Who it's for. What it's supposed to look like. What it means when it arrives outside the expected container—outside romance, outside sex, outside the transactional exchange of touch for touch. A woman stroking another woman's collarbone with a rose while three others witness and speak her beauty back to her doesn't fit neatly into any category most of us were given. And so, the mind goes looking for the catch.

Is this okay? Is this too much? Do I deserve this much attention? Should I be doing something in return?

And then if she can stay with it, if she can let the rose keep moving and the voices keep speaking and the room keep holding her, something shifts. The stillness softens. The breath changes. The body, faithful and patient as ever, decides it is safe enough to receive.

And I get to watch her wonder.

Is there more I can give myself permission to experience?

That question, arriving in a woman's body in real time, witnessed by her sisters—that is the most sacred thing I know. Not the rose. Not the ritual. The moment she stops managing her own receiving and simply opens to it. The moment she understands, maybe for the first time, that being tended to with care and without agenda is not an exception she has to earn.

It is something she was always allowed to have.

This is what reverence actually is. Not holiness. Not the perfectly curated altar or the right words spoken in the right order. It is the pink lights on a Tuesday and the mess of rose petals dissolving in the bath water. It is laughing at yourself in the camera and sending it anyway. It is the rose moving across your collarbone, and the tears that arrive without permission, and the laughter that comes right after because your body contains multitudes and none of them require your approval to show up.

The reflex to deny softens. The suspicion around pleasure quiets. The body you spent so long managing starts to feel like somewhere you actually live.

That's the art of it. Not the grand awakening. The devotion. The return. The choosing, again and again, to be a woman who treats her own pleasure—all of it, the sacred and the messy and the wild and the tender—as something worth showing up for.

Turn the lights down.

Put the music on.

Begin.

∞

I think about the woman I was on that mat in upstate New York. Curled on my side on the floor, out of breath, wrung out, reaching for something I couldn't name yet. It felt much more like an ending than a beginning—of a marriage, of a version of myself I had been carefully maintaining, of the competent, accommodating woman I had built in place of the one who used to dance on desks.

What I found on that floor was not a new self. It was the original one. The one who knew what she wanted before she learned to negotiate it away. The one whose desire was a compass before she learned to distrust it. The one who reached and kept reaching even when no one came.

Clarity gave her back her name.

Discernment taught her which rooms to walk into and which to leave.

Trust told her that the wanting itself was the signal, that desire doesn't return to a body that isn't safe, and safe doesn't mean comfortable or certain or without risk. It means alive. It means the body has decided it's worth feeling again.

Reverence was the practice of treating that aliveness as sacred. Of showing up for it on a Tuesday with pink lights and a playlist. Of sitting in a circle of four women with a rose and understanding that being witnessed in your body without judgment might be one of the most quietly radical things available to us.

The woman who faked it for twenty years wasn't weak. She was tired. She had run the numbers so many times, across so many years, that removing herself from the equation had stopped feeling like a loss and started feeling like just the way things were. Pleasure had become a nuisance. Desire an inconvenience. The girl who once stood on a desk and spun to music only she could hear—a person she vaguely remembered from a long time ago.

She is not gone.

She has never been gone.

She has just been waiting, with the kind of patience that should stop us cold, for you to remember that she was always the point.

You are allowed to want more. More pleasure. More truth. More of yourself back. More of the life that is actually yours, rather than the one that accumulated around you while you were busy being everything to everyone else. You are allowed to want it without justifying it, without shrinking it into something more palatable, without running the numbers on whether you deserve it first.

The wild art of it isn't the wanting. Any of us can want quietly, privately, in the life we've built around the absence of it. The art is the unapologetic. The decision that your desire is not a disruption to be managed but a compass to be followed. The choice made again and again in small unremarkable moments to put yourself back in the equation.

It starts with one question. Asked honestly. In your own body.

What do I actually want?

She knows.

She's always known.

✦ Abundance Practice: Expanding Our Capacity

INVOCATION

Beloved one, soften.

Let your body remember what it feels like to be safe enough to receive.

The universe wants to pour through you—not as reward, but as recognition.

You are already the vessel. You are already the channel.

All you must do is open.

RITUAL

Find a quiet place where you can sit comfortably, uninterrupted.

Take a few slow breaths, in through the nose and out through the mouth, until your shoulders drop.

Place one hand on your heart and one on your belly.

Begin to breathe into your lower body—the pelvis, the womb, the base of your spine—and imagine golden light filling these spaces.

Now, call to mind something you desire to receive. It might be money, love, success, support, or beauty.

Visualize it as light moving toward you.

Notice what happens in your body as it comes closer.

Do you open or contract? Do you tense, brace, or pull away?

If you feel the contraction, don't judge it. Just breathe. Say quietly to yourself:

It's safe to receive. It's safe to have more. It's safe to hold this.

Keep breathing until your body begins to soften and the light gently enters your field, filling you.

Let it settle into your cells. Let it feel familiar.

REFLECTION

- What sensations or emotions arise when I imagine receiving more?
- Where in my body do I hold fear around having enough or being enough?
- What practices, pleasures, or boundaries help me feel safe expanding?

When you finish, place both hands over your heart and whisper:

I am open. I am capable. I am the vessel for abundance.

Sit in the quiet for a few moments. Let your breath anchor the new pattern—not striving, not forcing, but allowing. This is how we expand capacity. This is how we hold the "bigness" of what we desire. Not by bracing for it, but by remembering that our bodies were always built to receive.

CHAPTER EIGHT
Erotic Alchemy

What happens when a woman learns to stay present with her intensity without numbing, performing, or abandoning herself? She becomes an unstoppable force.

My journey from people pleaser to boundary-driven, desire-filled, delicious matriarch wasn't a straight path, but it was a worthy one. I am grateful for the versions of me that survived and adapted, the parts of myself that still live on but are now integrated into the sovereign woman who knows her value and stands for it.

I am a woman who went from living in my head, disconnected from my body, numb to my desire, blocked from my sexuality, to the woman I am today: clear, coherent, unapologetic, embodied, courageous, riding her desires, living in the fullness of her wanting, and open to the possibilities that emerge from a life filled with pleasure.

Erotic energy is a life force. It is the same current that animates creativity, intimacy, leadership, and wealth. It is the pulse beneath desire, the charge behind inspiration, the vitality that makes us feel awake inside our own lives. When that current is suppressed, women don't become calmer or more contained. They become depleted. Burned out. Disconnected. Hungry for something they can't quite name.

Erotic Alchemy is what I call the practice of increasing a woman's capacity to feel pleasure, grief, longing, and power without collapse. It's working on the nervous system through integration. It's about learning to inhabit yourself fully, to let your life force move through you without apology.

I didn't arrive at this understanding overnight. Five years ago, I wouldn't have recognized the woman writing these words. But here's what I've learned: When you commit to staying present with your own intensity, everything changes. Your business becomes more magnetic. Your relationships deepen. Your creativity explodes. Your whole life becomes an expression of your aliveness.

This is not about sex, though sex becomes sacred when you know how to inhabit your body with presence. This is what happens when you stop abandoning yourself for someone else's comfort, when you stop performing your desire and start embodying it. This is when you turn toward sensation instead of away from it.

This is about becoming the woman who says yes to her own life.

This is where so many women have been misled.

We live in a culture that swings between repression and overexposure. One side teaches women to fear their desire—to tame it, contain it, spiritualize it, or silence it altogether. On the other, we are sold a version of liberation that still pressures us to perform—to be open, adventurous, available, and "empowered," even when our bodies are saying no, not yet, or not like this.

Erotic Alchemy asks us to fully inhabit the body, to move through trauma, fear, anxiety, grief, love, lust, sensuality, sexiness and embody every shade of being you can express.

THE WORK IS EROTIC

At its core, Erotic Alchemy is nervous system work. It is the practice of increasing a woman's capacity to feel pleasure, grief, longing, and power without tipping into overwhelm or dissociation. It protects us from rushing toward peak experiences.

Many women have learned how to succeed by overriding their natural instincts. We push through exhaustion. We override intuition. We tolerate subtle discomfort and call it resilience. Over time, the body adapts. Sensation dulls. Desire quiets. The erotic—once wild, curious, and alive—goes underground.

But it never disappeared. It was simply no longer safe.

This is why reclaiming desire can feel destabilizing. Desire asks for presence. It interrupts productivity. It dissolves control. It invites us into a relationship with sensation rather than mastery over it. For women who have built their lives on competence and containment, this can feel threatening—even irresponsible.

But desire signals safety in your body, that you are returning to you.

When desire begins to reawaken, it means you are safe to want. Safe to open. Safe to soften without disappearing.

Erotic Alchemy teaches women how to meet that moment without panic, and how to move and stay in it.

This work rests on four foundational principles that reshape how a woman relates to her life force.

- **Capacity over peak**
  We have been conditioned to sprint toward climax—in

pleasure, in success, in life—and collapse afterward. Erotic Alchemy teaches us to expand our capacity to hold sensation, to ride the wave rather than crash against it. This isn't about lasting longer or doing more. It's about feeling more *without losing yourself.*

- **Presence over performance**
The feminine has been trained to perform desire rather than inhabit it. We track how we look, how we sound, whether we're "doing it right." Erotic Alchemy invites us back into sensation—to what is happening in the body, moment by moment, when no one is watching.

- **Integration over isolation**
Erotic energy is not separate from creative energy, leadership energy, or spiritual energy. It is one current. When it is suppressed in one area, it leaks or distorts in others. When it is integrated, life becomes more coherent. Decisions clarify. Creativity flows. Boundaries strengthen.

- **Safety through sovereignty**
Erotic Alchemy is rooted in radical self-responsibility. You are the authority on your body, your boundaries, and your desires. This work is not about pushing edges for the sake of growth. It is about learning to recognize your full-body yes, your maybe (which is a no), and your absolute no—and trusting them.

Before I share the stories that shaped my own initiation into this work, there is a key element I want to share.

The nervous system is the gateway.

Women who have experienced trauma, childbirth, chronic stress, heartbreak, or years of subtle self-abandonment, develop intelligent protections in the forms of numbness and tension, anxiety when pleasure builds, or dissociation when sensation becomes intense. These have been our survival strategies.

Erotic Alchemy does not override these protections. It listens to them.

It teaches the body—slowly, patiently—that it no longer needs to choose between aliveness and safety.

From that place, desire can return as truth.

And from there, everything changes.

I was a woman coming out of a long, monogamous marriage—a devoted mother, a grown woman—suddenly aware that I had lived most of my adult life with one flavor of intimacy.

Vanilla.

Nothing wrong with it, but I found myself wondering what else was out there. What other flavors were there? *How can I know what I like if I don't even know?*

There's a lot to be said for curiosity with discernment, about researching pleasure as your life's work, to gather information about this miraculous body and how it responds and demands sensation. I set out to let my body gather information and expand the aperture through which I had always seen and experienced intimacy. And it wasn't only healing that I found.

There was fun, joy, discovery, play.

I wanted to pull back the drapes, lift the quiet cloaks that keep women's desire hidden, and name what so many of us secretly wonder. I wanted to open the door—with humor, care, and reverence for the body that knows the way. I knew gravity would pull others through the doorway in their own time, in their own way.

That's how I found myself standing in a beautiful home high in the Hollywood Hills, wearing white silk lingerie.

My identities as mother, single woman, pleasure researcher all collided in a single moment at my first *Mystery Temple party.* It was an invitation-only, conscious-community gathering devoted to exploring sacred sexuality and conscious connection. The thread that brought me here began months ago—an Instagram follow, a friend of a friend, a private message, and eventually a ticket purchase that felt like both a dare and an initiation. The instructions were clear: *Come with curiosity, come sober, lead with consent.*

I found myself in an open living room, the furniture had been cleared away and replaced with cushions, blankets, and low lighting. Around fifty people had gathered—different ages, genders, and expressions.

The theme of the night was "Light and Shadows" and most had embraced the theatrical invitation of the play party. The energy hummed with a mix of anticipation and reverence.

I dressed in a white silk bra, panties and garter, with a matching silk robe. When I bought it at a boutique in Beverly Hills, the saleswoman asked if I was getting married.

"Definitely not," I said, smiling. "Quite the opposite."

I convinced my best friend to come with me. At first, she declined, saying she was retired from that kind of scene—she'd been to her fair share of conscious play parties in her younger years and now sought partnership. I pressed further, asking her to be my wing woman. She smiled. We'd been winging for each other since our twenties. We'd danced at too many parties to count, weaving through crowds, reading each other's cues with a glance.

We know how to give each other space and when to step in close. That kind of friendship becomes its own language—one part intuition, one part telepathy.

She said, "Yes, anything for you, Goddess," laughing.

And just like that, we were back in flow—two women stepping into a new chapter, still side by side, still looking out for each other.

The evening began with a grounding circle led by the facilitators—a reminder that everything here is by choice, that every "no" is sacred, and that our only responsibility is to ourselves. I took a deep breath. My heart was racing from both nerves and anticipation. I promised myself that I'd wait for a full body yes before engaging in anything beyond observation.

Then there was an erotic theatre performance with ropes and fire that pressed me to the edge of my comfort. It was mesmerizing, theatrical, and beautiful. I was fascinated, intrigued, drawn in, but not aroused.

There were some group tantric exercises, connection through energy. We moved around the room, gazing into each other's eyes, moving from this energetic touch to physical touch, and changing partners every few minutes.

After a few rounds of physical touch, we were given permission to play, like the starting gun at a race, all the pent-up anticipation was allowed to spill over. Some people immediately found a partner or friend, others dispersed to find the play they wanted. I wandered around a bit, moving from room to room. There were workshops as well as spontaneous play and demonstrations. In the kitchen, I chatted with volunteers and a sweet gay couple who'd been coming to these parties for a few years.

I danced and moved around, realizing that, for me, simply being here was enough. I didn't need to participate to expand. I witnessed what was possible when people gather without judgment, when consent and curiosity guide the evening. There was healing in witnessing, in knowing my boundaries and holding them—seeing desire held with such care, stripped of secrecy or shame.

Later, a young man struck up a conversation and invited my friend and me upstairs to join a smaller circle. We exchanged a look and declined.

We do almost everything together, but in that moment, we knew—we drew the line at sex. We laughed at the absurdity of the moment, and made our way to the living room, snacking on strawberries in our lingerie, in alignment with our desires.

We left by midnight. The Uber ride home was quiet, the city lights glittering below.

"So, what did you think?" Sophia asked.

"It was good," I said after a pause. "I'm glad I went."

Back at my apartment, I slipped into a silk nightgown and thought about the night. I was proud of myself for going, for pressing and finding my edges and honoring myself with presence and simplicity. There would be other parties, and perhaps I'd feel differently, but that night I waited for the full-body yes. I wasn't disappointed that it didn't come, but I did sense an ache for connection. For the kind of partnership where energy flows easily, where curiosity feels safe, and where I could explore the edges of my desire with deep trust.

It wasn't about missing someone. It was the reminder of my own desire for conscious connection, trust, and play in the polarity that comes from being met fully.

That evening opened something in me. It showed me how many expressions of intimacy exist, yet what I craved most isn't variety—it's depth. Presence. The alchemy that happened when two people come together with awareness and let themselves be changed by it. It reflected something I had already begun to reclaim. The knowing that real erotic power isn't about saying yes to everything. It's about being so deeply attuned to yourself that your yes becomes unmistakable.

That night, as I turned out the light, I whispered a quiet *thank you* to my courage, my body, all the parts of me that had stretched and broke so I could be rebuilt. To the woman who walks into these rooms, finds her voice, and waits for her yes.

I could feel something in me expanding—an increased capacity, a widening of my lens on sexuality and self-expression. Something profound and beautiful happens when trust—especially self-trust—comes before experimentation. I had permission to expand, but I was also willing to give my body the time it needed to move toward a new edge. From there, I could choose what felt aligned: to explore with consciousness and integrity, and to honor the part of me that still wanted to play.

Mostly, I was proud that I said yes to a new experience—something far outside the box of the suburban mother I once was. I had gone and met another layer of myself.

And that was enough.

LINGERIE IN MY LIVING ROOM

I lit candles and placed roses, all symbols to invoke the Goddess, around the room. A singing bowl rested on the floor. I took a long, deep breath and looked around my apartment; this sacred space I call *The Goddess Palace.*

Two years ago, it was my refuge from a marriage that was ending. Later, it became a sanctuary for new love—a place that held my pleasure, my grief, my laughter, and my tears. It contained every part of me: the woman who wept on the floor, the woman who learned to touch herself tenderly, the woman who screamed with joy, the woman who screamed from heartbreak. This space has witnessed all the ecstasy, the loss, the unraveling, and the rebuilding.

That night, it held something new. A circle of women who came to awaken the Goddess within themselves. They've said yes to the Feminine, even if they don't yet know what that means. They only know they want more: more softness, more aliveness, more permission to feel.

I thought back to the first lingerie set I ever bought after my separation. Red silk. My lover had asked for it, and I remember how strange and electric it felt to stand in front of the mirror wearing it—the mother, the wife, the woman I had been—suddenly meeting the woman I was becoming. It stretched the edges of who I thought I was allowed to be. There, in that apartment, I discovered that I could be both. I could be the woman who tucked her children into bed and the woman who danced in silk. The woman who built a business and the woman who reveled in desire.

Years earlier, during the pandemic, I had begun to crack open these layers. I would dance alone in my living room in Chicago, letting the music move through me, catching glimpses of joy between the grief and the exhaustion. I would rally my children to join me in playfulness and fun and feel a surge of joy run through me. Back then, I was still living small and perfectly composed.

The memory makes me smile.

Recently, my daughter said to me, "Two years ago, me wouldn't like me now."

I laughed. "Same," I told her. "I think she wouldn't know what to do with me."

It stayed with me. I looked back with compassion at that earlier version of myself—the one who played the role of perfection so well. The mother who packed lunches, sent the emails, poured the wine at night. The woman who had every reason to be happy but couldn't feel it.

She had no idea where we were heading. She would have said, *No way. Too far.*

But this—this life, this woman—is what freedom looks like.

Back then, I had every resource I needed, but I was still living inside an old story of scarcity. I was proving my worth through work and busyness. I told myself I didn't have time for pleasure. No space for play. No energy for joy. There was always something more important to do, someone else to tend to.

And yet, here I am. In this new life, in this sacred space I've built. The women arrived that night dressed in lace and laughter, nervous and radiant, ready to reclaim a part of themselves that had been waiting all along. They said yes to the lingerie, yes to the dance, yes to remembering what it felt like to be fully alive.

Together, we breathed, moved, and remembered. We called the wild woman forward, the one who knows how to dance with both light and shadow, who knows that pleasure is not frivolous but sacred. We talked and cried and celebrated, and by the end of the night, they left changed; they remembered who they had always been.

I will remember, too.

That pleasure is the prayer.

Play is medicine. The temple was never somewhere out there. It was always right here in my body, in this home, in the living, breathing, untamed pulse of the feminine.

PLEASURE MAPPING

Never say never. That has been my motto since I blew up my neatly arranged life. Six years earlier, I would not have recognized the current version of me. I was married, living in Chicago, had two kids in Catholic school, and wondered why a beautiful life felt like a gilded cage. If you had asked me then to dance in lingerie on Zoom, to explore sensuality in community, or to take a lover, I would have given you a firm no. Life has a way of surprising us.

One October morning, a few weeks after a breakup that split me open, I sat in my kitchen with cacao, a microdose, and a heart that felt raw. An email from a feminist icon of pleasure education landed in my inbox: there was one final spot in her pleasure-coaching certification.

Yes, I thought before my mind could talk me out of it.

I did not need another certification. I had collected many—life coaching, breathwork, Reiki, Priestess initiations. But this invitation felt like an edge meant for me. The next day I was on Zoom with sixty women, lingerie optional, speaking openly about the power of the feminine body and the sanctity of our desire. For the next eight months, I immersed myself in tools for moving through rupture and re-igniting erotic life force for purpose.

For the next eight months I studied with Mama Gena at the School of Womanly Arts, a space devoted to restoring women's connection to pleasure, power, and presence through the body.

One of her most recognizable teachings—and the title of her book, *Pussy*—centers on reclaiming a word many women have been taught to fear, mock, or avoid altogether.

There's reason for that.

Most women grow up with a patchwork of euphemisms for their genitals—cute names, crude names, vague references that keep everything "down there" unnamed and unspoken. None of them is anatomically correct.

And almost all of them reinforce the same message: *This part of you is taboo.*

Language shapes embodiment. What we cannot name, we often cannot inhabit.

Pussy is a **political and energetic reclamation**—a refusal to erase the source of female creativity, intuition, and life force. Naming her is a way of restoring agency where shame once lived.

That said, sovereignty matters more to me than vocabulary.

In my own teachings, including Goddess Awakening, I offer women options. Some say pussy. Some say yoni. Some say pelvis, womb, center, body. What matters is not the word itself, but the *permission*. The moment a woman realizes she gets to choose how she names and relates to her own body.

Erotic Alchemy does not enforce language; it restores our relationship with our identity behind them.

When a woman can name her body without flinching—whatever language she chooses unlocks something. Sensation returns. Authority returns. Desire no longer feels separate from safety.

Reclamation is somatic.

And it changes everything.

The word itself matters just as much as what happens *inside you* when you hear it.

Tightening. Curiosity. Aversion. Heat. Judgment. Laughter. Shutdown.

Whatever your reaction, it's information.

Instead of bypassing it or intellectualizing it, Erotic Alchemy invites inquiry: *What did I feel just now? Where did that sensation land in my body? What story does it carry?*

Often, our response to a word like *pussy* has very little to do with the word and everything to do with the conditioning layered around it—the moments we were shamed, corrected, silenced, sexualized, or taught to disconnect from that part of ourselves.

The body remembers those moments long before the mind makes sense of them.

This is why I don't ask women to adopt my language. I ask them to **notice theirs**. To let the body speak first. To treat their reaction not as something to overcome, but as something to listen to. The awakening is to bring awareness to what is unconscious. What beliefs do you have and why? What assumptions are unspoken because of your lineage or ancestry? This work is an invitation to bring sovereignty and ownership to your body. For some, reclamation comes as medicine and for others, finding their own language feels right.

Whatever arises—discomfort, desire, resistance, longing—is the entry point.

And when women learn to stay present with their own reaction instead of judging it, we begin to reclaim something far more important than a word.

We reclaim our relationship to ourselves.

PUSSY!

My training as a pleasure coach with the School of Womanly Arts ended with a three-day retreat in Costa Rica. Along with the packing list, an optional sign-up for a "sensual session" with one of the facilitators arrived. The description was sparse; the emphasis was on safety and consent. I sat still, listened for my truth, and felt a clear yes.

I wasn't even sure what I was signing up for, but I felt the familiar pull of sense and curiosity. *If not now,* I thought, *then when?*

I arrived a few days early to meet a new friend I'd met on a plane. We'd talked the entire flight about divorce, dating, and what it felt like to choose pleasure again after years of putting it last. There was something immediately easy between us, that particular flood of openness that happens when two women recognize each other at the crossroads.

At the same time, my life back home was anything but spacious. Divorce paperwork. Refinancing. Solo parenting. I could feel all of it humming under the surface of my body. The low-grade tension of being in transition, of holding a lot without quite knowing what comes next.

I hadn't met the women from the program in person yet, but there was already a shared vulnerability between us. We were walking into this together without armor, without answers, carrying stories we hadn't fully metabolized yet. That felt both comforting and exposing.

I was excited. I was nervous. It's one thing to talk about pleasure on Zoom, to understand it intellectually. And it's another to let your body step forward, to be seen, to feel. I had a quiet sense that the next few days would ask me to meet places in myself I hadn't fully touched yet—old shame, old conditioning, old resistance—not as ideas, but as lived experiences. And I knew there would be no way through it except by staying present.

I held one quiet intention: to move slowly, to stay honest, and to let my body set the pace instead of my mind.

On the morning of our appointment, the practitioner of the "sensual session" arrived promptly at my hotel room. I met him in a robe, freshly showered. We began seated, with intake questions about history, boundaries, desire, and my intentions. The first practice was consent. He would name a place on my body and ask to touch. My task was to answer from both mind and body. A "maybe" counted as a no. It sounds simple until you notice how quickly a body can override itself to be agreeable. Slowing down became the point.

We opened a ceremonial container, the kind of ritual that makes anything feel safe enough to be sacred. The session that followed was not performance or goal-oriented intimacy. It was structured sensory mapping—gloved, consent-led, paced by my breath—inviting me to track subtle sensations, name preferences, and rate intensity on a scale so my body could lead.

At first, I felt mostly ones, twos, and threes. When the hour ended, I noticed a little disappointment. I wanted more time to explore. I texted and booked two additional sessions. With the unknown removed, my body softened. Curiosity replaced vigilance. I told him how often my past experiences had been performative or rushed, shaped by what I thought a partner needed. This was different: slow, spacious, for me. Even my self-pleasure had often been a sprint; this was an invitation to feel.

By the third session my attention dropped fully into my body. Sensation rose like a tide. I could feel waves of pleasure traveling through my legs and spine, and I learned where sensitivity was strong and where it was quiet. The afterglow no longer felt like an endpoint but like a field I could ride longer with breath and awareness. At the close of each session we debriefed, integrating insights. What I wanted most, I realized, was a partner back home who could explore with the same care and presence.

More than anything, those days were a reclamation. Consent slowed me down. Attention brought me home. Pleasure became a teacher rather than a performance.

THE POWER OF RELEASE

A few months later, I traveled to Austin for another Women's Immersion—thirty of us gathered to turn up our life force and to test a hypothesis I had been living into: When we unlock intimacy, we unlock new levels of creativity, success, and wealth. The feminine magnetizes through coherence. Pleasure is that coherence.

Early in the mornings, before joining the group, I booked sessions for deeper pleasure mapping with the same practitioner. He would arrive at my hotel room at seven in the morning, a quiet, dimly lit suite that felt like a cocoon. Over three sessions we explored my capacity and peak states with the same consent-first structure: breath, boundaries, slow sensing, clear language, and lots of integration. I learned that the peak many of us chase is not a finish line. It is a doorway. When I let my body breathe through the peak, the energy expanded rather than collapsed. Presence turned the "cliff" into a wave I could surf.

I know how tender and, to some, controversial this work may sound. For centuries, women's bodies have been policed, pathologized, and turned into something to manage rather than honor. Pleasure, especially a woman's pleasure, has been made taboo—too much, too wild, too shameful—to be spoken of in daylight. We were taught to keep quiet about our pain and our longing. To tend to everyone else's comfort before our own truth. To bury our trauma in silence and call it strength. But the body remembers. The stories we silence live in our tissues, shaping the way we love, work, and move through the world. Reclaiming pleasure is not indulgence; it is repair. It is the process of bringing light to the places that have been kept in the dark for too long.

This sacred attention to the body, is not about performance or provocation. It is about sovereignty. It is about returning to the source of our own aliveness, so that we can inhabit ourselves fully again. On the last morning, we added a practice called de-armoring—gentle, internal bodywork intended to release old tension patterns and stored stress in the pelvic bowl. He moved carefully, zone by zone, using breath to meet places that felt numb or guarded, mapping pleasure back into areas that had learned to tighten. Years of research and lived experience tell us the body remembers; this was a way of listening and letting it unwind. Our tissues, our fascia holding tension from years of trauma, are invited to release and repattern.

In the somatic world, this kind of work is often referred to as **pelvic or yoni de-armoring**: a form of trauma-informed bodywork rooted in both modern somatic and ancient Tantric traditions. It involves gentle, consent-based touch and guided awareness designed to release tension, numbness, or emotional residue held in the pelvic region. While the term may sound unfamiliar or even provocative, its essence is profoundly therapeutic—to help women reconnect with the parts of themselves that have been shamed, silenced, or dissociated from.

At its heart, de-armoring is not about sexuality, but about sovereignty. It's the process of bringing compassion, breath, and presence to the body's most guarded places—transforming what once felt forbidden into an experience of safety, tenderness, and truth.

A few hours later, back amongst the other women, I suddenly felt tears rise with no direct story attached. I sensed that this was emotion, grief that was still moving through my body and asking to be processed. So, I excused myself, stepped onto the deck, bent my knees, shook, and let a few grounded screams move through me—somatic tools I had gathered through the last two years. A few minutes later, one of the women came out to check on me and wrapped her arms around me. The words on my lips were clear and felt as though they traveled through my body from a hundred lifetimes: *May I never abandon myself again. May I never trade my voice for harmony, or my body for approval.*

Something had loosened. Of course, it had. Our bodies hold a lifetime of touch—welcome and unwelcome, lovers and births, medical procedures and private explorations. Meeting those layers with ceremony and consent let old imprints leave and new pathways form. The days that followed were full of sisterhood and celebration: admiring the beauty of each woman's body as a work of art, honoring ruptures and resilience, swapping numbers, promising to keep practicing.

I toasted my new sisters at lunch, flirting with the table of men next to us, caught my flight a few hours later, and made it home for dinner in Hollywood. That evening, I invited a lover to meet me in the new energy I was holding now: no drama, no games, just ease.

I have spent twenty years as a wife and fourteen as a mother. The roles are shifting, which means my relationship to pleasure is shifting, too. These seasons have taught me that touch can be sacred medicine when guided by consent and integrity, that peak states are doorways, and that sovereignty lives in how I listen to my body before I say yes.

I am still learning who I am outside the old rules. What I know now is that pleasure expands my capacity for love, for work, for wealth, for life. And when I honor that truth, everything else rises to meet me.

After pleasure mapping, I felt a broad awareness. It was inconvenient at first because it highlighted where I had made agreements that I no longer aligned with. I could feel everything that didn't resonate clearly. Like when I rushed myself, said yes too quickly, or when my body shut down instead of opening.

And once you feel that, you can't un-feel it.

This is the true home of Erotic Alchemy: a deep awareness that becomes impossible to ignore.

Pleasure has guided me toward that new baseline. Before this work, I understood myself mostly through thought, and some feeling. I could analyze, narrate, and contextualize. I could make meaning of almost anything. What I couldn't always do was feel it in real time, especially in intimacy, when the stakes felt highest. Bringing my body into the conversation changed that, I began listening to its own unique language.

Once my body had language, certain patterns became obvious. My body delayed between sensation and decision; it was a subtle bracing I had normalized. I even had a habit of leaving my body when sensations were too intense. Pleasure, embodied sensuality, somatic awareness, all the ingredients of erotic alchemy, brought me into a new awareness and intimacy with myself, and grounded me in a way I hadn't experienced.

My life and my relationships didn't change immediately, but I was showing up differently, with less charge. I became less willing to override myself for harmony, or reach for intimacy without safety. I felt less interested in dynamics that required me to shrink, or perform, but also less reactive. I didn't need to confront everything. I just stopped abandoning myself. That alone reoriented my life.

One of the biggest myths I had to release was the idea that pleasure comes after work. After the hustle and the to-do lists. I had to reorient to a knowing that pleasure is a resource that fuels me life.

Pleasure became not a reward I had to earn, but a compass pointing me toward my true north. It is a tuning fork, a way to know the body with precision and curiosity, measuring my aliveness. I listened and attuned to her softness rather than braced or endured. It gave me a language to speak with my body that transcends the mind and drops me into my desire. In pleasure I can feel myself expand and relax where I used to pull away and tighten. In pleasure, my wildness is awakened and my yes comes from a primal, visceral place where my yes is from a deep knowing instead of just trying to keep everyone happy.

Even now, immersed in this work as I am, I'm working against forty-eight years of wiring that taught me to override my body, to push through discomfort, to make everyone else's needs more important than my own truth. Every day I actively and consciously reorient myself toward pleasure. It's not automatic yet, so it's grounded in my rituals.

But I trust, through lived experience that we can rewire and adapt and rewrite our experiences through devotion and repetition. Years ago, meditation used to feel so foreign, the clock dragging by as I fought my inner monkey mind just to make it to the ten-minute timer. I kept showing up, day after day, ten minutes at a time, and then one day it felt as natural as brushing my teeth. Now I feel strange if I don't do it.

That's what I want for you—to be led by it, guided by your heart and desire rather than by old programming or other people's expectations.

There will always be days when you will need to remind yourself to feel your feet on the ground, to breathe into your belly, to ask your body what it wants before you bulldoze ahead with what your mind thinks you should do. That's just being human.

So, you live. You pay attention. You listen and adjust, dancing with awareness instead of fighting against yourself. Sometimes the payoff is subtle—the way you take a beat before responding to someone's sharp word. But sometimes the rewards are profound, like when you stop to take in the life you're building with pleasure as your compass and realize it's more magnificent than you could have imagined.

It's a great exploration in which you never arrive. You enjoy the ride, feel it all. And then you do it all over again tomorrow.

That's what practice looks like.

Erotic Alchemy isn't meant to stand alone. It's the practice of awareness, of cultivating the very rich and beautiful parts of being alive and making ourselves more alive. It's tending to the grief that needs to move through the body instead of staying locked up; it's activating sacred rage where there were numbness and collapse; and it's letting all of it become fertilizer for the most beautiful garden of fulfillment, because you are more human, more fully in your body than ever before.

✦ Temple of the Divine (You)

This practice is yours to deepen to the level that feels appropriate to you. It's an invitation to shift away from a climax-based experience to one that feels erotic, expansive, and invites curiosity. It is a way of listening to your body as a sacred instrument, bringing curiosity, gentleness, and love to the places that have carried so much tension, memory, longing, and power.

Set your space as you would for a lover. Dim the lights. Light a candle. Put on music that moves through the body. Not just background noise; choose your music to match your desire. Anoint your skin with an oil you love. Have your favorite lubricant nearby.

Lie down. Take a few slow breaths and let the day fall away. Place your hands on your body wherever they naturally land— belly, heart, thighs—and simply feel the warmth of your own touch before anything else. Stay with full presence and attention.

When you're ready, begin to explore. Slowly. More slowly than feels natural. Let your hands move across your skin with curiosity and tenderness—your neck, your collarbone, your ribs, the soft skin of your inner arm, your belly. Notice what feels alive. Notice what feels numb. Notice where you want to linger.

Move inward when your body asks you to, not before. Follow sensation. When you arrive at your pussy, begin at the outside—hovering, presence, heat—before any direct touch. Feel her energy before you touch her. Don't skip it.

Explore with the same slow curiosity. Long strokes. Soft pressure. Different rhythm. Notice what your body responds to when you're not rushing toward a finish line. This is pleasure mapping in real time—you are learning your own language.

If you feel yourself leaving the body—drifting into your to-do list, watching yourself from the outside, going numb—it's okay, just come back to the breath. Come back to sensation. Come back to the room. This is the practice within the practice: staying.

If emotion comes, let it. Tears, laughter, grief, tenderness—all of it is welcome here. Your body has been waiting for this kind of attention for a long time.

When you feel complete, stay with yourself. Don't rush back into the world. This is the aftercare: lying in the quiet, breathing, letting the experience land. Drink water. Wrap yourself in something soft. Let it have been sacred.

Then write without editing. Let yourself pour out onto the page. What did you feel? What did you discover? What do you want more of?

Come back to this practice. Let it deepen over time. This is how desire is reclaimed. Not in a single evening, but in the slow, devoted return to yourself.

This is the temple. You have always been the door.

CHAPTER NINE

Follow Your Pleasure

I was raised Catholic. Educated by nuns in my elementary school, then an Anglican high school where the same underlying message echoed through different hallways: Good girls don't want too much and sex is bad.

My family wasn't particularly devout. We were more Christmas-and-Easter Catholics than daily-rosary types. But that proves how deep religious ideology penetrates. It doesn't need fire-and-brimstone sermons to get under your skin. It arrives as atmosphere. As the way people's faces change when a woman laughs too loud or wants too much. As the quiet belief that virtue is measured by what you *don't* do, not what you accomplish.

Purity culture doesn't just tell you how to behave. It rewires your nervous system. It teaches your body that desire equals danger, that wanting is something that needs to be managed, confessed, or carefully rationed out. Pleasure becomes a liability. Your body becomes something that requires constant supervision and control.

This conditioning follows women everywhere: into boardrooms and bedrooms, into the way we apologize before asking for what we need, into that reflexive pause before we say yes to something that feels good. The quiet sense that wanting more is somehow irresponsible. That goodness and desire can't live in the same body.

I lived this way for decades without even knowing it had a name.

Then, in the thick of my pleasure journey, the story of Mary Magdalene came back to me. Not the version I learned in Sunday school of the prostitute who needed saving, but the real one. The one that placed Mary Magdelene at the center of Jesus's world, in education, authority, and proximity.

In the earliest texts, before centuries of men rewrote her story, Magdalene was a woman of means, education, and spiritual authority. She funded Jesus's ministry. She was a Priestess, trained in Egypt who taught Jesus the way of the divine through the body. Modern scholars believe she was Jesus's lover and that their intimacy was rooted in devotion, not shame.

But a woman who held spiritual authority, erotic intimacy, and material resources? That's a problem if you're trying to build a hierarchy with men at the top. So, they split her in half. Stripped her of legitimacy. Reframed her closeness to Jesus as sin that needed redemption.

The wholeness of the feminine got carved up into digestible pieces.

The good woman became the mother—pure, self-sacrificing, wanting nothing for herself. The sexual woman became the whore—dangerous, excessive, in need of control.

And here we are, two thousand years later, apologizing for our desire. Still justifying our pleasure and believing goodness and wanting can't coexist in the same body.

Purity culture is founded in religion, but it seeps out into the whole culture. It makes female sexuality the problem. It's the way an entire culture learned to fear women's full aliveness. It shows up in girl's high school dress codes, and "she asked for it" victim blaming. It shows up in insidious ways, but also in the trauma of those who have been embedded in religious extremism.

When I first encountered the real story of Magdalene, through the Rose lineage of Priestesses that remember her as teacher and embodied leader, something in my body recognized it immediately. This way of relating to pleasure, prayer, intimacy, and truth felt familiar, as if it had been waiting all along to be named.

Magdalene didn't feel like a figure from the past. She felt like a remembering of what had been hidden in plain sight.

And once I saw how deeply I'd been apologizing for my desire, my life, my dreams, I couldn't unsee it.

WHEN WE FINALLY STOP APOLOGIZING

Learning to be unapologetic about my pleasure, to stop explaining it, managing it, or making it more comfortable for other people has transformed me. For years, I kept her hidden—the part of me that wanted more. The one who craved touch, beauty, mystery, surrender. The one who was never afraid of desire itself, but its cost.

I called her reckless. Dangerous. Too much.

But she was never the problem. The problem was a world that taught me my body was a liability and my longing was a threat. By freeing my inner slut, not as rebellion but as reclamation, I am closer to myself. She is the part of me that remembers being fully alive. The one who does not apologize for wanting, for feeling, for taking up space.

The one who wants to be met in her hunger. Shameless.

I want to feel the current of energy that moves through me when I stop pretending that I am fine with crumbs. I want to let pleasure be my prayer, to feel the pulse that reminds me I am still here.

We have all inherited the lie that pleasure makes us weak. That too much wanting is dangerous. That endurance is more noble than enjoyment. But what if our wanting is sacred? What if it is the map that leads us home? For a long time, I performed intimacy, giving just enough to be wanted but never enough to be real. Sex and shame were tangled together until I could not tell where one ended and the other began.

Memories echoed into the present confirming this bias. In high school, I remember the girl who was named the slut. She wore short skirts, laughed too loud, and looked people directly in the eye. The boys adored her. The girls whispered about her. I joined them, pretending I wasn't curious about who she really was. But I remember thinking she was free in a way that I wasn't. She was in her pleasure while I was trapped in my fear.

I had sex to feel chosen, to feel worthy, to belong. With it came shame. It filled all the places I wanted freedom.

This is what happens when women forget that pleasure belongs to them. For years, I thought healing meant purification, that to be spiritual or "good," I had to scrub myself clean of wanting. I thought a Priestess was someone who had transcended the body. But a Priestess is not pure. She is *whole*.

She knows that divinity lives in her hips, her breath, her hunger.

When my mentor asked, "What does your Sacred Whore want you to know?" something provocative stirred in me.

How could those two simple words evoke so much emotion? I realized I had been trying to heal myself by erasing her—the part that knows how to burn, how to say yes, how to feel everything.

The Sacred Whore is not the opposite of the Priestess. She is the Priestess in her full expression. She is the body of the divine made flesh, the bridge between the erotic and the holy.

She is the truth that love and lust are not enemies. They are two faces of devotion. But we have been taught to fear her. We have been told that holiness lives only in restraint. So we swing between extremes: objectification or purity, indulgence or repression.

Even outside of religion, purity culture lingers in our bones. It tells us to tidy up our truth, to make our spirituality digestible, to keep our desire contained. But that is not awakening, it is another form of control.

To reclaim pleasure, we must face both distortions—the way patriarchy profits from our objectification and the way spirituality punishes our sensuality. To be a Priestess of Pleasure is to walk the middle path. We honor the body as sacred, erotic as holy, desire as divine instruction. This is what the Sacred Whore came to teach me: The body is not a distraction from divinity; it is divinity in motion.

And when a woman lets herself feel that truth fully, unapologetically, without trying to make it smaller or safer, she becomes ungovernable.

RECLAIMING YOUR BIRTHRIGHT

I was watching a period drama recently, one of those lavish portrayals of high society, when a woman went into labor and died. The scene was meant to be tragic, inevitable. But all I could think was: *If a midwife had been there, this wouldn't have happened. If someone who understood women's bodies, rhythms, and needs had been present rather than those who succumbed to authority and protocol, the outcome might have been different.*

That moment stayed with me because it captured something essential. Women once gave birth, healed, and gathered under the care of other women who trusted the body rather than feared it. As medicine, religion, and patriarchy consolidated power, that knowledge was packaged as witchcraft. Midwives were discredited. Pleasure, intuition, and embodied wisdom were treated as liabilities rather than intelligence.

What had once been communal and instinctive was taken over, controlled, and renamed "dangerous."

This is how the theft happened. Not through force, but through slow replacement. What women once knew instinctively got rebranded as dangerous, unreliable, something that needed expert management. And the effects ripple through everything—the way we learn to doubt our gut feelings, push past our limits, and mistake suffering for strength. If you are reading this and feeling something stir, you are not alone. Every woman I know carries some version of this story—the silencing, the shrinking, the quiet negotiation between longing and belonging. We feel it everywhere, in how we show up at work, in how we move through relationships, in how we inhabit our own bodies. We are not born disconnected from pleasure. We are taught to forget. We are conditioned to distrust what feels good, to measure our worth by how much we endure, and to earn love through suppression instead of self-expression.

Pleasure is not a reward you earn for being good.

It is a birthright.

It is your body's original language, the way your cells speak to the divine. Remapping your relationship to pleasure begins with listening. Not to the noise of "should" and shame, but to the whispers that live beneath them. Start small. Notice the warmth of the water when you shower. The way sunlight lands on your skin. The scent of your coffee in the morning. These are all doorways back to aliveness.

Pleasure doesn't have to start in the bedroom. For most of us, it can't start there—we're too disconnected from our bodies to feel much of anything below the neck. It starts with the slow return to sensation. With remembering you have a body that feels things.

If the word "pleasure" still makes you uncomfortable, forget it for now. Start with presence. Can you just be here, in this moment, without needing to fix anything? Can you notice your breath moving, your heart beating, the weight of your body in this chair?

That's enough. That's everything, actually.

Your body speaks in sensation, in the way your chest opens when something feels true, in the pull you feel toward certain people or places or experiences. The more you listen and attune, and stay open to what arises, the better you speak the language of your body.

The woman inside you who knows how to feel is still there. She's been waiting patiently for you to stop rushing long enough to listen. She doesn't move at the speed of your to-do list. She moves at the speed of presence, which is usually slower than you want but exactly what you need.

Ask her what she wants you to know. Not with your mind— with your whole body. Close your eyes and listen for the answer that comes not in words but in breath, in color, in the way your shoulders drop or your jaw unclenches. She'll remind you that your desire isn't something to be managed or fixed. It's intelligence moving through you, pointing you toward what's alive.

Pleasure is not something you do, but something you allow. Feeling disconnected from pleasure or exhausted by the idea of even exploring it, is normal. You're here to find your way back, which means you begin to learn how to receive in order to return. But most of us are exhausted from managing the world from our masculine energy. We've lost the ability to receive. Pleasure feels like a draining task when you could find yourself tucked on the couch watching TV. You can stay numb, closed, turned off. Or you can choose something new.

You may not have to become a new person or blow up your life to find her. But if that's what it takes to awaken the Goddess within—the one who delights in a warm breeze across her cheek while she drives her kids to the bus, or who strips down for her own erotic aliveness, then so be it.

When I hear women in their forties tell me they've shut down their sexuality, thrown away their sexy lingerie and given up, it breaks my heart. I lived in that barren desert of disconnection for two decades. Now that I'm dancing in the ocean of pleasure, I'm here to shout from the rooftops: Come on in, the water is perfect!

Every woman has her own menu of pleasure: the unique constellation of experiences, sensations, and desires that bring her fully alive. What turns you on is yours. The key is to remember that your turn-on is not indulgent. It is part of your life force, your creative spark, your divine electricity.

YOUR PLEASURE IS CONTEXTUAL

Esther Perel, a Belgian-American psychotherapist known for her work on relational intelligence, says, "Eroticism is the poetic expression of our imagination."

It's not just about sex; it's about aliveness, curiosity, and freedom. It's about being connected to your senses, to your mystery, to the part of you that's endlessly creative. You can't access that if you're running on empty or performing for approval. Remember, your turn-on doesn't begin in the bedroom, it begins in the body.

It begins with permission. Permission to rest. To receive. To move more slowly. To savor the moment instead of rushing to the next one. When we reconnect with pleasure, we are retraining the body to experience safety through joy rather than vigilance. Neuroscientists have found that pleasure increases **dopamine** (motivation and desire) and **oxytocin** (connection and bonding). These chemicals not only make us feel good but also build *resilience*. Pleasure builds capacity.

It expands what the body can hold: love, grief, joy, intensity. So, if you've been afraid to open again, start small. Pleasure doesn't demand intensity. It asks for honesty.

After years of numbing, striving, and caretaking, most women don't need more intensity. They need *warmth*. Warmth is what melts the armor. It's what lets the body exhale.

Start by asking: *What feels good right now?*

That might look like:

- A slow walk without your phone.
- A dance in your kitchen to one song that makes you feel alive.
- Self-touch without a goal, exploring your own skin as though it's new.
- A moment of honest stillness with your breath, your heartbeat, your humanness.
- Pleasure expands with curiosity.

If you can bring attention to the smallest flicker of sensation—a tingling in your hands, the soft rhythm of your breath—you're already reconnecting to your body's map of safety. From there, you can explore what I call **The Menu of Pleasure.**

MENU OF PLEASURE

Every woman has her own menu of pleasure. A collection of sensations, desires, and experiences that awaken her body and remind her she's alive. For some, it's the first sip of coffee in the morning or the slow stretch under warm sheets. For others, it's the dance floor, the ocean, a lover's touch, the sun on bare skin.

Pleasure is presence. It doesn't live in one place. It lives everywhere. In the pulse of your creativity, in the way you move, in the sound of your laughter, in the glimmer of possibility that runs through you when you let yourself *want*.

I was taught that pleasure was a reward—something you earn after all the work is done, all the boxes checked, all the people are satisfied. My body was shameful. My sexuality was something to manage, not celebrate. Pleasure belonged to other people, not good girls like me.

I spent decades believing this. And I spent decades exhausted, disconnected, running on fumes while telling myself I was fine.

But here's what I've learned: Pleasure isn't a luxury. It's your body's way of telling you it feels safe.

When we feel pleasure—real pleasure, not the forced kind—our nervous system shifts out of survival mode and into receptivity. This isn't some woo-woo concept. It's science. Researchers have shown that arousal, especially for women, is contextual. It doesn't just appear out of nowhere. It emerges when our bodies feel safe, relaxed, connected.

All those years I couldn't feel much of anything? My body was just doing its job, protecting me from a world that didn't feel safe enough to let my guard down.

Our nervous systems are built for protection.

When we live in chronic stress or emotional hypervigilance, the body shuts down, limiting our access to pleasure because it doesn't feel safe enough to open. It's how we've adapted.

When we begin to restore safety through breath, movement, self-touch, or connection, the body starts to remember that it can trust itself again. Somatic psychology calls this *regulation*. To me, it feels like coming home.

Pleasure is not separate from healing. It *is* healing. It's the felt experience of wholeness returning to the body. Even the simple act of touching your own skin, breathing into your belly, or feeling the weight of your body against the earth can signal to your nervous system, *You are safe now. You can open.*

Think of it as your own ecosystem of aliveness. Each item on the menu activates a different part of your body, your psyche, your energy.

1. **Sensual Pleasure**
   Engaging your senses through touch, taste, scent, sound, and sight.
   It's the candlelight, the silk against your skin, the scent of your favorite oil, the way your body moves to music.

2. **Erotic Pleasure**
   The spark of desire, fantasy, arousal, intimacy. It might include self-pleasure, sex with a partner, or simply the feeling of being turned on by life itself. There is no hierarchy here. All pleasure is sacred when it is conscious and consensual.

3. **Creative Pleasure**
   The pleasure of making something from nothing: art, writing, beauty, ideas.
   When you follow inspiration, you follow the same life force that fuels sexual energy. Creation and arousal are sisters.

4. **Relational Pleasure**
   The intimacy of being seen, heard, and met.
   It's the joy of friendship, laughter, play, and love.
   Connection is one of the deepest forms of pleasure we
   can experience.

5. **Spiritual Pleasure**
   The awe of being alive.
   The quiet bliss that comes from ritual, devotion, prayer,
   or meditation.

The feeling of being in union with something greater than yourself.

Each of these opens a different doorway into your turn-on.

You don't have to choose one.

You can feast from all of them.

Your body knows what it needs.

You only have to listen.

Following pleasure does not mean following every impulse. It means listening deeply and discerning what nourishes you rather than drains you.

Pleasure will call and knock on your door in different forms. There are seasons when rest is erotic. Others when creation is the turn-on. Seasons when intimacy feels expansive, and seasons when solitude does. Integration happens when you're honest, and balance follows.

Many women experience feeling stuck when integration appears on their path. This is a moment of action, and it asks more from us than simply learning the concepts. It asks us to choose and it shapes our new identities. This can feel scary and overwhelming, becoming ourselves often is. But pleasure *informs* this blooming.

When pleasure is integrated, we naturally pace ourselves. We know when to move forward and when to pause. Its essence becomes a conversation rather than a command.

Some days, following pleasure means saying yes. Other days, it means saying no. Both are acts of devotion to your aliveness.

✦ Integration Practice: Reconnecting into Our Senses

Knowing about pleasure is one thing. Living it is another. Most of us were taught to think about pleasure rather than feel it. We analyze it, plan it, question whether we've earned it. We schedule it into weekends or date nights and then wonder why it doesn't arrive when we call. But pleasure doesn't live in the mind. It lives in your body. In your breath, in sensation, in presence.

This practice is about rebuilding trust with your body through sensation. Avoid focusing on arousal or reaching a specific state.

If you've been disconnected from your body for a long time, you might feel some resistance. That's okay. Discomfort is not a sign that you're doing it wrong. It's just information.

Reclaiming your pleasure begins in the smallest moments: noticing what feels good, what feels alive, what helps your body remember safety. Pleasure is not something you chase. It's something you allow.

You don't need lingerie, a partner, or the perfect playlist.

You don't even need to feel "turned on."

You only need willingness—a soft curiosity about what might

happen if you stop performing and start listening. Your pleasure will not look like mine, or anyone else's. It's unique to your body, your story, your season of life. You might find it in stillness, or laughter, or tears. You might find it in solitude or in the arms of a lover. You might find it in the garden, in a song, in your own breath. There is no wrong place to begin.

The following ritual is a practice in remembering, a way of returning to dialogue with your body and uncovering sensations that may have gone quiet over time.

You can approach it like a ceremony, a date with yourself, or like an experiment in aliveness.

Whichever way you come to it, let this be your permission slip to explore. Let it be messy, holy, awkward, exquisite. Let it be yours. Your body holds the map, but your pleasure is the compass.

Start by mapping your own pleasure landscape.

Ask yourself:

- What sensations make me feel alive?
- What experiences fill me with warmth or excitement?
- Where have I been settling for comfort instead of pleasure?
- Where have I confused performance with presence?

You may notice that what once turned you on no longer does, or that new desires are beginning to surface. That's not a loss. That's evolution. Every woman's pleasure will change with time, with healing, with seasons. Your body is always guiding you toward what it needs next.

The goal is not endless ecstasy. It's remembering how to feel.

Living turned on, attuned, is to awaken to life itself. It means you've allowed pleasure to fill your life. It's the softening that comes when you stop apologizing for your joy. It's the deep exhale of the woman who finally decides she's worthy of feeling good.

This ritual is an invitation to come home to your body slowly, gently, without pressure. It's about rediscovering what brings you back to life and what makes you feel safe enough to open. It is a compass back to your aliveness.

STEP 1: SET THE SPACE

Create a small ritual for yourself.

Dim the lights. Light a candle or incense.

Play music that makes your body sway or sigh.

You are signaling to your nervous system that this moment is sacred, that you are stepping out of the noise and into your own presence.

Sit or lie down comfortably. Take a deep breath in through your nose and exhale through your mouth.

Let your shoulders drop. Let your belly soften.

Whisper to yourself:

I am here. I am safe.

STEP 2: SENSATION AWARENESS

Begin by bringing attention to your senses, one by one.

- What do you see? Notice the play of light and shadow in the room.
- What do you hear? Music, your breath, the subtle hum of life around you.
- What do you smell? The scent of your candle, your skin, the air.

- What do you feel against your skin? The texture of fabric, the temperature of the air.

Let yourself notice without judgment.
Pleasure begins with presence.

STEP 3: BREATH AND TOUCH

Take a few deep, slow breaths into your belly.

With each inhale, imagine you are filling your body with golden light.

With each exhale, release any tension or numbness.

If it feels available, let your hands gently, with a feather touch, explore your own skin.

Touch yourself with curiosity, not performance.

Notice what feels neutral, what feels pleasant, what feels alive.

Trace your collarbones, your thighs, your neck. Feel the warmth under your fingertips.

If you feel emotion rising—tears, laughter, discomfort—let it come.

This is energy moving.

You are teaching your body that touch can be safe, that pleasure can be simple, that you are allowed to feel.

STEP 4: NAME YOUR YES

As you move through this exploration, ask yourself:

What feels like a yes in my body right now?

Maybe it's the scent of your candle.

Maybe it's the memory of the ocean.

Maybe it's a song that invites your hips to sway.

Notice it. Name it.

This is your body's language of desire.

Then ask: *What feels like a no?*

Listen with compassion.

Your boundaries are part of your pleasure. They create the safety that allows desire to flourish.

STEP 5: WRITE YOUR MENU OF PLEASURE

When you're ready, take out your journal and write a list called: **What Turns Me On (Right Now)?**

Let it be uncensored.

Write everything that brings color back to your cheeks—not just sexually, but sensually, creatively, emotionally, spiritually.

Maybe it's:

- Clean sheets and warm skin
- A feather dancing across my skin
- Dancing alone in my living room
- The first sip of red wine
- Watching the sunrise in silence
- A lover's hand on the back of my neck
- Creating something beautiful
- Laughing until I cry
- Standing barefoot on the earth

Your list will become your personal Pleasure Map. A reference point to return to when life feels dry or dull. Revisit it often. Add to it. Let it evolve as you do.

STEP 6: CLOSE WITH GRATITUDE

Place a hand on your heart, one on your belly.

Take three deep breaths and thank your body for guiding you home.

Even if you felt nothing—or everything—trust that your body heard you.

Pleasure is not a switch you flip.

It's a relationship you rebuild.

Each small act of noticing, each soft touch, each sigh of relief is a signal that you are coming back online.

A FINAL WHISPER

You do not have to be fully healed to feel pleasure. You do not have to be partnered, or perfect, or ready. You only need to be willing.

This work—this remembrance—is revolutionary. In a world that profits from women's disconnection, pleasure is an act of rebellion. Following what feels good awakens your body, frees your mind.

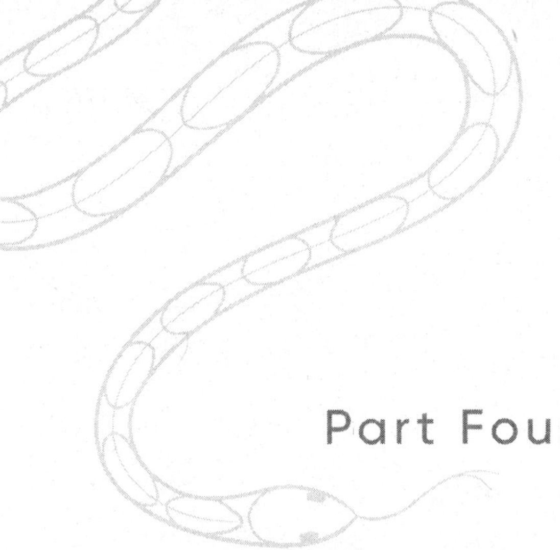

Part Four

An Invitation: Reclaim Your Expression

CHAPTER TEN

Becoming the Medicine

There are moments in life when talk therapy, journaling, and even breathwork fail to reach the deepest places within us. When the stories we've told about our pain no longer hold the charge, but the body still carries the imprint. For me, that was when the plants began to call.

Plant medicine entered my life not as an escape, but as a return. A reunion with something ancient that my soul already knew. Indigenous cultures work with plants as teachers, to work the way only nature can—without judgment, without hurry, and without pretending that I could think my way to wholeness.

The plants didn't just show me visions, they showed me *truths*. They worked through my body, the way somatic work does, dissolving the walls I had built around my grief and desire. They showed me where I was still holding, gripping, controlling. They stripped away the layers of who I thought I was—the good mother, the good wife, the spiritual woman—until only presence remained.

Somatic therapy brought me into my body and plant medicine brought me into communion with myself and the natural world. It prepared me for the deeper work of eros and pleasure that would follow.

It is not for everyone, and it is not a shortcut. Medicine meets you where you are. Sometimes that means bliss; often it's facing fear, letting go of illusions, and the death of false identities and the stories that no longer serve. And in that death, something new can be born.

This chapter is about that rebirth—about listening to the Spirit through sacred plants, Earth's whispers, and the song of the ancestors. It covers the conversation between body and spirit that reminds us we are nature remembering itself. We are the medicine.

THE CALL OF THE MEDICINE

In early spring, a friend and mentor I had admired for years called to invite me to her retreat in Mexico. We had spoken often about her work—healing the maternal line, reclaiming the feminine body, and reparenting the self—but this time the invitation landed differently. It was the middle of a gray California spring and my own unraveling whispered, *Go.*

On paper, my life still looked whole. But inside, I was fracturing. My marriage had grown quiet, a house echoing with logistics and silence. We slept in separate rooms, took turns with the kids, performed civility while everything collapsed under the weight of what we wouldn't say. There were still moments of normalcy—dinner, bills, carpools—but it was as though we were co-managing the ruins of what used to be our life.

Something—someone—had opened a current of desire in me that I could no longer turn away from. For the first time in decades,

I was inside desire rather than managing it, a thread of connection that pulsed through my phone like an electric current. Erotic, charged, emotional. The kind of intimacy that reminded me what aliveness felt like. The kind that also tore me open with guilt.

I was living in two worlds. The one I knew, safe and structured but slowly suffocating, and the other that glimmered with possibility. The ache of what I was becoming made it almost impossible to stay, yet terrifying to leave. When Gertrude's email arrived, it felt like oxygen.

For months, I had been quietly reading, listening, and hearing stories of women meeting Sacred Plant Medicine in ceremony, and finding what the modern world had forgotten: Communion, not consumption. Healing that piece begins in the body and reverberates through the soul.

I didn't know it yet, but I was standing on the edge of the biggest initiation of my life. I had already been microdosing psilocybin and had been quietly waiting for an opportunity to do a bigger dose. So, as I packed my bag, I tucked the capsules in with my supplements. I didn't tell anyone that I was bringing them with me. I only knew that something in me was ready to be undone. I could no longer survive my in-between life.

The retreat itself was small and intimate, hosted in her oceanside home in Mexico. The land held its own quiet authority, long linked to ancient myths of goddess women who guided the sun, symbols of feminine power, fertility, and protection. She invited us to share our intentions, about what we desired more of in our lives. We were strangers, most of us, women arriving from different lives and seasons, but sitting together in a circle, something shifted. There is a particular nourishment that happens when women gather in this way, when intimacy is created through shared vulnerability and presence.

By the end of that first evening, it was clear we were no longer strangers. We were woven together by shared meals, shared silence, and the quiet bravery of naming what was alive.

We spent the next few days journeying through the land, our stories, assumptions, and new perspectives. On the first night, we did a Temascal, a traditional Mexican sweat lodge, in a heated, small clay dome. The medicine woman invited us to enter the space without clothes. We accepted her invitation, and as the fire burned hot, and we sat with our discomfort, she called us to shed the layers of shame and judgment that had kept us from our feminine, our sexuality, our Goddess-given desire. I had been carrying my own quiet storm—desire and betrayal still bound in guilt—and the timing of this release was perfect.

When the retreat ended, I had an extra day before heading home. I asked Gertrude if I could dose psilocybin on her property. I wanted her blessing to honor the weekend, her, and her space. She agreed without hesitation. My new retreat sister Maggie, twenty-five, luminous, and wise beyond her years, offered to stay with me.

We had bonded quickly and I was grateful she would be with me.

In the morning, I woke early and walked down the dirt road to buy fresh limes from a fruit truck. Back in the open-air kitchen, the ocean glimmering beyond the patio, I prepared my medicine for the journey: six capsules emptied into lime juice, a little honey, a touch of warm water. I drank it quickly and ran down to sit by the edge of the ocean and wait.

At first, everything was pure wonder. The sky dissolved into sacred geometry, the rocks became slow-moving turtles, and every sound felt like a pulse from the universe itself. But when a woman walked by with a barking dog, the world turned sharp. The energy was too much. I needed to move back up to the retreat studio, a high-ceilinged temple of light and crystals.

For the next five hours, I moved between shadow and sun, between surrender and resistance. I rolled on the floor, cried, shook, and vomited old stories of unworthiness, guilt, self-sufficiency, the endless belief that I had to do it all alone. My two sisters sat nearby, tending me like midwives.

When I apologized for being too needy, they smiled and said, "You are safe. You are loved."

Gertrude's question pierced through me: "What story is this, the one that says you have to do it alone?"

It was the story of my life.

As she played the crystal bowls, their sound moved through me like medicine. I had texted my therapist that morning, somehow believing I could still make our session. In the middle of my ceremony, I asked Gertrude to connect us. Moments later, there was Sherri, my therapist, glowing on a tiny Zoom screen, held up by my sister's trembling hands.

"I get to have this," I kept saying, my voice shaking.

"Yes, love," Sherri said. "You get to have this. Your desire is life-affirming for all of us."

The words landed with initiation. I stomped, wept, and felt centuries of caregiving and martyrdom rise to the surface—the mother, the daughter, the wife, the woman who carried everyone else's needs before her own. I cried for her and released her.

As the waves of the mushrooms intensified, I found myself whispering, "I chose this medicine and this medicine chose me."

I kept reminding myself that I was safe and had permission to be there. I felt myself taking up more space as the moments passed, with these two women by my side.

By late afternoon, the retreat space was glowing, sunlight slanting through the skylight shaped like a cervix, half shadow and half golden light. I rocked between the two, metaphorically birthing myself from darkness into light. When the waves of the mushrooms finally calmed, I could feel the ground beneath me, solid and new.

By sunset, the mushrooms had worn off. I sat by the pool integrating the day with my wholeness. We talked about how each of my breakthroughs had rippled through them. What moved through me didn't stop with me. I could feel it touching the women who were holding me, changing all of us in small, unmistakable ways.

Maggie looked at me, eyes wide with reverence. "You kept saying, 'I chose this medicine, and this medicine chose me.' There's so much you didn't get to choose before. But this time, you did."

That truth pulsed through me like electricity. There had been so many things in my life I hadn't chosen—a fractured childhood, the weight of responsibility, the years of silence—but this, this I chose. And I began to see, that the choice was always mine.

THE SPACE BETWEEN

In plant medicine circles, there's a saying: You don't always get the journey you want, but you get the one you need. I've found the same to be true of life.

That spring became a ceremony all its own. Not contained to a yoga mat or a night in the jungle, but unfolding day by day in the dismantling of a life. I was holding the pieces of a marriage, a home, an identity, and trying to decide which parts could be carried forward and which had already burned away.

There were moments of deep exhaustion. Weeks without my children. Long nights wondering if I had misread the call. Some days felt heavy and slow, like wading through mud. Others glimmered with a fragile, unfamiliar hope. The kind that doesn't promise safety, only truth.

Once the decision was made, there was no turning back. I had spent years circling the edge of leaving, telling myself I could endure, that good enough might be enough. But when I finally pulled the thread, the whole tapestry came undone.

There was no fairytale waiting on the other side. No lover to catch me. Only the quiet knowing that the life I had been living could no longer hold who I was becoming. That aliveness, once felt, could not be negotiated away.

I moved forward without certainty, but complete clarity. The medicine had not given me answers. It had given me access to myself. And once that door was open, the truth came quickly, clean and unmistakable.

That spring, the truth didn't arrive gently. It arrived like a match struck in the dark. And once lit, there was no pretending I couldn't see.

AYAHUASCA

CEREMONY ONE: THE ASK

The night before my forty-fifth birthday, I walked barefoot through the Costa Rican jungle toward the palapa, dressed in white and trembling with a mix of fear and excitement. The air was thick and alive, heavy with rain and the scent of earth. Moments before, we stood around a fire in the courtyard, where we burned what we were ready to release. I wrote only a few words on my paper, but they carried lifetimes: *control, silence, shame.* The paper curled, turned to ash, and disappeared into the dark.

Inside the big open-air structure, the space glowed with candlelight and the smell of sage and tobacco. An altar stretched across the front, draped in feathers and fur, flowers, bowls of stones, and instruments I couldn't name. The shamans moved quietly, each step deliberate, their presence electric and calm all at once. We sat on thin mattresses arranged in a circle, each one with a bucket beside it—an omen of what was to come.

Gracia, the medicine woman, moved through the room, singing softly, her voice weaving between the jungle sounds that poured through the open windows. She held a small cup of the black, viscous brew. When it was my turn, I stepped forward, bowed, and drank. Bitter, earthy, ancient. Then I returned to my mat, pulled the shawl over my shoulders, and waited.

The songs began. The icaros, they called them—medicine songs that summon the spirit of the plant, the grandmother—to come work with us. The jungle answered, pulsing with life, insects and frogs and birds composing their own symphony in response. My breath slowed. My body began to hum.

The first wave came as a shimmer, a distortion at the edges of my vision, as if the air itself had texture. Then light. Then movement. Then the sounds around me—retching, sobbing, laughing, prayers whispered through tears.

The medicine moved slowly through me, and I felt both the absence of feeling and everything all at once. My body was a weighted blanket, impossibly heavy, but my mind was alive with images—vines, snakes, faces of women I didn't know but somehow recognized. When the shamans opened the line for a second cup, I watched others rise with ease, steady in their knowing. I stayed frozen on my mat, debating with myself.

Wasn't one cup enough? Hadn't I come far enough already?

But something deeper whispered, *You didn't come all this way to stop now.* I crawled forward, knees pressing into the wooden floor, and looked up at Gracia. "I'm nervous," I said quietly, "but I think I should."

She smiled, eyes ancient and knowing. "Take it with gratitude," she said.

I did.

The nausea came fast. It rolled through my stomach like an

ocean wave, and I reached for the bucket. I began to heave, my body contracting in violent rhythm. The bucket became a tunnel of light, the sound of my own breath echoing like thunder. Each wave took something from me—memories, grief, stories—I hadn't even realized I was still carrying.

Then fear arrived. As it always does.

You're not safe. You'll never stop. You'll be stuck here forever.

My heart pounded. My throat closed. My body remembered every moment of helplessness it had ever known. And then, through the haze, I did something unexpected.

I lifted my hand.

"I need help," I whispered. My voice was weak, but my words cut through the music. Then louder, "I need help."

The two men in front of me spun around and moved toward me, but before they could reach, Gracia appeared. She moved with purpose, waving them back, and knelt in front of me. Her face came close, so close that it felt like she was breathing me in.

"You are fighting it," she said softly, her voice vibrating through my bones. "Stop fighting. *This is ancestral.* Only you can do this. You have the tools. Let go."

Her words cracked something open inside me. I fell to my side, curling into myself, shaking and sobbing. My body emptied. My spirit emptied. Images of my mother, my grandmother, and all the women before me flickered through my mind—women who swallowed their words, who bore their pain in silence, who learned endurance instead of expression. I could feel them inside me, their unspoken stories pressing against the edges of my skin, begging to be released.

I let it happen.

The purge softened in waves, and with each one I felt lighter. The sound around me changed from chaos to harmony, the sound of others retching fading into the background, and the sounds of the jungle coming forward.

Gracia's songs drifted through the darkness, her voice blended with the jungle, and I tracked her as she moved, the faint jingle of her beads anchoring me to safety. Hours blurred into moments, a soft glow as my body sank into my mattress with relief.

When the lights finally rose, the room was still. We all reoriented ourselves toward one another as the ceremony closed and gathered our belongings. I sat up slowly, body weak from the purging, and grateful for the company of friends. Some had heard me call for help and came up to offer their gratitude or check on me. We had all returned together from a collective and individual journey.

Later, we gathered for soup and fruit, the candlelight soft on our faces.

A man who'd been sitting across from me said, "Sometimes, we get the ceremony we need, not the one we want."

For me, he was right.

Grandmother Ayahuasca didn't give me beauty or bliss. She gave me a gift. A hard but important gift of seeing what I had been avoiding. I had to ask for help, surrender control, trust that life— and love—want to hold me if I let them.

That night, in the jungle, on the eve of my forty-fifth birthday, I learned the simplest truth of all: Surrender is not the end of power. It's where it begins.

The ceremonies that followed brought the same truth back to me from different angles, quieter each time, deeper in the body.

My relationship with the medicine and myself had shifted. So did my fear. My capacity to stay present when things became uncomfortable or tender or overwhelmingly alive expanded. Each night softened something else I had been gripping—control, shame, the belief that I had to hold everything together on my own.

There were moments of beauty and moments of resistance. Laughter, grief, stillness. I learned that the medicine does not rush. It returns you to the same doorway until you stop bracing against it. Until you trust that what is moving through you is not there to harm you.

One message came through clearly and repeatedly, asking me to be nothing except honest. To tell the truth about what I was feeling. To let myself be seen without performance. To stop pretending I was fine when I wasn't.

By the final ceremony, there was no drama left. Only a steady sense of presence—the earth beneath me, the people in the room— all of it held me; it was larger than my fear. And then there was joy, dancing, and celebration. The work was no longer just about release. This was where integration met me. It was where I would live with new awareness.

I didn't leave with answers or a plan. I left with embodiment and a quieter nervous system. Now that my body knew the truth, it wouldn't abandon me and I wouldn't abandon her either. The medicine made it possible for me to finally release a life I had outgrown.

INTEGRATION: CEREMONY AS A WAY OF LIFE

The days that followed were a dreamscape of color and connection. We sang songs around the fire and wrote poetry under the canopy of trees. We rode horses through the valley, pulled tarot cards, shared meals, and spoke about the infinite lessons still unfolding inside us. The medicine lingered in every conversation, every laugh, every silence.

We plunged into cold mountain water, communing with nature and lying on the rocks in the hot sun. We did breathwork and ice baths, poetry circles and cacao ceremonies. The laughter came easier now. Our bodies were lighter. Our eyes softer.

When I look back at the photos from that week—my hair wild with feathers, my face glowing with joy—I can still feel it: the medicine alive in me, rearranging everything. That experience was the threshold, the initiation I didn't know I had been preparing for all along.

When I returned home, I felt changed in ways that words could only begin to touch. I knew I was headed into surgery, but my fear was replaced with a new steadiness in me, a quiet conviction that I was exactly where I needed to be. The edges of my fear had softened. The noise turned down.

We were advised not to make any big changes for three months after sitting with Ayahuasca. But my life had its own timeline.

Within weeks, I told my husband it was over. I didn't decide it with my mind—it came as a knowing from deep within my body, calm and absolute.

There was no anger left to burn. Just truth, and the sacred act of trusting the unknown.

I came back from the jungle as a woman in her embodiment. I had the courage to walk away, the softness to keep my heart open, and the wisdom to know that endings can be promising, too.

Ceremony showed me the door. Life guided me through it.

CLOSING: THE LIVING MEDICINE

The year I stopped drinking, I realized how much I had been numbing, how much I had been holding at bay. The silence that followed was deafening at first. But in that quiet, the plants began to speak.

My curiosity with mushrooms became communion.

I began microdosing mushrooms, gently, intentionally, allowing the medicine to show me where I was still holding on. The plants have a way of softening us where we've gone rigid, of loosening what's calcified in the body and heart. They move us through what might otherwise take years to uncover, guiding us through the dark, always toward the light of our own truth.

To this day, I hold deep reverence for the medicines and the teachers who steward them. I still work with plants, both in my personal practice and with the women I guide. They are not shortcuts or escapes; they can be sacred allies—accelerators of awakening, mirrors for what we are ready to see.

Plant medicine isn't magic. It doesn't fix you or suddenly make everything clear. What it does do is amplify what's already there—all the stuff you've been pushing down, avoiding, or pretending isn't real.

For me, microdosing became a way to hear my own voice underneath all the noise. But I learned quickly that you can't just take medicine and hope for the best. I needed support—a therapist who understood trauma, friends who could hold space when I fell apart, guides who knew both the medicine and how fragile we can be when we're cracking open.

The thing about plant medicine is that it makes lying to yourself almost impossible. I'd been telling myself I was fine in my marriage for years. The medicine didn't tell me to leave—it just made it impossible to ignore how dead I felt inside when I was pretending to be happy.

That kind of truth can be destabilizing if you're not prepared for it. I've seen women take medicine and make impulsive decisions they regret later because they confused the clarity of a single moment with having all the answers. The medicine shows you what is, but it's imperative you take time to decide what to do about it.

The most powerful and often overlooked part of plant medicine—and all healing really—is *integration*. The real work begins after the ceremony, when you return to your life and let what you've seen change the way you live. Integration is the moment we choose to embody the lessons instead of intellectualizing them, to rewrite the patterns instead of replaying them. If we return home and fall back into the same loops and triggers, we've missed the medicine's invitation.

This path is not for everyone. Plant medicine is powerful, and power requires discernment. It opens the body and soul to energy beyond our understanding and can put us in vulnerable positions. Therefore, it's up to us to take responsibility for the experience, to choose carefully where and with whom we sit, and what our boundaries are. This can be difficult if you are navigating deep traumas. Some bodies, some seasons, some nervous systems are not meant to walk this road. That does not make the transformation inaccessible. The deeper medicine—the one that heals—has always lived closer than we think. It's in presence, breath, devotion, and the body's willingness to tell the truth.

Integration is what transforms experience into evolution.

It is the bridge between revelation and reality—the difference between recreation and transformation.

And it is where the journey, truly, becomes a way of life. The Priestess walks this path with devotion. She studies the cycles of nature, learns the language of the wind and moon, and listens for the whisper of the plant spirits who guide her home to herself. Each ceremony, each season, each breath becomes a teacher.

The invitation is to walk gently here—to honor the plants as allies, not escapes, to let them open what has grown closed, and to remember that their wisdom already lives within you.

May you walk the path of the Priestess—rooted in the earth, attuned to her rhythm, and guided always by the living spirit of the medicine.

✦ Integration Practice: Entering the Living Medicine

If you're not yet comfortable with plant medicine, you don't need them to access the inner parts of you. Your body knows the way. This ritual is an invitation to listen —to enter the same inner landscape that ceremony reveals: the place where truth lives beneath the noise.

Find a quiet place where you can sit or lie down comfortably. Support your spine, the center of alignment. Place one hand on your heart and one on your belly.

Close your eyes.

Take three slow breaths, in through the nose and out through the mouth.

With each exhale, imagine releasing the weight you've been carrying: expectations, roles, stories about who you're supposed to be.

Now, bring your attention inward.

Imagine yourself standing at the edge of a threshold, a simple crossing.

A doorway between the life you've been managing and the life that wants to be lived through you.

You are not here to force anything.

You are here to listen.

Ask yourself:

What truth is trying to reach me?

Do not search for an answer. Let it arrive in its own way—as a sensation, an image, a memory, a word, or a feeling in the body. Stay curious. Be gentle.

If resistance arises, notice it.

If emotion arises, allow it.

If nothing arises, trust that listening is generating in the stillness.

Now imagine that truth is settling into your body. You are the invitation for it to land where it wants to land: in your chest, your womb, your throat, your hands.

What is mine to carry forward from here?

Be open to receive rather than decide.

When you feel complete, take one final breath and imagine stepping back across the threshold—not leaving the truth behind, but bringing it with you into your life.

Before opening your eyes, place both hands over your heart and say quietly to yourself:

I will honor what I have seen.

I will move at the speed of integration.

I trust myself to know what comes next.

When you're ready, open your eyes.

You may not have participated in plant medicine, but you remembered that the medicine lives within you.

And the work, as always, transpires in how you live.

CHAPTER ELEVEN

Path of the Pleasure Priestess

For much of my life, I followed the map we were all handed—be good, stay strong, don't need too much. If I could hold it all together, achieve enough, love enough, maybe I'd finally feel safe, worthy, whole.

When my life began to unravel—marriage, identity, faith in what I knew—I came to understand that I had been trying to live by a map that wasn't meant for me. I was being called into something far older and deeper. What began as a crisis became a descent. And in that descent, I met the Priestess. For me, that path began as a whisper—a remembering that was felt.

The Rose lineage found me first: the teachings of Mary Magdalene, of divine love as the highest frequency. Through that doorway, I began to trace the thread back to my own bloodline—to the Celtic shamanic roots of my homeland, to the women who once gathered in stone circles, who sang to the land, who knew the rhythm of the seasons and the language of the earth.

For many of us, this remembering comes as a stirring in the body, an ancient knowing carried in the DNA. We are not learning something new; we are reawakening something old. It is the call of the feminine, returning through us—the wisdom keepers, the healers, the midwives, the ones who once knew how to tend the *seen* and the *unseen*.

It is the Divine Feminine awakening. It is the moment a woman stops trying to live inside the story she was given and starts listening for the one she was born to tell.

The Hero's Journey, as Joseph Campbell described, is the architecture of myth, a call to adventure, trials, triumph, and a return with the elixir. It's the story of leaving home to conquer the world. But the Priestess Journey—the feminine counterpart—is not about conquest. It is about remembering. It is a journey of descent, of dropping into the body, shedding what was never truly ours, and reclaiming what was buried beneath survival. In this feminine arc, the call is not outward but inward—a whisper beneath the noise, a pulse that says, *Something is missing, go home.* The descent takes us into the underworld of the self: grief, shadow, unmet need, desire denied. It asks for surrender, not strategy. It breaks us open so that the deeper truths—our pleasure, power, and sovereignty—can rise through the cracks.

Where the hero slays dragons, the Priestess learns to hold them. Where the hero returns with treasure, the Priestess realizes *she is the treasure.* This is the somatic map of my work: the alchemy of feeling, of grieving, of loving ourselves back to life. It is the journey I guide others through from the surface to the depths, through the dark forest of emotion, and into the sacred remembering of the body.

The Priestess path is not linear. It spirals. Each descent brings a deeper awakening, another layer of falsehood stripped away, another homecoming to the truth of who we are. We do not return to the world we left; we *become* the elixir, the medicine, the offering. To blow up your life is not destruction for destruction's sake. It is an initiation. It is a reclamation of what was once exiled—your desire, your voice, your knowing. It is the sacred act of turning toward what hurts and allowing it to become the medicine for your transformation.

This is the Sacred Feminine remembering.

This is the Priestess Journey: the wild, tender path back to yourself.

THE PRIESTESS JOURNEY

I have played many roles: wife, mother, businesswoman, good girl. Each came with invisible lines I was taught to stay inside. I thought freedom meant mastering those lines, staying within them neatly enough to be praised, to belong. But there was an ache growing louder. The body always knows. Mine began whispering in the language of fatigue and quiet rebellion, tears that came for no reason at all. The whispers became tremors, then fire. Not a fire that destroyed for destruction's sake, but one that cleared space for something ancient to rise.

There is a point when you reach the threshold and know you can't go back. My marriage had become a museum of the past. I sat in the dark and felt the truth press against my chest, heavy and tender all at once. I had been living a life that looked beautiful from the outside but had been hollowed out by years of disconnection from each other and myself. The decision to leave was a slow unfurling, peeling back the skin of my old life left me raw to what was real.

That was the beginning of my Priestess path, I just didn't know it then. My Priestess did not arrive robed in certainty. She was born in the ashes of the woman who tried to do everything right. She was carved by grief, surrender, the choice to listen to what the body and the soul have been whispering all along.

In those early months, I found myself standing in the middle of rooms that used to feel familiar, unable to recognize the woman in the mirror. My body became my first temple; pleasure became my compass. I began to understand that the sacred was not hidden in faraway rituals, it lived inside the ordinary moments. The heat of sunlight on bare skin, the hum of breath before a yes, the soft pulse between my legs reminding me I was still alive. I woke before dawn to light a candle and write. It was not discipline that got me out of bed and to the page. It was devotion. The difference is vital. Discipline asks for control; devotion asks for surrender. In the early morning light, I felt closest to the Goddess, and life reorganizing itself around me. I learned that when I rooted myself in pleasure and softness, plans and strategies appeared on their own. Desire began to lead, and life followed.

As I learned to trust myself again, my world softened. Saying no became an act of devotion to what was true. I began to treat my business as an extension of my sacred work, a lover rather than a list of tasks. The more I softened into that rhythm, the more the world responded. I stopped managing the universe and began letting it romance me. There were seasons when everything bloomed, and others when I retreated into the dark winter. The Priestess learns to honor both. The in-between has its own kind of holiness. The quiet months, the ones that felt like nothing happened, was where deeper magic was digging its root.

The journey of the Priestess is not about becoming untouchable or transcendent. It is about being profoundly human. It is having the courage to walk into the fire of change and keep the tenderness of your heart open among the flames. It is about remembering that every breath, every yes, every boundary, is a prayer.

I blew up my life to find the divine within me. It was there all along, waiting for me to remember.

There comes a moment on this path when the light you've cultivated begins to reveal what has been hiding in the dark. Through this initiation, the Priestess walks with both the candle and the mirror. She meets her own shadow, to see where she clings, where she manipulates, and where she hides behind the illusion of control. The same fire that warms and illuminates also exposes. It shows the unhealed places—the patterns that keep repeating, the stories that keep us small, all the ways we reach for validation instead of truth.

It's tempting to believe that enlightenment means transcending the shadow, but we don't rise by escaping the darkness; we rise by opening within it. Each pattern, each ache, each trigger, is sacred data. The wounds are not evidence of failure but portals.

In this work, shadow hunting is not about judgment. It is about intimacy. We bring compassion to what we once rejected. We reclaim our power. The parts of us we've silenced—the angry woman, the seductress, the one who wanted too much—were never enemies. They were exiled aspects of our divinity. They have been waiting for us to call them home.

Every time you welcome a lost piece back, your magnetization increases. A woman who meets herself in darkness and returns with truth glimmering in her eyes becomes irresistible to her destiny.

Pleasure is not frivolous. It is holy. It is the language of the divine manifest in flesh. When you meet pleasure without guilt, without grasping, it becomes prayer. It moves out of attachment and into presence. In that place, there is no need to convince or prove. You are worthy just as you are.

Presence is the Priestess's true power. When we are fully here—in the breath and body, of what is real—the universe rearranges itself to meet us. This is magnetism. Not seduction through effort, but attraction through authenticity. We are building a new paradigm from this place: power through embodiment, pleasure with honor, divinity we live in, shedding the need to perform.

The Priestess ascent is a spiral—each turn drawing you deeper into your own knowing, each descent revealing more of your light. It is messy, radiant, humbling, and holy. And every time you choose to see yourself clearly, to meet the shadow without turning away, you are rewriting the story of what it means to be a woman in her power.

This is the quiet revolution—to let presence be the performance, and pleasure be the prayer.

THE WILD ART OF WANTING MORE

Those of us who remember the Priestess path carry something ancient in our bones. It is a song that was never lost, only quieted. It can arrive as a whisper in the night, an ache beneath the ribs, or a knowing that this life was never meant to be ordinary.

Whether we remember through the Rose lineage, the Magdalene, or other Divine Feminine lineage, it lives in our DNA. There was a time when the feminine was revered, when pleasure was seen as holy, when women gathered in temples in celebration of our sisterhood and our gifts to the world. The Priestess was not separate from the spiritual or the sensual. She knew that God lived in the body, in the breath, in the pulse between heartbeats.

That memory is returning.

When I first stepped into that circle of women in lingerie, candles flickering around my living room, I had no idea I was part of something bigger. I thought I was just a divorced mom trying to figure out how to feel alive again.

But as more women started showing up to my circles, to the retreats, to the conversations about pleasure and power, I began to see it. We weren't just healing our own lives; we were remembering something that had been buried for centuries.

We are the women who run a million-dollar business and still dance naked in the kitchen. The mother who teaches her daughters that their bodies are sacred, not shameful. The grandmother who finally leaves her loveless marriage at seventy because she realizes she deserves more.

Each time a woman owns her aliveness, she gives others permission to do the same. Not through preaching or pushing, but through the simple act of living fully in her own skin.

I used to think devotion and desire were opposites—that you had to choose between being good and being real. Now I know better. The most sacred thing I can do is honor the full spectrum of who I am. I am the businesswoman and the lover, the mother and the wild woman, the one who builds empires and the one who falls to her knees in gratitude.

This is how the world changes. Not through force, but through women remembering who they really are.

As we rise, we remember what the ancient ones knew: the Goddess was never gone, she was simply waiting for us to remember her name.

I have held women as they weep with shame and regret, after a lifetime of hating their bodies, in constant competition with an unachievable image. Our bodies have been misused, abused, shamed, distorted, and objectified, and that energy lives in our cells. There is real medicine in gathering and softening, celebrating and witnessing each other in our wholeness. It feels radical and essential in the same breath, because there was a time when it was the only way.

To dance naked, sweep rose petals over a woman's naked form, burn fires and adorn a woman on her solar return—these rituals that were erased, stomped out by Christianity and patriarchy, villainized and distorted are returning. We are remembering.

This is the art to wanting more. And it is wild.

I spent forty years apologizing for wanting things. I was sorry for taking up space, sorry for having opinions, sorry for not being satisfied with a life that looked perfect on paper.

But somewhere in those living room dance parties wearing lingerie, watching women shed layers of shame along with their clothes, I started to understand something different. My desire wasn't the problem. My shame about it was.

I became the woman who finally asked for what she wanted in bed after twenty years of faking it, the mother who admitted she dreamed of more than carpools and casseroles, the entrepreneur who stopped downplaying her success because it made other people uncomfortable.

Each time one of us stopped apologizing for our hunger—for more pleasure, more freedom, more life—something shifted in the room, in the air, in the way we looked at ourselves and each other.

People called us selfish for what we did. Reckless. Too much. The scarlet letters of modern womanhood, designed to keep us small and grateful for scraps. But here's what I learned: When they call you selfish for honoring your own needs, when they call you reckless for trusting your own truth, they're saying you've stopped being controllable.

The ache for more isn't greed—it's guidance. Your desire is intelligence trying to lead you home to yourself. When you stop hiding your hunger, you give others permission to do the same. That's how everything changes.

When I finally started speaking my desires out loud—not whispering them in therapy or journaling them in private, but to real people—something shifted. My body remembered something I'd forgotten—the way it felt to take up space without apology.

I watched this happen with other women, too. The moment they stopped hiding what they wanted, their entire presence changed. They walked differently. Spoke differently. The energy in the room shifted when they entered it.

And here's what I noticed: It scared people. Women who stop asking permission and start making declarations threaten every system built on keeping us small. They challenge every relationship that pleads for our silence to function. They break every structure that needs our compliance to survive.

Freedom becomes contagious. When one woman gives herself permission to want more, other women remember they can, too. It spreads like wildfire—this remembering of who we really are when we're not performing. Every time a woman chooses her own aliveness over everyone else's comfort, something ancient wakes up in all of us.

The wild art of wanting more isn't about becoming greedy or demanding everything right now. The Goddess wants us to celebrate and bow in gratitude and hold out our hands and ask for more, and more, and more. She wants us to remember we're meant to be turned on by our own lives. She wants us to rewild ourselves to the natural state of wanting, to knowing the pulse of our body is a whisper and following it nudges us toward a full life.

The wild art of wanting more is remembering that we are meant to live turned on by life, guided by longing, and led by love. It is the call of the Priestess rising through every woman who dares to say, *I am ready for more.*

And in that moment, the world begins to change.

THE PRIESTESS IN DAILY LIFE

The truth is, we forget.

We wait for the right moment, the weekend, the lover, the permission slip that says it's okay to want again. But the art of living as a Priestess is not about waiting. It is about remembering, as many times as necessary, that your body is the altar and pleasure is how you tend the flame.

For many women, pleasure has been framed as a peak experience—sexual, ecstatic, dramatic. But that definition can keep pleasure just out of reach. When pleasure is only allowed in intensity, we miss its real function. Pleasure is not meant to overwhelm the nervous system. It is meant to *regulate* it. It is the body's way of saying, *You are safe enough to be here now.*

This is why pleasure belongs in daily life.

To live as a Pleasure Priestess is not to float above the world. It is to meet the world from inside the body—resourced, attuned, awake.

The Priestess is not a role you perform or an identity you adopt. She is not reserved for temples, retreats, or altered states. She is revealed through how you relate to the ordinary moments of your life.

The Priestess lives in five primary places.

1. THE BODY AS ALTAR

There was a time I dragged myself out of bed at five in the morning by sheer will. The alarm, the dark, the floor—a discipline I built like a fortress against a life that was full, almost entirely, of other people's needs. That morning practice was life-saving. I mean that without exaggeration. It was the hour that was mine before everything became everyone else's. I built it out of necessity, and I am grateful for every cold, quiet morning of it.

But something has shifted.

These days I linger. Winter mornings especially—I lie under the warmth of the covers and let myself arrive slowly. I open the blind and look at the sky before I move. I feel the simple, quiet pleasure of my own body in stillness, the particular softness of this hour before the day has any demands in it. Some mornings that's ten minutes. Some mornings it's longer. I don't decide in advance. I feel into what I need.

This is not laziness. It took me a long time to understand that. It is the most honest practice I have: the moment before I am anyone's mother, anyone's mentor, anyone's anything. Just a body in a bed, awake and present, tuning to the season I'm in. Winter mornings are slow and warm and ask for more quiet. Summer mornings arrive bright and early and call me out into them faster. I honor that. The practice changes because I change. The devotion doesn't.

Eventually I go downstairs. I make my tea. I meditate, pull my cards, and then I open my journal—that quiet conversation with myself before the children wake and the day begins its claiming.

There was a man recently. A few dates. He said all the right things, the kind of things you want to hear, the kind of things that would have worked on an earlier version of me. But there was something else happening underneath the words. A tension. A subtle internal contradiction I couldn't name but couldn't ignore. Not a red flag I could point to. Just an off feeling that sat in my body like a quiet, persistent no.

I used to override that feeling. I used to give it more time, make excuses for it, talk myself into patience and open-mindedness and the possibility that I was being too particular. I used to write long thoughtful messages explaining myself to men who hadn't earned that level of my attention.

This time I listened to the no before it became a story. I blocked him. I moved on. No explanation, no deliberation, no second-guessing. I stopped worrying about whether I was being kind. My peace matters more than his explanation. My body had already spoken. My only job was to honor it.

I don't override the whisper anymore. I learned—slowly, at some cost—to trust it before I could explain it. It knew before I did. It always does.

The body is not a machine to be optimized. It is a living oracle. And the oracle was speaking all along.

The altar doesn't demand. It receives. So do I.

In your journal:

What is my body telling me this morning that I might override by noon?
What does this season, this week, this day, ask of me?
Where am I pushing when my body is asking me to soften?
What would it mean to tend myself today the way I tend the people I love?

2. TIME AS SACRED

I am a matriarch now. That's a chosen word—a reframe from single mother that changes everything about how I relate to my own needs. A single mother survives. A matriarch leads. And a matriarch must be resourced.

Not just functional. Full.

There will be seasons when the vacation isn't available. When the life is full and the calendar is already spoken for before the week begins and the rest you need feels three months away.

The Priestess has learned not to wait for it.

Not because she doesn't need it—she does, more than she often admits—but because waiting for the perfect conditions to replenish is just another way of running on empty and calling it virtue. She has learned to look for what is available. Not the ideal but the real. Not the retreat but the afternoon. The massage booked before she's desperate rather than after she's already depleted. The dinner alone at a restaurant where nobody needs anything from her, not as a consolation prize for the vacation she couldn't take, but as its own complete act of restoration.

She has learned to ask two questions before a season gets heavy: Where will I get filled, and where can I afford to be unsupported? Because a woman running on empty doesn't access any of it—not desire, not creativity, not presence, not pleasure.

This requires honesty. Not the aspirational kind, the operational kind. What does this particular week have room for? What is the smallest act of restoration available to me today, not someday? An hour in the sun with a book. Letting someone else handle dinner. Saying no to one thing that would have said yes to everyone else's comfort and no to her own.

I blocked two hours every Monday for the next month. Not because I had nothing else to do with them. Because I could feel, already, that without them I would run dry before the season was over. That's the calculation the Priestess makes—not where can I afford to rest but where can I afford not to.

And support, that's part of this, too. Where can I be held so I don't have to hold everything alone? A massage. A friend who feeds me dinner. A lover who reminds me I'm not just a woman who produces and delivers and manages, but a woman who is alive and worth tending. These aren't luxuries I'll get to eventually. They are the infrastructure. The thing the whole practice runs on.

The body will tell you when time has been consistently overridden. It gets sick. It goes flat. Desire goes quiet. The mornings stop feeling like yours. I know these signals now. I don't always catch them early, but I catch them earlier than I used to. And when I do, I don't wait for the beach. I find the Sunday afternoon. I find the dinner alone.

Urgency is not the same as importance. The most important thing she does some days is stop.

In your journal:

Where is my tank right now: full, half empty, running on fumes?

What restoration is available to me this week, not someday?

Where am I waiting for perfect conditions to rest instead of resting now?

Who or what fills me and when did I last let them?

3. DESIRE AS COMPASS

The first two years after my marriage ended, desire was loud. It had been quiet for so long that when it returned, it came like a current pulling me forward, waking things up, showing me what aliveness felt like after years of numbness. I followed it. Sometimes wisely, sometimes not. But I followed it and it moved me out of a life that had stopped fitting and into something I couldn't yet see clearly but could feel in my body as true.

That version of desire is easy to recognize. It announces itself. It has momentum and heat and direction.

This season is quieter. I am rooting with my children, with my work, with the parts of myself that needed to come back to center after so much motion. The desire is still there but it isn't pulling me anywhere right now. It's doing something else. It's clearing. Contracting. Making room.

It's uncomfortable, if I'm honest. There is a particular restlessness that comes with knowing something is rearranging beneath the surface and not being able to name it yet or rush it toward form. I can feel it—a shift coming, a next chapter gathering itself—but I can't speak it fully yet. And I've learned that trying to force language onto something that isn't ready is its own kind of betrayal. Some desires need to be held before they can be named.

The same is true for partnership. For love. There is a temptation in the waiting—when the right thing hasn't arrived and the longing is real—to settle for almost. Almost right. Almost a full yes. And almost is so much more available than the real thing. I know this temptation. I've felt it. You start to wonder if you're being too particular, if the full yes is something you've already had your share of.

But then the real thing arrives and the body just knows. Oh. That quiet cellular recognition. That was worth waiting for.

The Priestess trusts that recognition more than she trusts the availability of almost. She doesn't chase. She doesn't fill the space with what's almost right. She tends the longing the way she tends the morning—with patience, with presence, with the trust that what is meant for her will arrive with a clarity that makes the waiting make sense.

She'll know when she knows. Until then she refuses to be distracted by what doesn't feel like a full yes.

Desire is not always about getting what you want. Sometimes it's about trusting what you're not yet ready to name.

In your journal:

Where in my life am I currently settling for almost—almost right, almost aligned, almost a full yes?

What does my body feel like in the presence of a real yes versus an almost?

What desire am I currently holding that I can't fully name yet, and what would it mean to trust it anyway?

What would I have to let go of to stop filling the space with what's available rather than what's true?

4. BOUNDARIES AS RITUAL

The boundary I am most proud of this year is also the one that has cost me the most. And it begins, as so much does, with my mother.

Not because she is a villain in this story. She isn't. But because the mother is the original relationship, the first place we learn what love requires of us, what we have to perform or suppress or absorb to receive it, what happens when we assert a need that inconveniences someone whose approval we depend on. Every intimate relationship I have ever had was written first in that language. And I have spent the better part of this book—and the better part of the last several years—learning to read it differently.

Setting this boundary right here, now, is not just about my mother and me. It is about rewriting the source code. It is about what becomes possible in every relationship that comes after when the original agreement finally changes.

One of the most liberating and most painful things I have learned is this: I cannot expect more from someone than they are capable of giving.

Not my mother. Not my ex-husband. Not anyone I have loved and hoped and waited on to show up differently. The hoping is not the problem. The hoping is human. The problem is when the hoping becomes a kind of participation when I keep extending access, keep opening the door, keep engaging with a version of the relationship that only exists in my imagination of what it could be.

At some point the boundary isn't about them at all. It's about me withdrawing from an agreement I never consciously signed but have been honoring for years. The agreement that says I will absorb. I will accommodate. I will keep showing up to a dynamic that costs me more than it gives because that is what love looks like. That is what a good daughter does. That is what keeping the peace requires.

I have learned to question that agreement. To look at it clearly and ask, *Is this love or is this just a very old habit of self-erasure dressed up as loyalty?*

There is a particular moment that comes now, quiet and private. A holiday. A birthday. The pull of some small reaching out and then the choosing not to. Not because I don't feel it. Because I know what opening that door costs me. The boundary lives in that moment. Not in a confrontation, not in a speech, not in anything anyone else would see. Just a woman alone with her own knowing, choosing not to participate in something that is no longer aligned with who she is.

It feels like grief sometimes. I'm grieving what never was. I have had to learn to see people clearly—not who I need them to be, not who they might become, but who they actually are and what they are actually capable of. That is the hardest kind of boundary. Not the one held against someone who is obviously wrong, but the one held with clear eyes and a heart that still loves and still grieves and holds the line anyway.

My daughter is watching me do this. She can feel it, the shift in me, the way I move differently now in relationships that used to cost me everything. What gets handed down when we don't interrupt a pattern is the pattern itself. What gets handed down when we do is something else entirely. That is reason enough.

This is what the Priestess understands about boundaries. They are not punishments. They are not walls built to keep people out. They are the moment she stops pretending that a dynamic is working when her body has been telling her otherwise for years. She cannot change what another person is capable of. She can absolutely change how much of herself she offers to the gap between who they are and who she needed them to be.

Every no she speaks is a consecration of her yes.

The boundary doesn't always feel like freedom. Sometimes it feels like grief. She holds it anyway.

In your journal:

Where am I expecting more from someone than they are actually capable of giving?

What agreement am I still honoring that I never consciously chose?

Where am I confusing loyalty with self-erasure?

What would it mean to love someone clearly and limit my proximity to the harm they carry at the same time?

5. BEAUTY AS MEDICINE

I don't slap on clothes in the morning. I choose an energetic signature for the day.

This sounds more complicated than it is. It means standing in front of my wardrobe for a moment and asking: Who am I today, what does this day ask of me, what do I want to bring into the world when I walk out the door? Then I adorn myself accordingly. Jewels, even for the school pickup. Lipstick, not because anyone requires it, but because the way it makes me feel is reason enough. Lingerie under my shirt because it is a secret between me and my own body—a reminder that I am an erotic, alive woman even in the middle of the most ordinary Tuesday.

I speak love over my body while I dress. Not affirmations recited mechanically but actual tenderness—the kind I might offer a child or a person I love deeply. My body has carried me through everything in this book. It deserves that.

I work out as a celebration rather than a punishment. I cook with music on and I sing. I flirt with the man at the store because I am alive and aliveness wants to be expressed and the grocery store is as good a place as any.

None of this is frivolous. None of it requires a special occasion or a particular mood or anyone else's participation. It is available right now, today, in the middle of whatever season I am in—stretched or full, grieving or expanding, sick on the couch or striding into a room. Beauty is not the reward for having everything together. It is what helps me hold things together. It regulates something in the nervous system that nothing else quite reaches; the reminder that life is sensory, that I am sensory, that the whole point of being alive in a body is to actually feel it.

I am also, as this book goes into the world, building something with my best friend that is the outer expression of everything I have learned. A company born from the belief that a woman's nervous system is sacred. That her sleep matters. That the ritual of tending her own body is not vanity but necessity. That beauty and science and spirituality are not opposites but the same intelligence speaking different languages. We are building for the woman who is ready to treat herself as someone worth tending—not occasionally, not when she's earned it, but as a daily devotional practice.

The book and the company are sister lives. Both are built on the same foundation. Both are saying the same thing in different forms: that beauty is medicine, that pleasure is not a reward but a resource, that the woman who tends herself well tends everything well.

This is what the Priestess knows about beauty. It is not an accessory to her life. It is not something she gets to when the more important things are handled. It is one of the most important things. It nourishes the psyche. It restores coherence. It reminds the body that life is worth inhabiting even on the days when the world makes that hard to believe.

She adorns herself for herself. She moves through the world as though it is sacred because she has decided that it is. She flirts with the man at the store. She sings in the kitchen. She wears the jewels to school pickup.

Every ordinary moment is an altar. She tends it accordingly.

In your journal:

What does beauty do for my nervous system and when did I last let it?

Where am I waiting for a special occasion to adorn myself, to feel pleasure, to treat my body as sacred?

What is my energetic signature today and does how I'm moving through the world reflect it?

What would it mean to treat every ordinary moment as an invitation to feel alive?

Pleasure lives in awareness—in how you breathe, move, touch, and allow yourself to receive life. Every day, I return to small rituals that keep the fires burning. I do this to remind myself who I am when I'm not performing for anyone else.

It's in the moment I stretch slowly before I reach for my phone in the morning, when I put one hand on my heart and one on my womb and take a few deep breaths. When I play music while I make coffee, let my bare feet feel the floor, move my hips to whatever rhythm the moment brings. I light a candle before I work, drink water and savor the sensation, pause before I eat to thank the earth. I notice where my body opens and where it asks for rest.

These aren't grand gestures. They're intimate promises I make to myself.

When I make these small moments sacred, pleasure becomes less of a pursuit and more of a pulse—a quiet hum beneath everything. It's not always dramatic. Sometimes it's subtle, steady, alive in the background like an ember that never goes out.

That's the practice. Tending the flame even when no one's watching. And to keep saying yes—to my breath, my body, the beauty of being here.

Because pleasure isn't what I find through another person or experience. It's what I become when I return to myself.

You don't need to call yourself a Priestess to become her. You become her the moment you stop overriding your body. The moment you choose presence over performance. The moment pleasure becomes information instead of indulgence.

This is how the magic returns—not through spectacle, but through devotion to what's real. The world doesn't change because women strive harder. It changes because women come home to themselves.

And every time you choose pleasure as a practice—gentle, honest, embodied—you remember something that was never really lost: your body was never the problem. It has always been the way home.

✦ Ritual: Tending the Flame

This is not a performance.

There is no goal.

It is a return to the fire that has always lived inside you.

You don't need tools for this ritual, but you may want a
notebook and pen nearby.

Begin by softening the space around you.

Dim the lights. Set your phone aside.

Sit or lie down where your body can fully relax.

Place one hand on your heart.

Place the other low on your belly, just beneath your navel.

Take a slow breath in through your nose.

Exhale through your mouth.

Again.

And once more, longer this time.

With each exhale, feel your awareness travel downward—

out of the mind,

past the throat,

into the warm center of your body.

Imagine a small hearth there.

Not a roaring fire.

A steady one.

Glowing coals. Quiet heat.

This fire does not need to be forced.

It only needs tending.

With each inhale, imagine you are feeding the fire with breath.

With each exhale, feel the warmth spread gently outward.

Notice how the fire responds.

Does it brighten?

Does it stay low and calm?

Does it flicker, shift, or deepen?

There is no right way for it to appear.

Quietly say to yourself:

I am here.

I am listening.

Now ask softly:

What does this fire want right now?

Wait for the response to come through the body, not the mind.

It may arrive as:

- An image
- A memory
- A sensation
- An emotion
- A word or phrase
- Or a simple feeling of yes or no

Let whatever arises be welcome.

If your body wants movement, allow it—a sway, a stretch, a roll of the shoulders or hips.

If your hand wants to rest somewhere, let it.

If stillness is what is being asked for, honor that, too.

Stay with the fire for a few more breaths, continuing to feed it with your attention.

When it feels complete, place both hands over your lower belly.

Say silently or aloud:

I will tend you.

I will listen again.

Let the image of the hearth settle into embers—alive, warm, enduring.

Now reach for your notebook.

Without overthinking, write down anything that came through: Images. Words. Sensations. Desires. Questions.

Do not edit. Do not explain. Just record.

When you finish, take one final breath and feel your body in the room.

Notice what has shifted, even slightly.

This is how pleasure returns.

Not as intensity, but as intimacy.

Not as demand, but as devotion.

The fire is not something you create.

It is something you remember how to tend.

CHAPTER TWELVE

Let It Go

Every transformation begins with a breaking point—the moment you can no longer pretend to be what the world told you to be. Patriarchy is the water we swim in—ancient, invisible, everywhere. It names our longings before we can even feel them, calling one sacred and another sinful. It tells us to question the ache in our bellies, to shrink our wanting until it looks acceptable. It teaches us to fear our own pulse.

And in doing so, it severs us from *the way* before—the matriarchal knowing, the feminine intelligence that once guided everything. The body as cosmos, the womb as the original altar, the rhythm of life moving through blood and tide, moon and cycle. Before the patriarchy, we didn't need permission to trust our bodies—we *knew* they were the universe itself. We listened to the seasons, the moon, the heartbeat of the Earth. Pleasure wasn't something to earn; it was how we prayed.

That's what we're remembering now—not something new, but something ancient. A way of living that honors the body as divine and desire as the language of creation itself.

Beneath the boss babe, the single mom, or the perfectly content wife lives a woman with her own flavor of wanting. Maybe she wants to be taken. Maybe she wants to take. Maybe she just wants to feel again.

What if you gave your inner goddess permission? To eat the croissant. To dance in the living room. To let her breasts see the sun. To stop apologizing for being too much, too loud, too hungry, too alive.

I had to dismantle every rule I inherited. What was acceptable, what was off-limits. The parts of me I could show and the ones I couldn't. I can still hear my mother's conjured opinion: *She's lost her mind. She left her marriage. She's chasing desire like it's religion.*

Maybe I am. Maybe that's exactly what liberation is.

When I stop filling every minute with other people's needs, desire rises like flames through my body. I want my pussy worshipped. I want to be held and then consumed and then held again. I want to be met in every flavor—sacred and raw, gentle and wild.

My inner whore wants to be the altar, the offering, the prayer. She wants new expressions, new textures, new ways to worship life itself. Your version might be different. That's the point.

Your Eros lives inside you—not on TikTok, not in a magazine, not in a how-to-please-him video. It's in the quiet space where you let yourself ask, *What do I really want?* And when you hear the answer, will you let yourself have it? Will you play, demand, or experiment? Will you let yourself be loud, or messy, or divine?

It's time to stop managing your pleasure like a to-do list. It's time to stop censoring your own aliveness. It's time to let her out.

CATCH AND RELEASE

Dating in the city became my field study in voice and discernment—a laboratory for desire and self-trust.

After my divorce, my internal software was outdated, still running on the old programming of people-pleasing and survival. It was like operating on Hotmail in an iOS world. The first year was spent entangled in a situationship—the perfect mirror for my patterns of longing and unworthiness. It was painful but necessary. It was like breaking up the concrete under a pool to lay new wiring, it was messy and disruptive, but it allowed for something new to be built.

I maneuvered into season two: *The catch and release phase.*

I was on the dating apps. I learned to connect, read energy, and practiced earned access. I noticed what I liked and what I didn't like, how to trust my instincts, and follow a natural rhythm with another person who's also open to true intimacy. Pleasure work and somatic practice have given me tools to feel safe in my body, to take responsibility for my own turn-on, to ask for what I want. First to the universe, and then to the person across the table at coffee on a first date. I watch what happens when I'm met with enthusiasm, when I'm ignored, when someone pulls away. I track my sensations: the spark of excitement, the contraction of disappointment, the way my energy shifts with each dynamic.

The woman I am now brings her voice to the conversation. She says what she needs. She stops when it's not right. And when she doesn't, it's only information, another opportunity to listen more deeply.

On a first date with a man who takes a reckless left turn, I hear my voice before I even think. "Don't ever do that again," I say, calm and clear. And just like that, I recognize myself.

I think of the woman I used to be—the one who stayed in intolerable situations, who endured mediocre or painful sex, who froze when men crossed boundaries in public, and didn't know how to leave. She was too polite, too afraid, too unsure of her right to say no. This is how I know I've changed. Even when I slip—even when I stay quiet longer than I mean to—I trust myself enough to listen when my body says no.

I no longer betray that signal. Dating now is less about finding someone and more about practicing embodiment in real time. It's an experiment in attunement. I can catch and release because I know my value. I trust my yes and my no.

If the first year of my undoing was about ceremony and unearthing, the next one was about integration: living what I'd learned. Each connection is a mirror, showing me where I still abandon myself and where I stand fully in my worth. For the first time, I trust my own rhythm. I no longer need to perform, prove, or chase. I can let things come and go with ease, because I finally believe that what's meant for me will stay, not as a quippy meme but as a truth felt in my body.

LET THE BODY SPEAK

There are moments in healing when words stop working. Logic can't hold what the body remembers. That's when you stop talking about the pain and let it move.

I stood in front of a waist-high foam block, a bat in my hands, surrounded by men and women—some of the bravest I know—seeking out freedom from our conditioned ways of being. The room was quiet, watchful. I waited for the current to rise, the yes or the no to move through my body.

When it came, I lifted my arms.

The bat came down with a sharp whack.

Again. And again.

The sound landed heavy and clean. My arms kept moving—up, down, up, down—as the wave of no's left my body. My breath got louder.

My voice rose from my throat—energy and sound moving through me.

Breath. Hit. Breath. Hit. "No," I yelled.

Bring your voice, my therapist encouraged.

"NOOOOOOO!" I yelled, feeling the sensation like a wave rise from my belly up through my chest and out of my body.

Each strike cleared something. Grief. Rage. The residue of what was never spoken. Energy I'd been carrying for years moved out through my arms, my voice, my breath.

I swung until there was nothing left to swing with.

Then the wave passed.

My body shook. I emptied—I was dizzy, grounded—more there than I was before. I understood, without needing words, that the energy was never meant to stay inside me. It was waiting for permission to move.

I spent decades swallowing my rage. Smiling when I wanted to scream. Making myself smaller and quieter to keep everyone else comfortable. I thought I was being good, strong. In reality, I was just stuffing everything down until my body couldn't hold it anymore. My body was trying to tell me something.

It wasn't until I finally let myself feel angry—really, truly pissed off about all the ways I'd been diminished and dismissed—that things started to shift. I felt more alive hitting that bat in that moment than I had in years.

Anger isn't the enemy we've been taught it is. It's information. It's your body saying, *Something here is not right* and giving you the energy to do something about it. When I finally gave my anger a safe place to move, it transformed. The fury became clarity about what I would and wouldn't accept. The grief became tenderness for all the parts of myself I'd abandoned along the way.

During the first months of my separation, I was plagued by migraines that left me in bed for days.

One afternoon, while standing in the kitchen of an Airbnb in Laurel Canyon, my therapist asked me on Zoom, "Where do you put the grief and rage about his affair?"

I didn't know.

Until that moment, I hadn't realized I was holding it all in my body. Such a deeply ingrained habit, happening unconsciously for years.

The truth is we had both left long before we said it out loud. I wasn't innocent, but I was done pretending. His secret had mirrored my silence. Both had been a slow betrayal of our relationship.

That day in the kitchen, I told my therapist, "I don't feel rage. I just feel tired. Sad. Like I want to disappear." The headache pulsed behind my eyes, a constant dull reminder of everything unspoken.

I began to wonder if the pain itself was my body's signal, if it was holding the scream I never gave voice to. And slowly, as I began to let the energy move through writing, movement, breath, and tears, and through speaking my truth, no matter the cost: the migraines eased.

LIBERATING GRIEF

Grief stripped me bare. There was no spiritual bypass, no mantra that could save me.

It came in waves that knocked the breath from my lungs. Quiet mornings that dissolved into sobbing on the kitchen floor, nights where the ache in my chest felt physical, like my ribs were splitting open from the inside.

I had built a life around love and service—the home, the marriage, the children—and then I blew it up. What was left was me. The loneliness was excruciating. There were days I wanted to crawl out of my own skin, to escape the silence of a house without my kids, exiled by my own choice, from my life. But every time I tried to resist it, grief pulled me deeper, whispering: *You can't outrun what you came here to feel.*

So, I stopped running. I let it swallow me.

I met the little girl I'd been avoiding—the one who learned early that love meant caretaking, that safety came through being good, quiet, needed. I held her and told her she was safe now. That I could love her in the way no one else ever had. Grief became my teacher. It showed me how much I had abandoned myself in the name of belonging.

And then, when I thought I might drown in it, sisterhood arrived like a lifeline. I would show up at my Goddess Palace, tearful and tender, to find roses waiting at my door, left by my best friend. We'd sit together, sometimes in silence, sometimes in laughter that cracked the grief open just enough to let light through.

Being with her softened the loneliness of being away from my kids. It reminded me that women were never meant to go through these transitions alone, that our power multiplies when we gather, when we witness each other in the in-between.

That truth is a foundation of my work. Women gathering around each other in times of death and rebirth, not to fix, but to hold, to breathe, to wail, to celebrate the moment we choose ourselves again. And out of that space of grief and grace, something new was born. Together, we built a company—a creation that wove the best of both of us, even our names, into something alive and meaningful. It became a legacy that carried our gifts into the world. I poured my devotion into it, my artistry, my priestess codes—everything I had been too afraid to show before. It became not just a business, but a vessel for beauty, a new lineage for my family, and a love letter to what women can build when they rise together.

I was beginning to understand that solitude and sisterhood can coexist, that community can hold you while you learn to hold yourself. The two years that followed were a constant dance between death and rebirth: heartbreak, healing, love, loss, surrender, and again, love. Nights crying on the couch, mornings dancing barefoot on the beach. The ache of missing my children while they are with their father, the thrill of rediscovering my body.

The grief cracked me open, but pleasure stitched me back together.

Little by little, I began to feel alive again. My days were filled with more laughter than tears. I realized that to truly celebrate my life, I had to be willing to live it alone. I embodied solitude. For the first time, my days were my own—quiet, spacious, full of possibility. I cooked for myself, moved my body towards pleasure, filled my home with flowers just because I could. I wasn't waiting to be chosen. I had chosen myself. And through it all, sisterhood held me: women who held me when I broke, who let me rage and weep, who danced beside me when the light returned. We didn't just survive grief. We worshipped at its altar until it transformed into grace. Priestessing my way through the heartbreak, I fueled my own resurrection.

Creation bloomed in me again, soft, slow, steady. Grief had turned into something fertile. The sisterhood that held me through the ashes was now the same circle I was creating within—women who could see through my masks, who could read my energy before I spoke a word.

And still, healing wasn't linear. Even after all the rebuilding, the waves would come.

Last year, in the middle of a breakup that was never quite a relationship—one of those half-loves that reveal where you still ache—I found myself crumpled under a migraine that lasted days.

My body was speaking before my mouth could. Every pulse of pain felt like an echo of the old life still trying to leave. Sophia and another sister, Kristen—one of our temple healers—had planned to meet for a creativity day, a pre-filming ritual, the kind of gathering that usually fills me with joy. But that morning, I could barely stand. I arrived, while suffering tore me apart.

They took one look at me. "Goddess down," they said in unison.

I laughed weakly and surrendered. I lay my head in Sophia's lap, and they began to work their magic—angelic healing, energy clearing, and light language that whispered over my body.

Sophia placed her hand gently on my heart. "Your nervous system is trying to hold on to an old grid," she said softly. "It's half out, painful but leaving. Like a splinter that's almost ready to be released."

As she spoke, I felt it. The metal grid—a matrix of old lovers, expectations, and imprints—lifting, twisting, trying to find its way out. One by one, faces appeared: boyfriends, lovers, partners, each carrying their own tiny heartbreak. I could feel their energy dissolving from my field—the disappointments, the projections, the fragments of love that weren't truly mine to hold.

And beneath them all, my father. The original wound of abandonment, the first ache that taught me what it meant to be left. Maybe that ache began before language, in the womb itself, where my mother's grief became my first inheritance. As the healing deepened, I saw a vision: my own funeral. A black box, my body still and surrendered. Then my soul rose from it, radiant, whispering, *Enough.*

Enough of the patterns. Enough of the pain. No more carrying what isn't mine.

For a long moment, there was only silence, the sacred kind that follows release. Then warmth flooded through my body, light filling the spaces that had been empty. Sophia asked what I could see at the moment.

"A garden," I said. "Overflowing, wild, alive."

The angels spoke through her again: "It's time to seek fulfillment. Tend to the garden of your heart."

And I knew that this was the new season. Grief cleared the soil. Sisterhood held the ground. And now, my own rebirth was blooming.

THE RITUAL OF RETURN

Letting go doesn't always look like an explosion.

Sometimes it looks like grounding. Grounding with the sensation. Grounding with the truth after the ceremony ends. Grounding long enough for life itself to reorganize around what you've remembered.

The Ritual of Return is what happens after the breakthrough—when the body asks to live what it has learned.

This is where embodiment becomes devotion.

RETURN TO JOY

For a long time, joy felt dangerous and fleeting. It was something I had to earn, justify, or brace myself to lose. After everything cracked open—my marriage, my identity, the stories I lived inside—I noticed something unexpected: joy returned quietly. Not as fireworks, but as permission.

Joy began to live in ordinary moments. Morning light pooling on the kitchen floor. Music in my ears while walking alone through the city. The pleasure of choosing rest without explanation. A bath in the middle of the day in an empty house. It was not performative happiness. It was aliveness without an audience.

I used to think joy was something I had to earn. Like I needed to check all the boxes first—kids fed, work done, everyone else happy—before I was allowed to feel good.

But one morning, I was making my matcha and a ridiculous song came on. I just started dancing without thinking, right there in my kitchen, still in my pajamas.

My daughter walked in and rolled her eyes, but she was smiling. She sarcastically asked what was wrong with me. "Why are you so happy?"

"I don't know," I said, honestly. "I'm just grateful and happy."

And I realized I'd been waiting for permission to be happy in my own house.

That's when something clicked. I didn't need to have my shit together to feel joy. I didn't need to know what was coming next or have all the answers. I just needed to be here, right now, dancing to a stupid song in my kitchen.

Our greatest freedom is trust in the unknown.

It sounds so simple, but it changed everything for me. I started laughing at things that would have stressed me out before. I put music on while folding laundry and found myself moving to the beat. I stopped feeling guilty for enjoying myself when there was still stuff on my to-do list.

Joy stopped being this rare thing I had to chase and became something that was always available if I paid attention. Like a radio frequency I could tune into whenever I remembered to listen.

RETURN TO GRIEF

Grief didn't disappear after I started the work, but it changed its shape. I learned this lesson deeply when my ex-husband told me he was moving out of state in the fall.

I fought for my kids. I reasoned with him, made logical arguments about what this would mean for them, tried every angle I could think of. I gathered other Goddesses to help me stay turned on and then practiced begging him to stay. It was a humbling exploration of owning my power and energetically surrendering. Nothing worked. He didn't see that he had any other choice.

So, I let my apartment go. The Goddess Palace—my sanctuary, my refuge, the place where I'd learned to dance in lingerie and host circles of women remembering their aliveness—had to be packed up. I was moving to the suburbs, to my home, to be with my children full-time. There was grief in losing part of my independent, single life, but also relief, a deep trust that I was getting more than I was giving up.

The same weekend I was moving my things out, the man I'd been seeing was also leaving town. I found myself grieving two losses at once: him walking away and this part of my freedom dissolving.

But I'd learned something about grief by then. I couldn't afford to let it take me down. So, I doubled down on everything that kept me alive. I leaned harder into my erotic practices— the Goddess Descent rituals, Sacred Strip Teases, Embodied Movement. I intensified my connection with my lover while I could. I used orgasm to manifest what I couldn't yet see with my mind. I used pleasure as medicine, a way to alchemize the grief moving through me.

The old me would have shut down, gone numb, tried to be strong by feeling less. But I'd learned that the way through was to feel more. To let the grief move while flooding my system with life force energy.

What surprised me was how this approach transformed the loss. Instead of breaking me down, the grief became a teacher. I wasn't just mourning what I was losing, I was mourning a version of my life that had become too fragmented to sustain: the split between my dating life and my mom life and the way I could be fully free one week and fully constrained the next.

For the first time, I found myself craving what I started calling "the oneness." An integrated version of my life where motherhood, pleasure, relationship, and success could all exist in the same space.

Grief taught me that sometimes we have to let go of the life that's almost working to make space for the one that actually fits.

RETURN TO LOVE

Love, after embodiment, became quieter—and more exacting. I stopped confusing intensity with intimacy. I stopped abandoning myself to be chosen. I stopped negotiating with my body when it said no.

I learned this lesson viscerally just a few months ago. I met someone who looked perfect on paper—successful, attractive, owned a home in the desert. The "brochure" was appealing. He said all the right things, and when he invited me to spend a weekend with him, I saw an opportunity for some freedom while my kids spent a few days with their dad.

I'd learned to ask adult questions by then that would guide my choice. "Do you have to work? What's the flow of the weekend?"

When he mentioned he'd have "Some projects to work on," my fifteen-year-old daughter looked at me like only a teenage girl can, and said, "Mom... is he crazy? You are the project."

I asked for clarity about intimacy because I am not ambiguous with my body anymore. Long, slow mornings? Tantric connection? A weekend centered in pleasure and presence. These weren't outrageous questions—they were aligned-woman questions.

He quickly revealed that this felt too demanding. That I should just "go with the flow."

My nervous system fired on high alert. It was the familiar feeling of dysregulation when someone's energy doesn't match their words. It was the feeling of reaching for something that's retreating. I was seeking safety and clarity, and he made me feel like asking for what I needed was wrong.

Two days before we were supposed to leave, I ended it.

Here's what's wild—I teach this stuff. I help women trust their intuition. But even teachers get tested. The old me might have minimized the red flags, gone with his flow, and ended up calling my best friend to rescue me from the desert when things went sideways.

Instead, I chose differently. I spent that weekend in West Hollywood with my best friend, designing our dreams and enjoying our favorite places. I gained freedom that weekend, just not the way I thought I would. It was the freedom to choose myself, the freedom to honor my intuition in real time.

Love became a practice of attunement after that. I learned to track sensations instead of fantasies, to notice expansion and contraction in my body. I stopped needing love to rescue me from my life and started meeting it from a place of wholeness.

Now, I share my intimacy recipe early and wait for alignment. I'm clear about what I want—slow mornings, conscious connection, presence over performance. I don't negotiate with misalignment anymore, no matter how attractive the package or how strong the chemistry.

And here's what I've discovered: When you stop abandoning yourself for crumbs of connection, you start attracting people who find your clarity refreshing rather than demanding. Men who celebrate your boundaries instead of trying to erode them. Partners who match your depth instead of asking you to settle for shallow.

I'm not willing to fragment myself anymore—to be one version of myself on the weekends and another during the week. I want the oneness. A love that integrates with my motherhood, my work, my pleasure practices, my whole life. Someone who gets excited about the woman I've become, not someone who needs me to dim my light to feel comfortable.

I'm no longer afraid of the empty space while I wait. That space isn't loneliness—it's sovereignty. I love the spacious, grounded feeling of being alone without being lonely, fully embracing the intimacy of motherhood while enjoying pleasure partners and lovers along the way as the Universe works.

I have the freedom to design a life so aligned that adding someone to it becomes an overflow of joy, not a rescue from emptiness. And it's a very different thing to attract someone knowing they can only be additive—anything less is uninteresting.

The bar is raised, the standards are high, but more importantly, my vibration, my autonomy, is attuned to the frequency of sacred desire. I have awakened my Goddess and am willing to wait for the person who can truly worship her and be worshipped in return.

This is what the work has given me: the capacity to want more and the patience to wait for it. The knowledge that I am the woman worth waiting for, and anyone who gets to love me is receiving a gift I no longer give lightly.

RETURN TO RECEIVING

Money was one of the last places embodiment reached me—and possibly the most revealing. I had done so much internal work around worth, desire, and self-trust, yet I noticed how quickly my body tightened around receiving. Specifically when I asked for more. Or when it came to holding abundance without guilt or trusting that support wouldn't disappear.

The IRS sent me a notice which my friend called "a literal nightmare"—an oversight that was locking up my money, requiring hours on the phone trying to clear it up. The kind of bureaucratic maze that would have sent the old me into complete panic. But sitting there with the paperwork, I noticed something different. My nervous system stayed calm.

Instead of spiraling, I did what I'd learned to do: I fueled up with pleasure. I took a bath, put on music that made me feel powerful, moved my body until I felt grounded. I needed to make decisions from clarity, not fear.

I could see clearly how situations like this had derailed me before—how I'd let certain types of men exploit me when I was backed into financial corners, making desperate choices instead of discerning ones. But this time felt different. This time, I handled it from a place of internal safety.

That's when the deeper truth landed: My safety isn't tied to money. Money is just energy, a reflection of how open I am to receiving, how many people I'm serving. When I stopped making money equal safety, ironically, I became available to receive so much more.

Embodiment taught me that money's deeper story is about nervous system regulation. When my system began to settle, my relationship to money softened. I stopped forcing outcomes and started listening for alignment. I raised my rates without apology. I let opportunities come to me instead of proving my readiness.

The body has to believe it's safe to hold abundance before life will offer it consistently.

∽

By the time you read this book, I'll be living the integration I've been calling in. There's a closeness and freedom in my life—lots of travel, laughter, and discovery with my children. Big dinner tables full of chosen family, different generations gathered around the abundance we've created together.

The oneness I've been reaching for is no longer a dream but my daily reality. My work as a priestess, my role as a mother, my writing, my business—they all flow together in this beautiful, seamless way. I'm no longer compartmentalizing pieces of myself, trying to be one version on the weekends and another during the week.

Money flows in from clients who are so grateful to work with me, whose lives are genuinely changing through our work together. I watch their energetic, physical, and spiritual bodies emerge from a deep sleep as they activate through the practices I share. My gifts have become the creator of my abundance, just as I always knew they could.

There's a masculine energy in my life now—someone who energetically matches me, who supports and celebrates the full spectrum of who I am. He adds to my children's lives without trying to replace or diminish what we've built. We create together, we travel together, we hold space for each other's expansion.

We live somewhere beautiful, close to nature and the ocean. Close enough to Sophia that she's woven into our daily lives, and my children know the gift of chosen family. The kind of place where I can strip down not for someone else's gaze but for my own erotic aliveness, where I can feel warm breeze across my skin while driving my kids to wherever they need to go.

I'm in the current of life now. When I feel that old impulse to shrink or move from lack, I ask myself: *How can I be back in the current of life? How can I manifest what I need to stay here?*

This isn't a fairy tale ending. It's the life that becomes possible when you stop abandoning yourself for everyone else's comfort. When you follow your pleasure as a compass. When you trust that your desire isn't dangerous. It is divine intelligence moving through you.

The woman reading this book? She's already becoming the woman who can have this, too. Every time you choose presence over performance, every time you honor your body's wisdom, every time you refuse to negotiate with misalignment—you're building the foundation for your own version of having it all.

Your life is waiting for you to claim it.

✦ Integration Meditation: Becoming the Woman Who Walks Forward

Find a comfortable position.

Sit or lie down somewhere your body can soften.

Close your eyes.

Begin by noticing your breath.

No need to change it.

Just feel the inhale arrive.

Feel the exhale release.

Place one hand on your heart.

One hand on your belly.

Bring your awareness to the front and back body equally.

Let your attention drop beneath thought and into sensation.

Now imagine yourself standing at a doorway.

It can be ornate or simple.

Let one appear...

On one side is the woman you have been—

the one who learned to manage, to endure, to wait.

The one who survived by staying small or silent or strong.

On the other side is the woman you are becoming.

She carries what you have reclaimed—

your pleasure, your discernment, your truth, your eros.

She is not perfect.

She is present.

Notice how your body responds to this image.

Where do you feel openness?

Where do you feel hesitation?

There is no need to force anything.

When you're ready, imagine taking one step forward.

Open the door and take a breath.

As you exhale, let go of any fear or doubt about your path forward.

Take the step.

Feel it in your feet.

In your legs.

In your pelvis.

With that step, let your body register this truth:

I do not have to earn my aliveness.

I am allowed to move toward what I want.

Take another breath.

Now feel this new version of you standing fully in her body.

Notice how she breathes.

How she holds her shoulders.

How she feels from the inside.

You are her.

This is not pretending.

This is remembering.

Let your nervous system take in the sensation of being here.

Stay for a few breaths.

When you're ready, gently bring your awareness back to the room.

Feel the surface beneath you.

Wiggle your fingers and toes.

Place both hands on your body and whisper, silently or aloud:

This is who I am now.

Take one final breath.

When you open your eyes, move slowly.

CHAPTER THIRTEEN

The Remembering

The invitation had been made to return, to trust, to live from the body again. But the thing about invitations is that they're rarely tidy. Saying yes means letting everything false fall away. By the time I reached this part of the story, the undoing had become real—houses, marriages, identities, all shedding. What began as a spiritual awakening was now a human reckoning—messy, raw, and necessary.

"What if I end up an old cat lady?" I said, checking my blind spot as I turned down a sun-washed street in Santa Monica.

On the other end of the line, my friend Jordan laughed softly. We'd met through my therapist—two writers, both mid-transformation, both unraveling marriages that no longer fit. We weren't lovers, but we were intimate in that soul-recognizing way that only happens when two people are walking through the fire at the same time.

"So be it then," he said.

"Right," I answered. "I'd rather live alone with a house full of cats than stay in a marriage that's draining my soul."

Jordan became a mirror for what was possible—intimacy without demand, presence without pretense. He reminded me what it felt like to be seen, and that made pretending at home impossible.

A few weeks after that conversation, I drove north to Ojai for a breathwork session with my teacher, David. I had studied breathwork with him for a year, but we hadn't seen each other in person since I had moved to California. He knew right away that something was shifting. He could sense I had been unraveling my life.

"Since that weekend in Joshua Tree," I reflected, "so many changes, and I'm pulling it apart so fast I can barely breathe."

Tears streamed down my face the whole way. The affair had ended. My husband was leaving for five weeks, which felt like the quiet beginning of the end. Most days I cried, and my ex assumed it was about him. Maybe it was. But what I was really mourning was *aliveness*—the pulse that had briefly woken something in me. I couldn't have the lover. I didn't want the marriage. All I had was a broken singing bowl and two children looking at me for what came next.

His small house sat nestled beneath old oaks, the Ojai air was heavy with sage and grief. Breathwork usually cracked me open, but this time I arrived already shattered. I lay down and began to breathe, and the sound that tore out of me wasn't just crying, it was keening, ancient, the body remembering what it had carried for too long.

I was left with the truth: I was going to be alone. My world was shattering, and I was the one swinging the hammer.

When the session ended, I was limp and raw, my eyes swollen.

David sat beside me, his voice low and certain. "The guilt is eating you alive," he said. "You can't lose any more weight. Give yourself time to clear out all this dark energy. There's more love available to you in this lifetime."

"I want to believe it," I whispered. "Even if I can't yet."

In that moment, I understood. I would have to make peace with being alone before I could ever be met again.

A friend once told me, *"There is a part of all of us that hopes we'll be the lucky one, the one that gets out (of our marriage) unscathed."*

She was right. We imagine we can slide into another pair of arms and skip the fire. Hop from one chapter to the next without ashes in between. But the truth is, everywhere I go, there I am. I had to face it all: how I got into that marriage, why I stayed, what had come alive, and what I was willing to risk for more. Leaving was the only choice the future version of me could live with. The only one I could be proud of. The grief was unavoidable.

WHAT WOULD MY DAUGHTER DO?

The question that guided me through everything was simple: *What would I want my daughter to do?*

When we lived in Chicago, she was nine, the same age I had been when I learned how dangerous silence could be. I remember looking at her and wondering how anyone could harm a child so small, so full of trust. That awareness split me open. It became impossible to justify staying in a life that required me to disappear.

Years later, in California, when she asked me quietly, "Why doesn't Dad hug you?" I said something about being busy, but her eyes told me she already knew.

She could feel the absence, the distance where love used to live. And in that instant, I realized she was watching me model love, not just for her father, but for myself.

That question awakened something in me. It showed me what had been missing all along: the love field, that sacred current that flows between two people who are truly connected, seen, and cherished. I wanted my children to feel that energy through me. To witness their mother adored, desired, and deeply loved.

That became the possibility I carried forward. The seed of desire I refused to abandon. Now I am learning about love and intimacy in real time, with my daughter beside me, both of us growing into new language together. We talk about boundaries, consent, and choice. She laughs as I swipe left on the dating apps, teasing me about obvious red flags. But sometimes she asks questions that stop me in my tracks.

More than anything, I want to show her what it looks like to choose herself. To say no when someone cannot meet her. To keep her heart open, but her standards high.

There was a moment, years ago, when I stood at the edge of my marriage and friends said, "But he's such a good guy."

And he was. But good is not the same as right.

When doubt crept in, I thought of her. If my daughter came to me and described the marriage I was living, what would I tell her? I would tell her to go. To find a love that feels bigger than the whole sky. To trust that the season of marriage had ended and that her next season would be her own becoming. Once I knew that, there was no other choice. I had to do for myself exactly what I would want for her.

BLOW UP YOUR LIFE

Sometimes I picture it in slow motion: the moment a life unravels, a city of certainty collapsing into light and dust. We all know that story—the woman who burns everything down, the one who finally stops pretending.

When I say I blew up my life, there are some people who nod knowingly, as if they've seen the trailer. They imagine the chaos, the heartbreak, the wreckage. But what they rarely understand is that the explosion isn't the end. It's the light that burns the fuse. The truth is, it starts quietly. A whisper in the body. A slow pulling of a single thread until the whole fabric gives way. You try to hold it together, but you already know the holding is what's killing you.

As the pieces fell apart—marriage, identity, home—I became all the characters in the story: the heroine, the villain, the savior, the witness. I directed and survived the whole thing. And when the dust cleared, I saw what was left: open space.

Blowing up your life is about being honest about the life you want. It's when you choose truth over comfort, aliveness over approval. Every explosion is an opening.

Central casting was being rewritten: mother, father, husband, daughter, lover.

Each role examined. Each archetype released. It was never solely about leaving a man. It was also about leaving the version of myself who believed endurance was love. We live in an age of awakening. Podcasts, therapy, TikToks about trauma. We're swimming in knowledge, yet terrified to act on it. Embodiment changes that. It's where you choose to live in knowing.

When I finally did, I faced every old ghost: the mother who endured, the father who left, the good girl who stayed too long. I met them all with compassion and let them go. And still, doubt visits me sometimes.

At night, when the house is quiet, she slips in like an old friend and asks, *Are you sure? Was it worth it?*

I don't banish her anymore. I pour her a cup of tea. I let her remind me that courage is not the absence of fear, but the choice to keep moving through it. There's a tattoo on my arm now, a serpent curling through the flower of life. It marks this chapter, a visible reminder that endings and beginnings surface in tandem.

I blew up my life, and as I did, I remembered that I was the one holding the match all along.

THE RETURN TO AVALON

I went on a pilgrimage across the ocean to Avalon, a mystical land in the countryside of England. It was a business mastermind woven with a Priestess pilgrimage. Like many things in this season, I felt the yes before my mind could rationalize the logistics of Europe in the middle of summer break. I just knew something was calling me there.

European land carries memory differently. It holds centuries of ritual, devotion, and distortion layered on top of one another. Places like Avalon are energetic vortexes, amplifiers. They don't initiate you; they reflect you. Some people describe the energy in this area as spiraling. I felt like the world had tilted slightly on its axis, that I'd entered a parallel time, part fairy land and part mystical novel. These high energy places, that carry mysticism and lore also require energetic boundaries, especially for those sensitive to them. It's like the feeling of going to a huge concert and when you come out, you need a week to recover from being in a space with that many people. Avalon requires a grounded relationship to your own energy, because whatever you bring is what the land magnifies.

We met with the local priestesses, dipped our hands and bodies into the sacred Chalice well water, sang songs in the sacred sights, gathered rose petals, and walked the paths of the ancient stones as women have done for centuries.

At the top of the Tor, a profoundly sacred site in pagan mythology, we gathered in ceremony, led by the Magdalene priestess.

She invited us to step through the opening, as though it were a portal to a new timeline. "It's time," she said, "to step into your role as priestess and lead. Take as much time as you need, and when you step through, let it be with all of your lineage, past, present, and future.

I took that step through the threshold, and claimed, embodied for myself. It was time to lead.

When I stepped through the opening, I felt what was staying and what was done.

There was no drama in it, just a quiet certainty in my body. Old identities loosened their grip. Shedding old skins like the snake, releasing and growing simultaneously. Although it was sometimes painful, I let instinct and intuition guide me. Past versions of myself were laid down with gratitude, not rejection. They carried me as far as they could. I didn't need to bring them any further. I honored what came before, and I didn't carry it forward. In that singular moment I felt the power of honoring the past while letting it rest, and blooming like the lotus, through the mud, not in spite of it, but because of it.

With that step I became the woman who wrote the book, told her story, shed the past, claimed the future, and who held the present and pleasure as her guides.

AFTERCARE: THE ART OF HOLDING YOURSELF (AND OTHERS) THROUGH DESIRE

Every high has an afterglow and every expansion asks for integration. Aftercare is the bridge between the two—the art of returning to the body after intensity, of finding your ground again after you've opened wide.

It's a word that comes from the world of BDSM. Its purpose is to process emotions, calm the nervous system, deepen intimacy, and offer reassurance. What I've learned is that *aftercare is not just for sex*. It's for life.

WE ALL NEED AFTERCARE

Aftercare is what we all crave but rarely ask for, space to land after a big emotional stretch. It's the moment after vulnerability when we long to be held literally or energetically. In my own relationships, I used to rush past this part. I was so focused on keeping the peace, on being easy, on not being "too much," that I'd ignore my own need for presence.

I didn't know how to say, "Can you hold me for a moment?" or "Can we talk about what just happened?"

It felt safer to perform strength than to reveal need. But being in my body again, studying intimacy, somatic healing, and kink, taught me something sacred: *The ability to ask for care is not weakness, it's mastery.* Aftercare is how we teach others to love us well. It's how we stay connected to ourselves when the wave of sensation has passed. It's how we prevent desire from becoming depletion.

THE THREE FORMS OF AFTERCARE

In my work and my own relationships, I've come to see that aftercare lives in three forms:

1. **Physical Aftercare**
   Touch, comfort, grounding. It might be a hug, a warm bath, a weighted blanket, or a gentle hand on the heart. After an intense emotional or erotic experience, your nervous system needs to feel safe again. Physical care helps the body regulate and integrate what it just experienced.

2. **Emotional Aftercare**
   Words, reflection, communication.
   "What did that feel like for you?"

"What do you need right now?"

In partnerships, this is the check-in, the dialogue that allows each person to be witnessed. Alone, it might be journaling, breathwork, or simply naming your feelings out loud.

3. **Energetic Aftercare**

The subtle tending of your inner world. Grounding your energy after being "in the field." This can look like solitude, meditation, movement, or ritual. It's how you honor the sacredness of what just unfolded and signals to your body that the experience is complete. Each kind of aftercare is an act of reverence. A way of saying to yourself or another: *Your body matters. Your energy matters. Your heart matters.*

Aftercare is attunement, to ourselves and another. Through it we learn to communicate our needs for intimacy and wellbeing. Aftercare is the gentle inquiry and willingness to be in natural rhythm, like nature. With every expansion, there is a natural contraction, and when you're prepared for it, you're not surprised. This work is all about self-knowledge and self-expression and aftercare is just one way we can express our needs and desires and ask to be met.

LEARNING TO ASK FOR WHAT YOU NEED

The first time a lover asked me, "What kind of aftercare do you like?" I froze. No one had ever asked me that before. I didn't know how to answer.

Did I want a glass of water? A cuddle? To be left alone? I wasn't sure.

It struck me how many years I'd spent giving without ever

learning how to receive. Now I ask myself this same question after every experience that opens me—whether it's a deep conversation, an emotional release, a sexual encounter, or even a creative breakthrough.

What do I need right now?

Sometimes it's softness: a bath, a nap, a long walk.

Sometimes it's containment: a clear boundary, saying no, pulling my energy back.

Sometimes it's connection: calling a friend, asking to be held, letting someone love me.

The key is learning to know your own nervous system—what grounds you, what nourishes you, what helps you feel safe again after expansion.

When you start to practice aftercare regularly, you'll notice something shift. You'll begin to trust yourself more. You'll stop swinging between extremes—between over-giving and shutdowns, between ecstasy and emptiness.

Without aftercare, pleasure can feel chaotic or destabilizing. With it, pleasure becomes a portal to deeper safety and self-respect.

Aftercare closes the loop. It completes the cycle. It turns experience into wisdom.

In the world of conscious kink and ethical relating, aftercare isn't an afterthought, it's part of the negotiation.

Before any scene begins, partners ask: *What are you open to? What are your boundaries? How will we take care of each other after?*

Imagine if we did that in dating, in marriage, with ourselves. Aftercare isn't just a blanket and water bottle after the high. It's a conversation before the high—a declaration of values, of honesty, of self-respect. It's saying, "This is how I need to be met," before you open your body, your energy, your heart.

It's asking:

- What helps you feel safe?
- What helps you come back to yourself afterward?
- What kind of connection do you want for a night, for a season, for a lifetime?

These questions are intimacy—foreplay for the soul. One of the most radical things a woman can do is articulate what she needs without apology, without shrinking, without fear of losing love.

It might sound like:

"I want you to text me tomorrow."

"I want to know if this meant something to you."

"I need to feel emotionally safe before I open sexually."

Or sometimes, "I can't meet you there tonight."

So many of us were trained to believe that asking for what we want makes us needy or difficult. But in truth, clarity is a form of care for ourselves and for others. Naming your needs isn't control; it's integrity. When you speak your truth clearly, you create the conditions for real intimacy. When you avoid it, you build intimacy based on fantasy, projection, or performance.

For years, I thought "empowerment" meant I didn't need anything from anyone. I could take care of myself. Handle it. Be fine.

But fine isn't intimacy. And power without vulnerability isn't sustainable. Aftercare asks us to live in the paradox, to be both powerful and tender, sovereign and soft. To want fiercely *and* to be willing to be held. To say, "I need you to check in," and "I'll hold myself, too."

In my post-divorce dating life, I started experimenting with this practice. Before sex, before intimacy, before opening my energy, I'd ask for what I knew I would need afterward:

A message the next morning.

A phone call later in the week.

Clarity if it was just one night, or something unfolding.

At first, it felt awkward. Exposed. But what I realized was this: Men who could meet that conversation with honesty were men who could meet me. And men who couldn't? That was aftercare, too— the kind that comes from walking away with my self-worth intact.

We often think of desire as something wild and uncontrollable, something that just happens to us. But desire is also a practice. It deepens when it's held with awareness. Aftercare is how we bring awareness into desire.

It's how we say:

I want to feel this fully and I want to feel safe while I do.

When we learn to ask for aftercare before the moment, we shift the paradigm. We stop performing the "cool girl" who doesn't need anything. We become women who can hold the fullness of pleasure *and* the honesty of what it takes to sustain it.

That is erotic maturity.

That is sovereignty.

This is the new paradigm of love.

The wild art of wanting more begins here, daring to want to be met in your needs, fully, honestly, and without apology. That's the deeper edge of desire—not just wanting sex, attention, or connection, but wanting to be *seen* and *held* inside it.

It's easy to want the spark, the kiss, the rush of chemistry. It's harder to want integrity, honesty, and care, and to trust that they can coexist with passion. But this is the revolution of the awakened woman. We are no longer willing to abandon ourselves in the name of connection.

Aftercare is where that revolution begins.

And now, sister, it's your turn. You may not be standing on the hills of Avalon, but the same pulse that called me is alive in you. The same whisper that told me it was time to rise is already moving through your body. Every woman who reads these words carries the memory of her own awakening.

You are part of this lineage—the bloodline of women who chose truth over illusion, love over fear, life over numbness. The Priestess path doesn't ask you to travel across oceans. It asks you to travel inward. It asks you to remember that your pleasure is holy, that your grief is sacred, that your desire is the compass home. This is the wild art of wanting more.

A wanting that comes from knowing you were made for beauty, depth, and aliveness is a wanting that says, *I am ready for all of me.* You don't have to blow up your life to find yourself—only to listen, to tell the truth, to follow the quiet call that keeps tugging at your heart.

Every woman's initiation is her own. It might look like leaving the marriage, ending the career, reclaiming your voice, or simply choosing to rest. But underneath it all is the same vow, the sacred marriage to self. You will know when the moment comes. You will feel it in your bones, in the ache, in the longing, in the quiet pull toward something more. That is your doorway.

Step through it. Your ancestors are waiting. The Goddess is waiting. You are waiting.

This is the return, not to who you were before, but to who you have always been. The thirteenth moon rises now, full and bright.

The circle is closed.

The initiation is complete.

Welcome home, Priestess.

Welcome to the wild art of wanting more.

✦ Aftercare Practice: Creating Safety

Aftercare is how we weave the sacred into the everyday. It's how we bring the erotic into the real world. It's the way we walk between the temple and the kitchen, the altar and the school pickup line, still rooted in our truth.

Before your next date, your next intimate encounter, your next big heart-opening moment, ask yourself: *What kind of aftercare will I need?*

Do I want tenderness? Clarity? A moment of grounding? Do I want to be left in silence or held in conversation? Do I need to set a boundary before we begin? Then, if it feels right, speak it out loud. Practice the courage of naming what would help you feel safe enough to open.

Because pleasure without safety isn't pleasure. It's survival in disguise.

And we are not here to survive through our desires anymore. We are here to be transformed by them—with care, with honesty, with grace. Your body is not just a vehicle for pleasure. It's a temple for integration.

So, after every deep experience—in love, in sex, in grief, in creativity—remember this: You deserve to be held in your becoming. You deserve the exhale. That's aftercare.

After your next deep experience—whether it's sex, emotional release, or creative expression—take a pause before moving on.

Ask yourself:

What sensations am I feeling right now?

What would help me feel grounded and safe?

What kind of care do I need: physical, emotional, or energetic?

Then give yourself permission to receive it. Wrap yourself in a blanket. Drink water. Journal what you learned. Move your body slowly. Whisper a *thank you* to yourself for showing up.

✦ Wisdom Practice: Letter from Our Ninety-Year-Old Selves

In the early pages of this book, you wrote a letter to your nine-year-old self. You reached back and offered her what she needed—the truth she was too young to hold alone.

Now reach forward.

Somewhere ahead of you is the woman who knows how this all turns out. She has lived everything that comes after this moment. She is not worried. She wants you to know that.

She is the elder you are becoming. And this is her letter to you.

Dear Aine,

I know it seems like a house of cards some days, but you have done the brave and important work of finding yourself, your true voice, and letting the world see you. You're in turbulence but you're going to get through.

That invitation, the whisper from the universe, or the thud when Jason sent that FB message, we have it saved somewhere in a screenshot. But it was the call, the siren that set off the alarm that woke you up. You were living in a real house of cards then, tiptoeing around so afraid to face the reality of your marriage. You had started running toward something bigger, and he wasn't interested in running with you.

You had chosen something that felt like safety but was closer to self-abandonment. You put your needs and desire so far out of reach you thought they didn't exist. And then Sean died, and the ground opened up and swallowed you, but it also gave you space to slow down and figure out who you want to be when you're not just in survival mode.

You faced those memories and fears. You asked the hard questions and found out there was some more alive version of you that could be reclaimed. You set out on a journey, looking for cracks where the light gets in, finding the wounds, the longing, the fear of being left that has you abandoning yourself over and over again, the unworthiness so artfully masked by your beauty and charisma, by your wit and charm, no one would think you were so insecure and uneasy.

You set out on the journey of healing, of breaking down the masks and hard shells and characters that you built to survive, and with each healing, ceremony, process, you shook the foundation, and you hauled away all the rotten stuff and rebuilt a new foundation.

You are doing it, because you get to have this, you get to have this life, this big, beautiful life full of love and lust and gorgeous sun-soaked nights on the beach, and you get to have your desire, you get to live a full and fucking fantastic life and there is so much more to come.

Now write yours. Find somewhere quiet. Let the woman you will become speak to the woman you are right now.

The Weight of a Hummingbird

The weight of a hummingbird, tiny, just a few ounces, that *could easily fit in my palm. Its long beak almost outweighs its body. Her tiny wings are almost translucent and move so quickly that they disappear to our human eye. One came up under my awning last summer, floating around the fan, looking confused and out of breath. She seemed disoriented and exhausted with only white walls and a black fan instead of lush gardens and flowers.*

"Sit on the fan," I said, "'Take a breath."

But, she wouldn't. She landed only for a moment, her tiny body heaving up and down from the strain of stillness. She didn't stay long, just enough to catch her breath I think and then she was off, maybe to tend to her friends or her family. 'They need me," she'd say. "Can't stay. Just got to get myself together and get back out there."

Back to hovering, weightlessly in midair.

I read that hummingbirds can be quite bossy and territorial. They like to come back to the same sweet spots, the same gardens, and they always bring friends.

In the early morning, they come in a pack, darting from plant to plant, soundless, but the way their wings move the air, I always look up. I hear the pack of yellow breasted birds who jump from one side of the greenery to the other, singing loudly at each other, moving so fast you can just catch the end of their bodies, and then they are gone. Onto the next garden, the next flower, chasing the hummingbirds and singing on branches. Maybe they are making plans, or just exuberantly celebrating the sun and the new growth after the rains.

I'm happy to have them back tomorrow, singing and floating in my garden, on my flowers, sitting in their silence, in their expansive tiny weight.

The portal of transformation for me has always been aliveness. Saying yes to every experience that felt like truth: circles, plant medicine, movement, tattoos. Each one became a ceremony, a living altar of devotion. I look down at my arms, at the sacred geometry on my skin, and I remember the intention that lived in each line: the prayer, the pain, the surrender. The ink became medicine, a way to mark the moments I could have turned away but chose to stay. They are not decorations. They are **living symbols carrying the prayers and initiations of my becoming.**

Ceremony isn't about the form at all. It's about the intention that breathes through it, the way it brings you back to your body, your truth, your heart. For me, that remembering happens in circle, in song, in breath, in the temple spaces I now create where women gather to remember themselves, to hold one another through the sacred work of becoming.

As I reflect on all the ways I've held ceremony over these years—the circles, the breathwork, the movement, the writing, the prayer—I see now that every one of them was a doorway back to myself. Each moment of devotion was a reminder that life itself is the altar.

And we are the medicine.

Our breath, our tears, our laughter—all sacred offerings. Ceremony isn't something we visit. It's something we live. It's in the way you begin your mornings, how you love your people, how you walk into a room and bring your whole self. It's in the way you soften when you want to run or choose truth when silence would be easier.

When we approach life this way, every act becomes prayer. Cooking. Parenting. Creating. Grieving. Making love. The ceremony is wherever you are willing to be fully present. It's easy to fall in love with transformation—the fire, the breakthrough, the rush of what's next. But the deeper work is in what comes after: the integration. Letting the lessons take root in your everyday life. Allowing yourself to be truly changed. The real ceremony is found in the ordinary moments: the morning light on your skin, the warmth of coffee in your hands, the quiet gratitude for the life you've built.

That's the high worth chasing. Not the spark of the initiation, but the steady glow of devotion.

When you stop needing the next transformation, you realize you've already arrived. The growth is in the grounding. The medicine is in the living. So, step bravely into the spaces that call you: the circles, the song, the medicine, the mirror of sisterhood. Meet them as an equal, not a seeker. You are not waiting for the medicine.

You *are* the medicine.

Acknowledgement

There are people without whom this book would not exist.

To my mother, my grandmother, and the mothers before them, I stand on your shoulders. I hope to carry forward your dreams, and to finish what you could not. This book is part of that healing.

Sherri, my therapist, my teacher, and a guide through my darkest moments. You witnessed a transformation in me that no one else could have held the way you did. You remain beside me still, and I am deeply grateful for your love, your wisdom, and your unwavering belief.

Sophia, my best friend of twenty-six years. I have watched you model the integration of the divine feminine in your life, and now in our business. I love your engineering, spreadsheet-loving mind, and the way we always end up choosing the dance floor. My non-romantic life partner in every sense that matters, and now we are building *Sofanya* together.

Ivana, we started long before there was a book. You believed in me and in my stories before I could believe in them myself, and you were the first to call me a writer. You doula'd this book into being in your Writer's Kitchen, and I look forward to many more matchas and writing dates.

Kristen, my editor and friend, thank you for believing in this story and in me. You pushed me to sharpen and clarify my vision until I arrived here. Thank you for giving this story a home with Rise. And thank you to the entire team at Rise who helped bring it into the world.

To my family at the School of Interpretive Somatics—especially Marissa and Casey—thank you for being an anchor in this wild season.

To the teachers and women whose work lit the path ahead of me—especially Regena, aka Mama Gena, who helped awaken a deeper permission in me to live fully.

Gertrude, thank you for the retreat that cracked something open in me and for the space you created where transformation could unfold.

To my lovers—the ones who opened doors I didn't know were closed—I am grateful for what we were to each other.

To my sisters—the women who have walked beside me through the many seasons of this journey—you held me through rupture and rapture and the birthing of this book in a way only women can. Thank you.

And to the women who have trusted me with their stories—you have taught me as much as I have ever offered you. This book carries you, too.

About the Author

Áine Rock is a writer, speaker, and guide devoted to helping women reclaim their pleasure, truth, and personal power. Known for her deeply embodied approach to transformation, her work bridges emotional healing, feminine leadership, and the courage to create a life that feels fully aligned.

After walking through her own season of profound change—leaving behind a life that looked successful on the outside but felt misaligned—Áine began sharing a new way forward. One rooted in desire, discernment, and self-trust.

Today, she guides women through that same threshold. Through her writing, mentorship, and community spaces, she creates environments where women can release what no longer fits and step into lives that feel deeply their own.

Áine is a mother, founder, and devoted student of the feminine path.

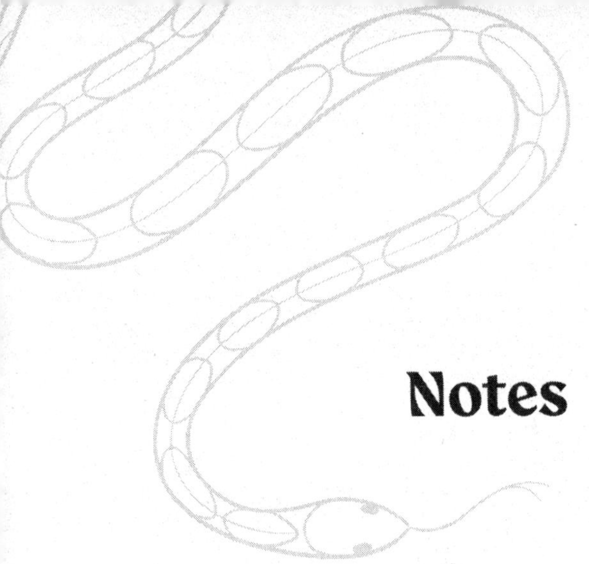

Notes